History of Technology—quantify its ^{KC} call
existance—Newspaper
Gilded Age Thought   Directories & Phone
Letters etc   Books
The Eunthreprenuer
The Speculator

History of the West
Becoming the Mid-West
The Significance of
the change of name
econ
Pol
Soc
Rel

Economic history of
Region — extra-urban
forces J. Commons

Theories of Regional economies
and history

The Historian and the City

This book is one of a series published under the auspices of the Joint Center for Urban Studies, a cooperative venture of the Massachusetts Institute of Technology and Harvard University. The Joint Center was founded in 1959 to organize and encourage research on urban and regional problems. Participants have included scholars from the fields of anthropology, architecture, business, city planning, economics, education, engineering, history, law, philosophy, political science, and sociology.

The findings and conclusions of this book are, as with all Joint Center publications, solely the responsibility of the contributors.

The Historian and the City

EDITED BY OSCAR HANDLIN AND JOHN BURCHARD

The M.I.T. Press

MASSACHUSETTS INSTITUTE OF TECHNOLOGY
CAMBRIDGE, MASSACHUSETTS, AND LONDON, ENGLAND

Fourth Paperback Printing, 1977

ISBN 0 262 58006 3 (paperback)

Library of Congress Catalog Card Number: 63-18004
Printed in the United States of America

Preface

The spread of urbanization is one of the characteristic features of our civilization. However the concept is defined, the phenomenon, in every part of the world, has shown dramatic strength and persistence. Few cultures have resisted the trend which took form in western Europe two centuries ago and has since transformed the essential elements of man's environment.

The peculiar conditions of life created by the aggregation of large numbers of people early attracted the attention of social scientists. The unique features of the economy that sustained men so organized, of the political forms by which they were governed, and of the social and cultural institutions by which they ordered their existence have posed distinctive problems for scholars and managers. The practitioners and students involved in the construction and the physical shape of the spaces men occupied have been even more directly implicated.

Yet the historical development of the city has received only sporadic attention. Archaeologists and historians have devoted time and effort to the reconstruction of urban forms and have given us a reasonably accurate description of the evolution of physical layouts at various periods. But the reasons for the development of those forms and their relation to the life conducted within them have rarely been treated adequately. The general works on the subject have often been interesting, but usually also speculative and tendentious; and they have neither rested on adequate data nor been rigidly disciplined in method. On the other hand, occasional monographs of value have lacked continuity and the unifying focus of common problems.

The deficiency is comprehensible. History as an academic discipline has not been oriented toward immediate problems. It has followed lines of inquiry which were mostly marked out in the nineteenth century, when the development of the city seemed incidental to other, more important trends—the rise of the nation state, industrialization, and the secularization of culture. Indeed, even now it is difficult to define the subject matter of urban history, to disentangle that which is peculiar to the evolution of the city from that which is characteristic of the culture as a whole. But a growing number of scholars have become aware both of the necessity and the complexity of studying the urban past.

The desire to confront some of these problems induced the Joint Center for Urban Studies of the Massachusetts Institute of Technology, Harvard University, and the Harvard University Summer Session to convene a conference, in August, 1961, that would consider the city in history. The sponsors of the conference sought to bring together historians who had examined some aspect of the subject and men who had dealt with the contemporary city, both as students and as practitioners. It was hoped that the meeting of those familiar with historical data and those involved in present-day problems would provide a basis for a fruitful exchange. The results of that conference are contained in this volume.

It seemed desirable to approach the subject through a general consideration of the place of the modern city in history. It was hoped thus to outline the distinctive characteristics of this environment and the social and personal problems it created. It was clear that the city had to be treated both as an entity in itself and as a force operating in history. To appraise the impact of the city on the wider world in which it was located it was necessary, on the one hand, to understand its role, past and present, in technological innovations and economic development and on the other, to estimate its influence in the history of ideas. Even when viewed from within, as an artifact, the city reflected in its physical features the views that man held of its functions and purpose.

The present volume assembles some of the papers delivered at the conference, together with additional essays prepared by participants either by way of commentary or formally to elaborate points raised in the course of a lively discussion. Space did not, however, permit publication of the full proceedings of the sessions, interesting as that was to those who heard it.

Oscar Handlin's introductory analysis aimed to outline the general problems which occupy the historian of the modern city. There was no effort here either to sketch a chronology or to catalogue the important work already done; the emphasis rested rather upon definition of the significant questions that arise in the study of the urban developments of the past.

The discussion of the city in technological innovation and economic development centered upon the thoughtful papers of a medieval historian and an economist. Robert S. Lopez probed the trading function of the town, particularly as exemplified in Genoa, and Shigeto Tsuru outlined the economies and diseconomies of urbanization. Alexander Gerschenkron's comments introduced a critical discussion of both papers. Sam B. Warner's account of Philadelphia supplied a supplementary case study from a later period; and the contributions of Aaron Fleisher and Richard L. Meier treated the economic role of the city from the point of view of present-day practitioners.

The city as a factor in intellectual life has been a less familiar subject of historical study; yet the novel environment certainly influenced the ideas of the men who resided in it. A philosopher and a historian incisively sketched those reactions. Morton White took as his subject the critical response of intellectuals in the United States, while Carl E. Schorske dealt with their counterparts in Europe. The formal comments by Frank Freidel and Sylvia L. Thrupp pointed to the existence of countertraditions, in the one case, that of the American booster, in the other, that of the city as the citadel of social order. The implications of these analyses were brought home to the conference by two papers which dealt with the significance of the city in contemporary life. The economist Kenneth Boulding speculated on the place of the city in social evolution and the historian Denis W. Brogan set forth his thoughts on the necessity for discarding agrarian myths and accepting the imperatives of the historically given job of urban citizenship.

Sir John Summerson provided a useful approach to the analysis of the city as artifact in an essay which focussed on London and examined the significance of the physical forms of urban growth. Anthony N. B. Garvan's study of proprietary Philadelphia, to the same end, investigated the influence of the founder's values upon the city's plan. The prepared comments of Walter L. Creese and Henry Millon explored the implications of efforts to deal meaningfully with the visual material of the city's history.

Finally, two summary papers attempted to assess the operational tasks of urban history, that by Christopher Tunnard, from the point of view of the city planner and that by Eric Lampard from the point of view of a scholar anxious to broaden the scope of the subject in its relevance to the social sciences. Frederick Gutheim and Atlee E. Shilder added comments on the building blocks of urban history; and John Burchard's summation captured the spirit of the immediate reactions to the proceedings.

The papers presented at the conference and here reprinted did not aim to arrive at positions of agreement with reference to any of the questions they treated. They intended, rather, through a review of material oriented to the historic past, to clarify the problem of the evolution of the city and thus to establish a basis for understanding the contemporary urban world.

The contributors, of course, are responsible only for the views expressed in their own papers. All, however, are grateful to other participants, whose comments in the discussion were stimulating and perceptive. These included:

Oscar Handlin   PROFESSOR OF HISTORY, HARVARD UNIVERSITY

Robert S. Lopez   PROFESSOR OF HISTORY, YALE UNIVERSITY

Shigeto Tsuru   PROFESSOR OF SOCIAL SCIENCE, UNIVERSITY OF ROCHESTER

Alexander Gerschenkron, Walter S. Barker   PROFESSOR OF ECONOMICS
HARVARD UNIVERSITY

Sam B. Warner, Jr.   INSTRUCTOR IN HISTORY, HARVARD UNIVERSITY

Aaron Fleisher   ASSOCIATE PROFESSOR OF CITY PLANNING
MASSACHUSETTS INSTITUTE OF TECHNOLOGY

Richard L. Meier   ASSOCIATE PROFESSOR, SCHOOL OF NATURAL RESOURCES
UNIVERSITY OF MICHIGAN

Morton White   PROFESSOR OF PHILOSOPHY, HARVARD UNIVERSITY

Carl E. Schorske   PROFESSOR OF HISTORY
UNIVERSITY OF CALIFORNIA AT BERKELEY

Frank Freidel   PROFESSOR OF HISTORY, HARVARD UNIVERSITY

Sylvia L. Thrupp   ASSOCIATE PROFESSOR OF SOCIAL SCIENCE
THE UNIVERSITY OF CHICAGO

Kenneth E. Boulding   PROFESSOR OF ECONOMICS
THE UNIVERSITY OF MICHIGAN

Denis W. Brogan   PROFESSOR OF POLITICAL SCIENCE
UNIVERSITY OF CAMBRIDGE

Sir John Summerson   CURATOR, SIR JOHN SOANE'S MUSEUM, LONDON

Anthony N. B. Garvan   PROFESSOR OF HISTORY
UNIVERSITY OF PENNSYLVANIA

Walter L. Creese   PROFESSOR OF ARCHITECTURE, UNIVERSITY OF ILLINOIS

Henry Millon ASSISTANT PROFESSOR OF ARCHITECTURE
MASSACHUSETTS INSTITUTE OF TECHNOLOGY
Christopher Tunnard ASSOCIATE PROFESSOR OF CITY PLANNING
YALE UNIVERSITY
Eric E. Lampard
ASSOCIATE PROFESSOR OF ECONOMIC HISTORY
UNIVERSITY OF WISCONSIN
Frederick Gutheim PRESIDENT, and Atlee E. Shidler, DIRECTOR
OF EDUCATIONAL ACTIVITIES
WASHINGTON CENTER OF METROPOLITAN STUDIES
John Burchard DEAN OF THE HUMANITIES AND SOCIAL STUDIES
MASSACHUSETTS INSTITUTE OF TECHNOLOGY

Contents

xi

I
Introduction

The Modern City
as a Field of Historical Study

OSCAR HANDLIN

Seen from above, the modern city edges imperceptibly out of its setting. There are no clear boundaries. Just now the white trace of the superhighway passed through cultivated fields; now it is lost in an asphalt maze of streets and buildings. As one drives in from the airport or looks out from the train window, clumps of suburban housing, industrial complexes, and occasional green spaces flash by; it is hard to tell where city begins and country ends. Our difficulties with nomenclature reflect the indeterminacy of these limits; we reach for some vague concept of metropolis to describe the release of urban potential from its recognized ambit.

Contrast this visual image with that of the ancient or medieval city. It is still possible, coming up the Rhone, to see Sion in the

Valais much as it looked four hundred years ago. From a long way off, one can make out its twin castles jutting into the sky. But the vineyards and orchards, the open fields and clumps of woodland, reach along the roadside to the edge of town. There, we cross a boundary to enter another universe, one which is whole and entire to itself. The record of sieges that lasted for months on end confirms the impression of self-containment. It is much so that Paris must once have been, and Athens.

The cities of the past were, of course, vulnerable to external assault and to disruptive changes that emanated from without. Wars, shifts in patterns of production and trade, and cultural innovations gathered force outside their walls and yet decisively altered their history. But even when they held agricultural lands and even when some residents tilled the soil, those earlier communities possessed an individual life of their own in a sense that their modern successors do not. The ancient world had been a world of cities, but each had been a world unto itself. The towns of the Middle Ages and the Renaissance, even those of the eighteenth century, were self-contained entities walled off from their surroundings, with which they had only precisely defined contacts. They provided a marketplace for the products of rural craftsmen and husbandmen; but the main lines of their trade ran to distant, often overseas, places. They were centers of administration. But the governmental and ecclesiastical functionaries existed apart in detachment. The distance between London and Westminster, between Paris and Versailles, even between Milan and the castle of the Sforzas, was more than symbolic; it measured the genuine isolation of the life of the bourgeois.[1]

On the map today London and Paris and Milan occupy the same sites as did the places which bore those names three hundred years ago; and subtle institutional and cultural ties run across the centuries. But it would be a mistake to regard the later communities as merely, or even primarily, the descendants of the earlier ones. The modern city is essentially different from its predecessors, and the core of the difference lies in the fact that its life is not that "of an organism, but of an organ." It has become "the heart, the brain, perhaps only the digestive stem, of that great leviathan, the modern

[1] Max Weber, *The City* (Translated and edited by Don Martindale and Gertrud Neuwirth; Glencoe, [1958]), 70 ff.; Raffaele d'Ambrosio, *Alle Origini della città le prime esperienze urbane* (Napoli, 1956); A. Temple Patterson, *Radical Leicester* (Leicester, 1954), 3, 165.

state." Its history cannot be understood apart from that of the more comprehensive communities of which it is a part.[2]

(The distinctive feature of the great modern city is its unique pattern of relations to the world within which it is situated. Large enough to have a character of its own, the modern city is yet inextricably linked to, dependent upon, the society outside it; and growth in size has increased rather than diminished the force of that dependence. Out of that relationship spring the central problems of urban history—those of the organization of space within the city, of the creation of order among its people, and of the adjustment to its new conditions by the human personality.)

It is, of course, perfectly possible to approach the history of these communities in a purely descriptive fashion—to prepare useful accounts of municipalities, markets and cultural centers on an empirical basis. But such efforts will certainly be more rewarding if they are related to large questions of a common and comparative nature. These introductory remarks aim to define some of those questions.

(The forces that made the modern city what it is took form outside its own limits.) Hence the increases were always unexpected and unanticipated. (In the sixteenth and seventeenth centuries London, the first truly modern city, was repeatedly forbidden to grow; men who knew it as it was could not conceive what it would become.) For the same reason, projections of future trends—whether prophetic or scientific—almost without fail fell far short of actuality, even in the most optimistic cultures. It was rare indeed that the facilities of a community anticipated its later needs, as those of Los Angeles did (The direction and rate of expansion were not foreseen because the generative impulses were not contained within the older urban society of merchants, artisans, and functionaries.) They sprang from three profound and interrelated changes in the society external to them—the development of the centralized national state, the transformation of the economy from a traditional, household, to a rational, capital-using basis, and the technological destruction of distance.[3]

[2] George Unwin, *Studies in Economic History* (London, 1927), 49.
[3] Norman G. Brett-James, *Growth of Stuart London* (London, [1935]), 67 ff., 105 ff., 296 ff.; Walter Besant, *London in the Time of the Tudors* (London, 1904), 83; Boyle Workman, *The City that Grew* (Caroline Walker, ed., Los Angeles, 1935), 266 ff.

The political changes were first to show themselves; here the medieval cities were at their weakest. Few of them had ever disposed of substantial military force. Venice and Ragusa were unusual in this respect, perhaps because of their relation to the sea. Most other towns, at best, found protection from a stadtholder, or at worst, remained the victims of *condottieri* or feuding barons. Often they welcomed the security of monarchical authority, but they had no illusions about the extent to which that would increase their own power. In the face of any assertion of royal or national will, they could only acquiesce.[4]

That dependent situation has persisted to this day. (Despite their wealth and their critical economic position, the great cities do not control themselves; indeed most of them remain underrepresented in their ability to influence state policy.) Their subordination in the polity has decisively shaped many aspects of their development.

The economic metamorphosis from which the modern city emerged is conventionally referred to as industrialization—an inappropriate designation because factory production was only slowly, and late, incorporated into the urban economy and was, in any case, only one aspect of a more general development. (The eye of the change occurred outside the city rather than within it. First in agriculture and then in industry, old household-oriented modes of production gave way to large-scale rationalized forms, ultimately mechanized, that immensely increased output. The need to distribute the products to territorially wide, rather than to local, markets directly implicated the city.)

The influence of technological change upon communications needs little comment. The evidences are all about us; and the development that led from the early roads and canals to the railroad, the telephone, the wireless, and the airplane permitted the speedy concentration of goods, messages, and persons at the focal points of ever wider areas. (The simultaneous acceleration in managerial skills that permitted the organized deployment of great numbers of men and materials was equally impressive. The pace of innovation was particularly rapid in the half century after 1875 when the character of the modern city was most precisely defined.) Why there should have been so striking an outburst of creativity in those years

[4] William A. Robson, *Great Cities of the World Their Government, Politics and Planning* (New York, [1955]), 78 ff.; Société Jean Bodin, *Recueils*, VI (1954), 265 ff., 367 ff., 434 ff., 541 ff., 612.

is as elusive a question as why there should have been so striking a failure of creativity thereafter.

The centralized national state, the new productive system, and vastly improved communications created the modern city. Together they increased its population, they endowed it with novel economic functions, and they imposed upon its way of life a fresh conception of order.

The initial manifestation of the change was a rapid growth in urban population. The centralizing tendencies of the emerging states of the sixteenth and seventeenth centuries brought significant groups of newcomers to the capitals and to regional subcenters. Operations, formerly dispersed in particular units of administration, were now concentrated; and the steady growth of state power created many additional places. Numerous functionaries carried on the expanded volume of government business and brought with them their families and retainers. Moreover many noblemen found it necessary to live close to the focus of authority, either through choice to be near the source of favors as in Bourbon France, or through compulsion to be subject to control as in Tokugawa Japan. Ancillary educational and religious institutions gravitated in the same direction. All the people thus drawn to the city created a market for trade, crafts, and services which swelled the economy of their place of residence.[5]

These developments had subtle, long-term effects. Channels of communication with the rest of the country were established that deepened through use and that conditioned the routes of later railroad and telephone lines. In some places the extensive fiscal transactions of the central government laid a basis for subsequent banking developments. As important, the seat of power acquired a symbolic value that later acted as a magnet for other detached elements in the society; and national citizenship facilitated their free entry.

Urban population expanded preponderantly by immigration. Cataclysms of many types outside the city borders precipitously swelled the streams that flowed into it. A stroke of fortune such as the discovery of gold near San Francisco and Johannesburg, or population pressure in the hinterland, or a disaster such as the

[5] See, e.g., Franklin L. Ford, *Strasbourg in Transition 1648–1789* (Cambridge, 1958), 159 ff.; Lewis Mumford, *The City in History. Its Origins, Its Transformations, and Its Prospects* (New York, [1961]), 386 ff.; *Golden Ages of the Great Cities* (London, 1952), 192.

migrations into Bombay and Calcutta after partition quickly raised the number of residents. Colonial trade contributed to the same effect in London and Amsterdam. Most important of all, structural changes in agriculture and industry involved a total reorganization of the labor force and effectively displaced great numbers of human beings for whom the city was the only refuge.[6]

From these sources was derived the rapid increase in numbers characteristic of the metropolis. Through the nineteenth century the pace accelerated, with the very largest places growing more rapidly than the smaller ones. In 1800 the twenty-one European cities with a population of 100,000 or more held, in all, somewhat more than four and a half million souls, one thirty-fifth of the total. In 1900 there were 147 such places with a population of 40,000,000 or one-tenth of the total; and thirteen and one-fourth million lived within the narrowly defined political limits of the six largest cities. Were there means of estimating the true size of the urban districts involved, the number would be larger still. The same cities in 1960 had a population of about 24,000,000—again a gross underestimation of their genuine numbers. Meanwhile places of comparable dimension had appeared in America and Asia. In 1961 well over 85,000,000 persons lived in the world's twenty largest cities, each of which contained 2,500,000 or more residents. And the process was not yet over.[7]

Mere accretions of population, however, changed the funda-

[6] Adna F. Weber, *The Growth of Cities in the Nineteenth Century* (New York, 1899), 230 ff.; Besant, *London in the Time of the Tudors*, 226 ff.; Walter Besant, *London in the Eighteenth Century* (London, 1903), 213 ff.; Percy E. Schramm, ed., *Kaufleute zu Haus und über See Hamburgische Zeugnisse des 17., 18., und 19. Jahrhunderts* (Hamburg, 1949), pt. II; Emile Vandervelde, *L'Exode rural et le retour aux champs* (Paris, 1903), 39 ff.; Robson, *Great Cities*, 112 ff., 141, 683.

[7] *Information Please Almanac, 1961*, 658; Edmund J. James, "The Growth of Great Cities," *Annals of the American Academy of Political and Social Science*, XIII (1899), 1 ff.; Weber, *Growth of Cities*, 20 ff., gives extensive nineteenth-century statistics. See also for more recent data, International Urban Research, *The World's Metropolitan Areas* (Berkeley, 1959); Kingsley Davis, "The Origin and Growth of Urbanization in the World," *American Journal of Sociology*, LX (1955), 429 ff.; Norton S. Ginsburg, "The Great City in Southeast Asia," *ibid.*, LX, 455 ff.; Robert I. Crane, "Urbanism in India," *ibid.*, LX, 463 ff.; Donald J. Bogue, "Urbanism in the United States, 1950," *ibid.*, LX, 471 ff.; Irene B. Taeuber, *Population of Japan* (Princeton, 1958), 25 ff., 45 ff., 96 ff., 126 ff., 148 ff.; Kingsley Davis, *Population of India and Pakistan* (Princeton, 1951), 127 ff.; Vandervelde, *L'Exode rural*, 16 ff.; Edmond Nicolaï, *La Dépopulation des campagnes et l'accroissement de la population des villes* (Bruxelles, 1903); R. Price-Williams, "The Population of London, 1801–81," *Journal of the Statistical Society*, XLVIII (1885), 349 ff.

mental character of the city but slightly. New people came in, but their presence in itself called for few radical accommodations on the part of the old residents who generally prospered from the increased demand for their services. The city spread through the addition of new areas to its living space. But the organization of life for some time remained much what it had been earlier. <u>Growth to great size was a necessary precondition, but did not in itself bring the modern city into being.</u> Edo (Tokyo) in 1868 is said to have had a population of about a million, London in 1660 held more than one-half million people; yet these places were but extended towns which functioned according to patterns set long before. Their nobility, mercantile pursuits, and artisans' handicrafts formed larger aggregates than before, but they were aggregates of units that were essentially unchanged. Characteristically, in such places the building trades occupied a large part of the total labor force, and they altered but little with the passage of time. Other pursuits remained much as they had been earlier. The number of smiths and tailors, of drapers and merchants grew; but the mere multiplication of stalls and shops did not change the character of the bazaar, of the lane or of the exchange.[8]

Nor did the new needs thrust upon the city by the transformation of agriculture and industry after the eighteenth century alone give it its modern identity. Viewed simply on the economic plane, there was nothing inherently novel in the relationship of the city to these changes. It had long been accustomed to receiving the placeless men who sought its shelter and it had always provided a market for the products of the countryside. What was new was the desire, and the ability, to impose a rational order upon the relations created by the new productive system. The evolution of that order not only brought the city into intimate dependence upon the surrounding society; it also entailed a thoroughgoing transformation in the urban way of life.

Earlier markets had been dominated by the characteristics of the fair; buyers and sellers had approached in the expectation that they might meet one another, but the actual encounters had been shot through with chance. Monopolies and other political controls, various systems of correspondence and intelligence, and numerous other devices had aimed to impart some regularity to these transac-

[8] For the population of earlier European cities, see Roger Mols, *Introduction à la démographie historique des villes d'Europe* (Louvain, 1955), II, 502 ff. See also M. Dorothy George, *London Life in the XVIIIth Century* (London, 1925), 155 ff.

tions, particularly in the exchange of the great staples—wine, wool, and later, spices, tea, tobacco, and sugar. But distance and the vagaries of household production had limited the utility of these efforts. In effect, the movement of goods came to a halt, started and stopped, within the city, and that discontinuity gave the entrepôt a considerable degree of autonomy.

That situation ceased to be tolerable after the eighteenth century. The new techniques resulted in a large and growing capacity for production far beyond local need; they involved heavy capital investments and considerable risk; and they entailed difficult administrative problems. The success of any enterprise hinged upon the ability to anticipate with some precision a favorable relationship between cost of production and selling price. It could only survive by planning, however primitive the means by later standards; and planning required dependability and predictability in access both to markets and to supplies.

The city supplied the essential mechanism: from it radiated the communications network—increasingly more extensive and more rapid—and within it were situated the facilities for transshipping, storing, and processing commodities on their way from producer to consumer. Here, too, was the apparatus of accounting and credit that made the movement of goods possible. The task of the city was that of speedy transmission. The more sensitive communications became, the more thoroughly the city was entangled in a mesh of relations that deprived it of autonomy and integrated it into a larger economic and social whole.[9]

The new role had profound consequences for the internal life of the city. Its effectiveness in the productive system of which it was a part depended upon its ability to create an appropriately functioning order within its own boundaries. The pressures toward doing so were critical in its development.

One can discover premature efforts to create such novel economic relationships in the role of Milan in Lombardy and in the experience of other Renaissance cities with their hinterlands. Such developments were abortive, not only because of their restricted territorial scope and because of technological limitations, but also because the corporate life inherited from the middle ages survived,

[9] Robert M. Fisher, ed., *The Metropolis in Modern Life* (Garden City, 1955), 85 ff.; Weber, *Growth of Cities*, 170 ff. For earlier market relations see, "La Foire," Société Jean Bodin, *Receuils,* V (1953), *passim.*

indeed grew stronger; and that life significantly inhibited further changes. The seventeenth-century syndics who sat for Rembrandt's corporation portraits were custodians of communal organizations which resisted untoward changes. The destruction of their way of life was the necessary preliminary to the creation of a new urban order more in accord with the developing productive system.[10] Where that corporate life was weak or nonexistent to begin with, as in the United States, the process was all the faster.

Destruction of the older way of life was achieved through a convergence of political and economic forces. The national state eroded traditional elements of control and created new loci of power that dominated the city from outside it. The local aristocracy dwindled in importance; the old corporations were drained of influence; privileges were reshuffled; and new people rose to prominence. More generally, the national state undermined all traditional affiliations. It recognized only the indiscriminate relationship of citizenship. In its eyes there were only individuals, not members of clans, guilds, or even of households.

The changes in the productive system redistributed wealth to the advantage of men who could cast aside inherited modes of action to capitalize on fresh opportunities. The new economy encouraged the pursuit of individual profit rather than of status within a defined community; and the city housed a pack of people seeking after gain:

> Where every man is for himself
> And no man for all.[11]

The result was a new concept of orderly city life, one that no longer rested on a corporate organization of households, but instead depended upon a complex and impersonal arrangement of individuals. The process was already at work in the sixteenth century in England; it was immensely stimulated by the American and the French revolutions and was complete by the end of the nineteenth century.

[10] See Douglas F. Dowd, "Economic Expansion of Lombardy," *Journal of Economic History*, XXI (1961), 143 ff.; *Storia di Milano* (Milan, 1957–1960), VIII, 337 ff., XIV, 835 ff.; Jakob Rosenberg, *Rembrandt* (Cambridge, 1948), I, 70 ff.; Weber, *The City*, 91 ff.; Mumford, *City in History*, 269 ff., 281 ff.; Société Jean Bodin, *Receuils*, VII (1955), 567 ff.; Schramm, *Kaufleute*, 185 ff.
[11] Robert Crowley, quoted in Mumford, *City in History*, 343.

We shall better be able to understand the character of the inner order of the modern city by regarding some of its specific manifestations.

An entirely new pattern for disposing of space appeared. The layout of the old city was altogether inappropriate. The population had already spread beyond the encircling walls and waters but it was inefficiently organized by a cumbersome and anachronistic plan. Churches, palaces, and other monumental structures occupied central places; squares and plazas pockmarked the limited area; and the streets ran but the short distances between nearby termini.

There was no reason why they should do more, for men had little need to travel since the household was both residence and place of work. Various districts were differentiated by occupational, class, or religious distinctions. But in each case, the basic unit was a self-contained familial entity that had a precisely defined place in the corporate life of the city. An increase in numbers was accommodated by multiplying the units, not by altering their character. In those unusual situations, as in the ghettoes, where space was constricted, the buildings rose upward and expansion was vertical. More frequently, where room was available, new clusters of settlement split off from the old and expansion was lateral. But until well into the nineteenth century growth in most places had simply multiplied the number of clusters; it had not altered their essential character.[12]

Reconstruction of the city plan depended upon the differentiation of living and working quarters. Such specialized use of space, reflecting the growing impersonality of business and its separation from the household, became prevalent everywhere except in professions like medicine, and in the service crafts where a personal relationship survived. Elsewhere, the dispersal of the population went hand in hand with the destruction of the household and was eased by the engulfment of suburb after suburb. The father and mother and children lived together but their life was detached from work. The categories of experience they shared in the home were unrelated to those of the job. Each individual left after breakfast to take up a separate task in the counting house or the shop or on

[12] Gideon Sjoberg, *The Preindustrial City Past and Present* (Glencoe, [1960]), 100 ff.; Martin S. Briggs, "Town-Planning," Charles Singer, *et al.*, eds., *History of Technology* (New York, 1957), III, 269 ff.; *Golden Ages,* 31–34, 67, 230; Mumford, *City in History,* 299 ff.

the scaffold, to return in the evening to his residence some distance away, for each was an integer subject to a separate reckoning in the accounting of the productive system.[13]

(The division of function was economical. Every productive or distributive operation became more efficient when it selected the individual employee according to his talents or cost apart from considerations of kin and clan, of family or ethnic grouping.) Of course, no society fully realized the ideal of total fluidity that permitted its population to be sorted out in this manner; but the separation of work from residence encouraged an approach in that direction. The fact that single men and women always constituted a large proportion of the migrants into the city stimulated the trend as did related alterations in the behavior of settled families.

(As a result space was released from all sorts of traditional expenses. The enterprise no longer had to bear the charge on land of high value, of wasteful drawing rooms and gardens. Precious urban acreage was withdrawn from farming.) And the distribution of population by income levels permitted a rational valuation of space in terms of an abstract, calculated, rent. (Speculation was the incidental by-product, rather than the cause, of this development.[14])

Specialization required and facilitated the construction of an entirely new urban plant, a good part of which was built with the aid of a remarkable burst of innovation that began shortly after 1820 and which reached its peak between 1875 and 1925. Space was reallocated with an eye toward its most profitable use; and buildings directed toward a single function—trade, industry, or residence—went up with ruthless efficiency. (The process of differentiation created demands for services which theretofore had been unneeded or had been supplied within the household, for fresh foods, milk, water, waste disposal, light, transportation, and recreation.) In the frenzy of construction, the city was entirely recast and its ties to the past obliterated. Even topography ceased to be an obstacle; hills were razed, marshes and lakes filled in, and shore lines extended to make way for the limitless grid. Goethe could still make out medieval Frankfurt in place names, markets, build-

[13] See Otis D. and Beverly Duncan, "Residential Distribution and Occupational Stratification," *American Journal of Sociology*, LX (1955), 493 ff.; R. P. Dore, *City Life in Japan. A Study of a Tokyo Ward* (Berkeley, 1958), 91 ff.

[14] Mumford, *City in History*, 421 ff.; Fisher, *Metropolis in Modern Life*, 125 ff.; Weber, *Growth of Cities*, 322 ff.

ings, fairs, and topography. By 1870, hardly more than a few of these monuments and ceremonies survived.[15]

Now begins the time of travel, at first on foot. Dickens' characters still walk across London, and at about the same time a resident of Tokyo thinks nothing of tramping five miles to and five miles from his destination every day. Even in twentieth century Rio or Tokyo an inefficient transport system compels workers to spend six hours a day between home and job.[16] But in cost-conscious societies speed is an important consideration; in its interest new streets are driven through the city, straight and wide to carry an ever heavier stream of vehicles—at first horse drawn, later, motor propelled. The wheels roll above and below as well as on the ground and inconvenient rivers are bridged over and tunneled under. The critical breakthrough comes with the appearance of the common carrier. At the beginning of the nineteenth century, every conveyance still bears the appearance of the personal or family carriage or litter—even the long distance stages that take fare-paying passengers. It is not at all clear, when the first railroads are built, that they will follow a different line of development. But the carriages are thrown open for all to enter; mass travel becomes possible; and the meanest laborer moves on wheels.

The pace and ingenuity of this work were impressive by any standard. That the subways of London, Paris, New York, and Boston were built faster than those of Moscow, Stockholm, or Rome fifty years later must mean something, although it would be hazardous to try to make the meaning precise. Any such comparison is to some degree arbitrary and perhaps far-fetched. Yet the standard of achievement certainly was not lower a half century ago than now, if we take into account the presumed improvement in technology since then. Travelers to New York today are aware that it will take seven years (1957–1964) to reconstruct La Guardia Airport and that Idlewild has been more than a decade in the building. Their predecessors fifty years ago were likely to reach the city through one of the largest buildings ever theretofore constructed at one time, one covering eight acres of ground, with exterior walls of one half a mile. They could enter through two tunnels under the Hudson River and four under the East River

[15] *The Auto-Biography of Goethe. Truth and Poetry: From My Own Life* (John Oxenford, transl., London, 1948), 3, 4, 7–10, 12 ff.
[16] Fukuzawa Yukichi, *Autobiography* (transl. by Eiichi Kiyooka, Tokyo, [1948]); Robson, *Great Cities,* 510; Brett-James, *Stuart London,* 420 ff.

extending more than eighteen miles from Harrison, New Jersey, to Jamaica, Long Island. Work on this project began in June 1903; the Hudson tunnels were finished in three years, the East River tunnels in less than five and the Pennsylvania station in less than six. In September, 1910, the whole complex was in operation.[17]

The modern city demanded an immense number and variety of new buildings. Already in the eighteenth century architects like Claude-Nicholas Ledoux were compelled to devise new shapes for warehouses, for banks, for other commercial structures, and for dwellings appropriate to various classes of residents. Considerations of cost compelled them to adhere to the rule of geometry, and to stress functionalism and the rational organization of materials and space. In doing so they struggled against counterpressures toward tradition and individualism, against counterpulls toward exoticism and a romanticized view of nature. By the second half of the nineteenth century, they had begun to work out the styles that accommodated the life of the modern city.[18]

Certainly the New York tenement block of 1900 was an unlovely object. Having dispensed with the old central court, it could pile its residents up in suffocating density. The reformers of the period were altogether right to attack overcrowding there and elsewhere and to complain that the cities had not adequately met their housing needs. Only, one must remember that overcrowding and need are relative concepts; and few later efforts have been notably more successful.[19] Comparison with the experience of Moscow in the 1930's, to say nothing of Calcutta in the 1950's, puts the achievements of a half-century ago in better perspective.[20]

The altered situation of the city called also for a new conception of time. In the rural past, years, months, days, and hours had been less meaningful than seasons, than the related succession of religious occasions, than the rising and setting of the sun. Small communities had their own flexible conceptions of chronology.

[17] Pennsylvania Railroad Company, *The New York Improvement and Tunnel Extension of the Pennsylvania Railroad* (Philadelphia, 1910).
[18] Emil Kaufmann, "Three Revolutionary Architects," *Transactions of the American Philosophical Society*, XLII (1952), 494 ff.; Helen Rosenau, *The Ideal City in Its Architectural Evolution* (London, [1959]), 79 ff.
[19] Mumford, *City in History*, 465 ff.; Dore, *City Life in Japan*, 40 ff.; Reinhard E. Petermann, *Wien im Zeitalter Kaiser Franz Joseph I* (Vienna, 1908), 128 ff.
[20] Alec Nove, ed., *The Soviet Seven Year Plan* (London, [1960]), 75 ff.; Harry Schwartz, *Russia's Soviet Economy* (2 ed., New York, 1954), 453 ff.; Robson, *Great Cities*, 384 ff.

Such habits had extended to the city as well. Each household had a large margin within which to set its own pace, for the tempo of all activities was leisurely. An analysis of the course of an eighteenth-century merchant's day, for instance, revealed long disposable intervals so that even when he was busy, it was upon terms he could shape for himself.[21]

The complex interrelationships of life in the modern city, however, called for unprecedented precision. The arrival of all those integers who worked together, from whatever part of the city they inhabited, had to be coordinated to the moment. There was no natural span for such labor; arbitrary beginnings and ends had to be set, made uniform and adhered to. The dictatorship of the clock and the schedule became absolute.[22]

No earlier human experience had made such demands. The army camp, plantation labor, and the ship's crew which came closest to it were coherent, closed societies, the members of which lived close together and in isolation from outsiders; the tasks involved had a rhythm of their own that regulated their budgets of time. But the modern city could not function except under the rule of a precise and arbitrary chronological order which alone could coordinate the activities of thousands of individuals whose necessary encounters with one another were totally impersonal. By the same token, literacy or some alternative code of signals was essential to the coexistence of people who did not know one another.

The new uses of space and time were indicative of what order meant in the modern city. Its complex life demanded myriad daily contacts of such sensitivity that it could not depend, as earlier, upon well-established and static connections among the stable households and the fixed corporate groups in which its population had been distributed. Instead it required its residents to behave individually and impersonally in terms of their function, and it assured regularity of contacts by rigid allocations of space and time.

That order made it possible to bring manufacturing, like other large-scale activities, into the cities. The planners of the early great factories thought of the only models of disciplined activity familiar to them, the barrack and the army camp; their sites—visionary or

[21] Arthur H. Cole, "The Tempo of Mercantile Life in Colonial America," *Business History Review*, XXXIII (1959), 277 ff.; *Golden Ages*, 44, 45.

[22] On the problem of time, see Pitirim A. Sorokin and Robert K. Merton, "Social Time: A Methodological and Functional Analysis," *American Journal of Sociology*, XLII (1937), 615 ff.

actual—were therefore invariably in the countryside, where the tolling bell from the clock tower of the mill replaced that of the village church. The similarity in design of factories and prisons was by no means coincidental.[23]

(The urban factory was conceivable only well in the nineteenth century when it was possible to imagine that a labor force would come to work regularly and dependably. The process of transition in actuality took a number of forms. Some factory centers, like Manchester, grew into cities. In other cases, as in Pittsburgh or Zurich, a commercial center expanded to engulf nearby industrial communities. Elsewhere industry was drawn in by the attractions of superior transportation facilities, or by the presence of an abundant labor supply, as in Berlin, or Chicago; or the shift was a product of conscious government decisions as in Moscow after 1928. But whatever the immediate impulse, the necessary condition was the order that permitted the factory to function.[24]

The way of life of the modern city created grave social and personal problems. Any increase of size had always complicated the police of the community. But so long as the family, the clan, or the guild remained accountable for the behavior of its members, so long as the normal ambit of activities was restricted to a familiar quarter, the primary danger of deviant behavior came from strangers. When the decay of the household weakened the sense of collective security, the initial response was to control or exclude outsiders, to arrive at some accommodation with violent elements, and to maintain the isolation of the district within which its residents felt safe. At the end of the eighteenth century, as large a place as London had not moved beyond this point.

But these expedients were not long useful. The modern city was no *colluvies gentium*—a fortuitous accumulation of unfused populaces—as were ancient Rome, or Alexandria. Extended travel and promiscuous contacts were essential to it; and the frequent mingling of men unknown to each other generated the need for holding each individual responsible for his behavior. The ultimate goal was some sort of total index that would precisely identify and infallibly locate each person so that he could be called to account for his obligations and punished for his delinquencies. The steady

[23] Kaufmann, "Three Revolutionary Architects," 509 ff.; Rosenau, *Ideal City*, 121, 133.
[24] See, e.g., Catherine E. Reiser, *Pittsburgh's Commercial Development 1800–1850* (Harrisburg, 1951), 28, 191 ff.

The Modern City as a Field of Historical Study / *15*

development of governmental power, the contrivance of numerous devices for registration, and the appearance of a professional corps of administrators were steps toward an approximation of that goal.

More was involved than the containment of criminality. The urban resident had positive as well as negative responsibilities. He had not merely to refrain from such actions as were injurious to others; he was expected, in ways that were difficult to define explicitly, also to contribute to the total well-being of the community by civic actions. The collective tasks of the old household and guild could not be left in abeyance. Someone had to provide care for dependent persons, education for children, facilities for worship, media for cultural and sociable expression, and commemorative monuments and objects of awe and beauty. The police of a city thus included a wide range of functions connected with its health and security. The state assumed some of these obligations, but the scope of its activity varied widely from country to country. Although we cannot yet explain convincingly the differences in the depth of its involvement, it is clear that it nowhere preempted the field entirely. Much remained to be done through other forms.[25]

It was not possible, although men often longed to do so, to revive the old corporate institutions or the solidary rural communities from which so many residents had migrated. The modern city contained too many disparate elements, too often thrown together, and in too fluid a pattern of relations to permit such regressions. Instead, where abstinence by the state left a vacuum, the characteristic device of a voluntary association, directed toward the specific function, met the need. The rapid proliferation of such organizations drew together memberships united by common interests, common antecedents, or common point of view. The wide expanse of the city and the continuing migration which peopled it, shaped such groupings. In some places the effective modes of organization fell within territorial, neighborhood lines; the *quartier*, ward, *ku*, or *favela* was the matrix within which associations formed. Elsewhere cultural or ethnic affiliations supplied the determining limits of cooperative action.[26]

[25] Louis Wirth, "Urbanism as a Way of Life," *American Journal of Sociology*, XLIV (1938), 20 ff.; Patterson, *Radical Leicester*, 222 ff.; Dore, *City Life in Japan*, 71 ff.

[26] See, in general, Lloyd Rodwin, ed., *The Future Metropolis* (New York, 1961), 23 ff. For specific illustrations see Louis Chevalier, "La Formation de la population parisienne au XIXe Siècle," Institut National d'Etudes Démographiques, *Travaux et Documents*, X (1950); Alphonse Daudet, *Numa Roumestan—Moeurs*

(For a long time, the cost of this adjustment was recurrent, overt conflict.) Leadership was effective only within limited circles, and there were few means of resolving the frequent crises that led easily into outbreaks of violence. (Bread riots in the West and rice riots in the East expressed the desperation of the uncared-for elements in the community; and racial or social antipathies, smoldering beneath the surface, erupted at the least disturbance.[27])

(By the end of the nineteenth century, the instruments for controlling such dangerous disorders were at least available,) if not always effectively used. The reconstruction of the great cities permitted a strategic disposition of power to contain the mob. (The maintenance of an armed police force deterred overt lawbreakers. Moreover, by then a complex of philanthropic, religious, educational, and cultural institutions had begun to elicit the acquiescence of the urban masses through persuasion. Thereafter conflicts took more negotiable forms, in the bargaining of labor unions and employers, and in politics which was less a partisan contest for power than an instrument of group accommodation. Disputes were increasingly subject to conciliable resolution through the mediating efforts of recognized leaders.) However, the issues which could be confronted on the municipal level were limited and concrete; and the deeper economic and emotional grievances of the population were likely to be displaced into other channels.[28]

(The life of the modern city created subtle personal problems. Here were distilled many of the general effects of change in the past two centuries: the break with tradition and the dissolution of inherited beliefs, the impact of science and technology, and the transformation of the family and of the productive system.) In the city, as elsewhere, such decisive innovations were a source of both release and tension in the human spirit. Only, concentrated as they were in their urban form, these new impulses were far more volatile than elsewhere. Furthermore, the man of the city passed

parisiennes (Paris, 1881), ch. iii; Dore, *City Life in Japan*, 255 f.; Alexander Campbell, *The Heart of Japan* (New York, 1961), 3 ff.; William A. Jenks, *Vienna and the Young Hitler* (New York, 1960), 4.

[27] Société Jean Bodin, *Receuils*, VII (1955), 398 ff.; J. B. Sansom, *The Western World and Japan* (New York, 1958), 242; J. D. Chambers, *Nottinghamshire in the Eighteenth Century* (London, 1932), 40 ff.; Besant, *London in the Eighteenth Century*, 475 ff.; George Rudé, *The Crowd in the French Revolution* (Oxford, 1959), 232 ff.

[28] Robson, *Great Cities*, 210 ff.

The Modern City as a Field of Historical Study / *17*

through experiences unique to his setting. The number and variety and speed of his contacts, the products of an original conception of space and time, the separation from nature, the impersonality and individuality of work all were novel to the human situation.

Evidence of the negative consequences was painfully abundant. On the Bowery or in Brigittenau drifted the uprooted masses who had lost personality, identity, and norms and who now were trapped in every form of disorder. The deterioration of man to bum was all too familiar in every modern city. Even the less desperate were heedless of the restraints of church and family; in London, Berlin, and New York of the third quarter of the nineteenth century, a majority of marriages and burials were unsolemnized by the clergy. The most prosperous tore at each other in vicious competition except when they indulged in fierce and expensive debauchery. High rates of mortality, suicide, alcoholism, insanity, and other forms of delinquency showed that men reared in one environment could not simply shift to another without substantial damage to themselves.[29]

At the high point of change, in the half century after 1875, there were two distinct, although not contradictory, interpretations of the effects of the modern city upon the human personality. Those who focused their attention upon institutional developments, like Georg Simmel, Emile Durkheim, and, to some extent, Max Weber, took particular note of the decay of old forms which left the individual unsheltered, unprotected, and isolated, and therefore prone to deterioration. The later exaggerations of Spengler and Mumford distend these insights into a vision of imminent catastrophe.[30]

Exaggeration was easy because personal disorders were more visible in the city than in the country. But these observers were also limited by a fixed preference for what the city had been, a total systematic unit comprehending a defined order of institutions that no longer existed. It is significant that their views mirrored somber

[29] See Petermann, *Wien*, 331 ff.; Jenks, *Vienna and the Young Hitler*, 11; George, *London Life*, 21 ff.; Besant, *London in the Eighteenth Century*, 140 ff., 263 ff.; Fisher, *Metropolis in Modern Life*, 18 ff.

[30] Georg Simmel, "Die Grosstädte und das Geistesleben," *Jahrbuch der Gehe-Stiftung zu Dresden*, IX (1903), 187 ff.; Kurt H. Wolff, ed., *Georg Simmel, 1858–1918*, (Columbus, Ohio, [1959]), 100 ff., 221 ff.; Emile Durkheim, *De la Division du travail social* (5 ed., Paris, 1926), *passim*, but especially the preface to the second edition; Oswald Spengler, *The Decline of the West* (New York, 1950), II, 92 ff.; Mumford, *City in History*, *passim*. See also Wirth, "Urbanism as a Way of Life," *loc. cit.*, 20 ff.

predictions, made long before. Rousseau and others had already warned of the inevitable results of urban detachment from nature before the process had even taken form. "Of all animals man is least capable of living in flocks. Penned up like sheep, men soon lose all. The breath of man is fatal to his fellows. . . . Cities are the burial pit of the human species." [31]

The personal hardships of adjustment to city life were genuine but they were distorted when examined in the perspective of the corporate, rural past. Other observers, whose gaze was fastened on the residents as human beings, made out a somewhat different pattern. "What can ever be more stately and admirable to me," asked Whitman, "than mast-hemm'd Manhattan?" Observing the curious procession of the ferry riders leaving work behind for their thousands of homes, he felt and expressed the wonder of their each being a person.[32] This was often the response of compassionate onlookers. At first regard, the city was totally inhuman; jungle, wilderness, hive, machine—these were the terms of the metaphors that sprang spontaneously to mind(But those sensitive enough to look more deeply found marvelous assertions of the human spirit even under these unpropitious circumstances. Here life was real and hard, and tested the human heart and mind so that emotions were deeper and reason more acute than elsewhere) Social scientists influenced by Darwinian conception of the survival of the fittest readily assumed that the city was the new environment within which a new, superior man would develop. And some who began half to understand the character of that life were tempted to idealize and romanticize even its least lovely aspects, the slums, the ruthless competition, and the grinding order.[33]

(The two responses were not irreconcilable; indeed, in retrospect, they seem almost complementary, or perhaps, they were but different ways of describing the identical process. The decay of familiar institutions was another way of saying the release from traditional restraints; the unsheltered individual was also the liberated individual. The breakdown of the household and the attenuation of all the relationships formerly centered in it were the condi-

[31] J[ean]. J[acques]. Rousseau, *Emile ou de l'éducation* (Paris, 1854), Book I, p. 36; Robert A. Kann, *A Study in Austrian Intellectual History* (New York, 1960), 63; see also the point of view implicit in such novels as E. M. Forster, *Howard's End* (London, 1910).
[32] Walt Whitman, *Complete Writings* (New York, 1902), I, 196.
[33] See also Weber, *Growth of Cities*, 368 ff., 441 ff.

tions of the liberation of modern man to all his painful tensions, all his creative opportunities.)The hard stone of the city streets provided the stage for this drama; and it is the task of historical scholarship to explain its triumphs, its defeats, and its conflicts.

(The modern city provided the scene for great outbursts of cultural creativity. Georgian London, Paris in the first decades of the Third Republic, Vienna toward the end of the reign of Franz Joseph, and Berlin of the 1920's were the settings of great achievements of the human spirit, in literature, in art, in music, and in science.) Yet these were also, and at the same time, the scenes of bitter struggles for existence, of acute hardships suffered by hundreds of thousands of ill-prepared newcomers beaten down by insoluble problems. John Gay and William Hogarth, Anatole France and Honoré Daumier, Robert Musil and Berthold Brecht, and Charlie Chaplin and René Clair compiled a record of personal disasters, of moral disintegration, of human costs so high it could only be contemplated under the palliative gloss of humor. The laughter of their audiences did not conceal, it recognized the harsh truth. (Yet the withering away of traditional guides to life, so debilitating in many ways, also set the individual free, left room for spontaneity and discovery, brought together selective new combinations of people, ideas, and forms, that permitted man to catch unsuspected glimpses of an unknown universe and an unfamiliar self.)

Every aspect of the development of the modern city generated conflicts not resolvable within its own boundaries; that was a condition of its intimate relations with the society beyond its borders. The urban residents were divided among themselves, and they had to reckon with outsiders in their midst and beyond the walls, whose interests were intimately bound up with their own. Disputes of great importance were the result.

The city plan was therefore never simply the realization of an abstract design. Even in places created entirely afresh, as in Washington or St. Petersburg, it was the product of inescapable compromises.(Within the city, the primary interest of the entrepreneurial groups and of the laboring population was to economize on the use of space. They wanted low rents, an efficient, functional allocation of the resources, and speedy interior transportation)

Such people met the determined, and sometimes effective,

resistance of other elements, whose conceptions were still dominated by the static images of the rural landscape. The aristocracy—genuine and putative—wished to bring with them the commodious features of their landed estates. They expected the city to provide them with elegant squares to set off their homes, with picturesque monuments, and with parks and boulevards that would supply a back drop for the May Corso, for the Spring Parade, for the *ausflug* or Sunday excursion, for the gentleman on horseback and the lady in her carriage. Public transportation concerned them not at all.[34]

Immigrants who prospered to a lesser degree clung to the rural village as the model of home; they built wasteful villas in the sprawling suburbs and sought a restricted transport system that would take them conveniently to their desks and counters, yet prevent the city from engulfing them. Often their dogged struggles for autonomy hopelessly complicated any effort at urban reorganization, a problem as troublesome in Vienna, Leipzig, Manchester, and Liverpool in 1890 as in Boston and Nashville in 1960.[35]

The persistence of the rural model prevented these people from thinking of the city as a whole and as it was. From Robert Owen, Fourier, and the utopian socialists, to Ebenezer Howard, Frank Lloyd Wright, and Lewis Mumford, a good-hearted but illusory plea went forth for the rebuilding of urban life in garden cities or multiplied suburbs, where adults would not be tempted to squander their resources in the pub or music hall, nor children theirs in the sweetshop; and all would have access to the salubrious and moral air of the countryside.[36]

To such pressures were added those of agriculturists and industrialists in the hinterland concerned only with lowering the cost of transshipment, and of the state, increasingly preoccupied with security against insurrection or lesser threats to order. The great planners, like Baron Haussmann in Paris, found room for maneuver in the play of these forces against one another. But rarely did they

[34] See Percy E. Schramm, *Hamburg, Deutschland und die Welt* (Hamburg, [1952]), 350 ff.; Mumford, *City in History*, 395 ff.

[35] Robson, *Great Cities*, 30 ff., 60 ff., 75 ff.; Sam B. Warner, *Street Car Suburbs* (Cambridge, 1962); Weber, *Growth of Cities*, 469 ff.; H. J. Dyos, *Victorian Suburbs* (Leicester, 1961).

[36] Rosenau, *Ideal City*, 130 ff.; Robert Owen, *Book of the New Moral World* (London, 1842), II, 16; Ralph Neville, *Garden Cities* (Manchester, 1904); G. Montague Harris, *The Garden City Movement* (London, 1906); Mumford, *City in History*, 514 ff.

find the city material they could mold into a unified and coherent whole.[37]

(Urban elements were at a disadvantage in the determination of both municipal and national policies.) The level of tariffs in the 1880's and 1890's, the routes of canals and railroads, and the character of the banking system vitally affected all cities. Yet their influence was perilously weak, underrepresented in the councils of state and divided, while the rural interests were monolithic and well entrenched. Paris, Rio, Rome did not govern themselves; and voices from the Platteland or Upstate were more likely to command than those from Johannesburg or New York. (The political power of the country generally outweighed the economic power of the city.[38]

(The clash of interests took its most subtle and most significant form in the contact of the diverse cultures that converged on the modern city.) The folk traditions of the old bourgeois did not survive the disintegration of the corporate bodies in which it had been embedded; it was totally disrupted by the pressure from both above and below of alien elements.

The aristocracy surrendered its isolation and shifted some of its activities to the city. Still stabilized by its landed estates, it also drew support from new wealth and, in the nineteenth century, began the quest for a uniform, hierarchical culture at the peak of which it could stand. It wished more than indulgence in a lavish style of life; it wished also general acquiescence in its position. (Indeed, to some extent it flouted the conventions of inferiors precisely in order to demonstrate its superiority.) Legally recognized rank as in England and Prussia, the pretense of ancient lineage as in Austria and France, or arbitrary registers of inclusion as in the United States, asserted its claims to pre-eminence. In addition, it transformed the theater, the opera and the museum into institutions to display its dominance. (The aristocracy turned music into classics, art into old masters, and literature into rare books, possessions symbolic of its status.[39])

[37] David H. Pinkney, *Napoleon III and the Rebuilding of Paris* (Princeton, 1958), 25 ff.

[38] Robson, *Great Cities*, 685; Schramm, *Hamburg*, 187 ff.

[39] Oscar Handlin, *John Dewey's Challenge to Education* (New York, [1959]), 33 ff., George D. Painter, *Proust; the Early Years* (Boston, 1959), Robert Musil, *The Man Without Qualities* (London, 1953); Hans Rosenberg, *Bureaucracy, Aristocracy and Autocracy* (Cambridge, 1958), 182 ff.; Hannah Arendt, *The Origins of Totalitarianism* (New York, [1951]), 54 ff.; Norman Jacobs, ed., *Culture for the Millions?* (Princeton, 1961), 43 ff.; Kann, *Austrian Intellectual History*, 146 ff.

The problems of other migrants into the city were of quite another order. The mass of displaced peasants were eager to transplant their inherited culture but the soil was inhospitable. Folk wisdom, inappropriate to the new conditions, took on the appearance of superstition; and folk art, detached from its communal setting, lost much of its authenticity. However these people fared, they were driven by anxiety—to retain the rewards of success, to avoid the penalties of failure. Some escaped through alcohol; others found moments of relief in the excitement of the yellow press, the music hall, and the popular theater.[40]

Above all, they needed to interpret their lives by seeing themselves as actors in a meaningful drama, and since it was inconceivable that they should be conquering heroes, they most readily visualized themselves as victims.

Of whom? Rarely of the aristocrat. Peasant and gentleman had a long history of accommodation; and their roles in city life engendered few direct conflicts. The lowly felt no compulsion to ape the high born, and gaped at the splendor of the carriages on the way to the opera without envy.

More often the villains were the capitalists, big business, whose wealth was abstract, was located in no communal context, and was attached to no responsibilities of position. Or sometimes, the enemy was the stranger—the Slav or the Jew or the Catholic or the Protestant Masons or the barbaric foreigner—who could be blamed for the ills of the city. Inhuman materialism, disregard of traditional faith, sensuality and obscenity were crimes against man; and for crimes, criminals were responsible; and they who came were guilty so that we who left home were but the innocent victims.[41]

The factory workers and craftsmen who held places in disciplined organizations found belief in socialism; the class struggle explained their present situation and offered them the hope of an acceptable future. But millions of placeless men could not so readily tear themselves away from the past. The shopkeepers and clerks, the casual laborers, the chaotic mass of men without function did not want the future; they wanted the security of the homes and families and blood communities they had never had or had lost in migration. That is, they wanted a miracle; and in their eagerness they became the gullible victims of nationalistic, racist, religious

[40] Jacobs, *Culture for Millions?* 64 ff.
[41] Oscar Handlin, *Adventure in Freedom* (New York, 1954), 174 ff.; Kann, *Austrian Intellectual History*, 50 ff., 109 ff.

The Modern City as a Field of Historical Study / 23

and quasi-religious fantasies of every sort. There is a particular interest, in Europe, in the ease with which these people allied themselves with some sectors of the aristocracy under the banner of a universal faith—Ultramontane Catholicism, pan-Germanism, pan-Slavism. Drumont and the royalist officer corps in France, Luëger and Prince Alois Liechtenstein in Austria, illustrated the attractiveness of tradition and authority for the demagogue and his mob. Perhaps analogous elements were involved in the revival of Shinto in Japan after 1868; they were certainly present in the history of fascism.[42]

The true miracle, however, was the emergence of a sense of civic consciousness connected with the old burgher traditions but responsive to the new character of the modern city. Its characteristics were tolerance to the point of latitudinarianism, rationalism, cosmopolitanism, pragmatism, and receptivity to change. It attracted the settled middle-class elements of the city, the leaders of organized labor and even demagogues suddenly charged with responsibility, as Luëger was in Vienna and La Guardia in New York; its essence was a creative reaction to the problems of the place; its achievement was the monumental building of the city to which I earlier referred.

Some decades ago—and I am deliberately vague about the date—a significant change appeared. The immediate local causes seemed to be the two wars, the depression, and new shifts in technology and population. However, these may be but manifestations of some larger turning in the history of the society of which the modern city is a part.

The differences between city and country have been attenuated almost to the vanishing point. The movement of people, goods, and messages has become so rapid and has extended over such a long period as to create a new situation. To put it bluntly, the urbanization of the whole society may be in process of destroying the distinctive role of the modern city. It is symptomatic of this change that, in western societies, most migrations now originate, as well as terminate, in the modern metropolis.

This change may be related to a general slackening of urban spirit. The worldwide movement to the suburbs is not in itself

[42] Dore, *City Life in Japan*, 291 ff.; Arendt, *Origins of Totalitarianism*, 301 ff.; Jenks, *Vienna and the Young Hitler*, 40 ff., 74 ff., 126 ff.

new; this was always one of the ways in which the city expanded. What is new is the effective motivation—the insistence upon constructing small, uniform, coherent communities, and the surrender of the adventure of life in the larger units with all the hazards and opportunities of unpredictable contacts. Increasingly the men who now people the metropolis long for the security of isolation from the life about them. They strive to locate their families in space, with a minimum of connections to the hazards of the external world.[43]

(Finally, there has been a perceptible decline in urban creativity. The regression to private transportation is indicative of what has been happening in other spheres as well.) Despite other advances in technology and despite refinements in methods, the last thirty or forty years have witnessed no innovations to match those of the thirty or forty years earlier. We have done little more than elaborate upon the inherited plant; nowhere has there been an adequate response to the challenge of new conditions.

We console ourselves with the calculation that if the modern city has ceased to grow, the metropolitan region continues to expand. What difference that will make remains to be seen. In any case, it seems likely that we stand at the beginnings of a transformation as consequential as that which, two hundred years ago, brought the modern city into being.

Therein lies the historian's opportunity to throw light on the problems of those involved with today's city, either as practitioners or as participants. His task is not to predict, but to order the past from which the present grows in a comprehensible manner. He can illuminate the growth of the modern city from the eighteenth to the twentieth centuries to make clear what was permanent and what transient, what essential and what incidental, in its development.

Such an account as this essay has presented has perforce touched upon a few themes abstracted from a large number of cases. Yet the historian must deal with particulars, not with generalities. Certainly the stress, laid here upon the connections between the modern city and the surrounding society points to the decisive role of political, cultural, and economic variants, widely different from place to place.

[43] Mumford, *City in History*, 511 ff.; Louis Wirth, *Community Life and Social Policy* (Chicago, [1956]), 206 ff.

Comparisons crowd immediately to mind. Did the differences between Washington and St. Petersburg in 1900, new capitals of expanding nations, emanate from the hundred-year disparity in their ages or from discernible differences between the United States and Russia? Did Shanghai and Singapore become what they did because they were perched on the edge of Oriental societies or because they were colonial enclaves? Did a tropical situation set the experiences of Rio and Havana apart from those of cities in the temperate zone; did their European population distinguish them from other tropical cities? Why did some cities fail to grow as others did, why were some more successful than others in resolving their problems?

No amount of theorizing about the nature of the city will answer questions such as these. We need fewer studies of the city in history than of the history of cities. However useful a general theory of the city may be, only the detailed tracing of an immense range of variables, in context, will illuminate the dynamics of the processes here outlined.[44] We can readily enough associate such gross phenomena as the growth of population and the rise of the centralized state, as technological change and the development of modern industry, as the disruption of the traditional household and the decline of corporate life. But *how* these developments unfolded, what was the causal nexus among them, we shall only learn when we make out the interplay among them by focusing upon *a* city specifically in all its uniqueness.

In the modern city, the contest between the human will and nature assumed a special form. Here man, crowded in upon himself and yet alone, discovered his potentialities for good and evil, for weakness and strength. Compelled to act within a framework of impersonal institutions, he was forced to probe the meaning of his own personality.

In the balance for two centuries now has lain the issue of whether he will master, or be mastered by, the awesome instruments he has created. The record of that issue deserves the best energies of the historian.

[44] Weber, *The City*, 11 ff.; Wirth, "Urbanism," 8 ff.; Sjoberg, *Preindustrial City*, 4 ff., 321 ff.

II

The City in Technological Innovation and Economic Development

The Crossroads Within the Wall

ROBERT S. LOPEZ

In the earliest handwriting that we can read, hieroglyphic, the ideogram meaning "city" consists of a cross enclosed in a circle. The cross represents the convergence of roads which bring in and redistribute men, merchandise, and ideas. This convergence entails a quickening of communication which is nearly always a great advantage, but may become a handicap if speed grows so frantic that the city has no time to keep its share of the incoming goods and to impress its mark on the goods it re-exports. The circle, in the hieroglyph, indicates a moat or a wall. This need not be materially erected so long as it is morally present, to keep the citizens together, sheltered from the cold, wide world, conscious of belonging to a unique team, proud of being different from the open coun-

27

try and germane to one another. The wall, too, may become an obstacle if it is too high and tight, if it hinders further growth, above all if it frustrates the opportunity for exchanges beyond it.

No other definition seems more fitting than the Egyptian one, the oldest of all. Communication plus togetherness, or, a special aptitude for change combined with a peculiar feeling of identity: is not this the essence of the city? Technological innovation and economic development are bound to come when such a combination is put to good use. The use depends, however, on the quality of the citizens. To quote another, although far less ancient authority, "not houses finely roofed or the stones of walls well-builded, nay, nor canals and dockyards make the city, but men able to use their opportunity." These were the words of Alcaeus of Lesbos, the Greek poet and friend of Sappho, about 600 B.C.

Students of urban history, however, do not always agree with Alcaeus or with one another. Cities are hard to single out. They do not differ from other agglomerations as men from dogs or black from white. In between, there is a broad grey area of inhabited centers that meet some but not all of the tests.

To Henri Pirenne, the supreme test was whether or not a locality acted as a center of distribution of wealth; without a market he said, one could not speak of a city. This was the definition of an historian of medieval economics, a master in my own field. It corresponded roughly to the crossroads of the hieroglyph but made nothing of the wall, that rampart of oneness that urges all citizens, not only the merchants, to work together like the cells of a living body. Nor did it fit snugly the glory that was the Greek and Roman city, where the center was the public square, that openair ancestor of the town hall, which, according to Aristotle, "must not be dirtied by merchandise, should not be a thoroughfare for craftsmen and workmen."

If Pirenne's definition seems too exclusive, some other economic and social definitions are too inclusive to be of much use. One often repeated in Marxist circles is that the citizen body feeds on agricultural surpluses it is able to consume without having produced them. True, but so does the feudal lord with his retinue, in a fortress which has a wall but no crossroads; so do certain communities of ascetics, whose roads have no terminus on earth. Moreover, many medieval towns included peasants and shepherds, some of whom took active part in the exchange of wares and ideas. Again, it is often said that a city contains a diversified society, a variety of occupations. Indeed it does, but the case of the village inhabited by farmers or fishermen alone does not occur unless the agglomeration is obviously too small to be called a city. Even the Carolingian manor had smiths, carpenters, at least one clergyman, and normally a lord or his representatives. How various must variety of occupations and ranks be for a place to qualify as an urban center? Is Hartford less of a city because so many of its inhabitants are insurance dealers? The grey area, under these terms, becomes almost limitless.

Legal definitions are certainly crisper, perhaps too crisp to be true. For the historian, they have the advantage of originating in the minds of the very people who adopt them. A city, according to many Islamic political scientists of the Middle Ages, existed always and only when there was a mosque with a Friday preacher, a bazaar, and a public bathhouse. The West was less concerned with bathing, but it was often stated that a set of walls, or an episcopal see, or the presence of a count, or a royal charter of incorporation was the necessary and sufficient condition for a city to be a city. But walls may merely enclose a castle, a cathedral without faithful is not a temple. Even Isidore of Seville, that shaky torchbearer in the Dark Ages, realized that, when he said in his *Etymologies* that a city is not made of stones but of men.

Law, however, is usually born old. Either it puts its official seal on something already existing and evident, or it runs contrary to fact and cannot be enforced. It was not enough for Pope Pius II to rebaptize "city of Pienza" his native village, to give it a bishop, and to persuade his cardinals to build palaces at the dead end of a country road. Nowadays, the only visitors of those mansions, erected by one of the greatest Renaissance architects, are tourists and chickens. On the other hand, Paris never got a charter from the French King, but managed without it. Frederic Barbarossa destroyed the walls of Milan and spread salt on its smoking ruins, but could not destroy the crossroads and the moral wall of Milanese determination. In fact, legal fences, because of their propensity to formalize the past without foreseeing the future, are often a nuisance. Many cities which got the concurrent recognition of walls, a charter, a bishop, and a count were involved in tangles of conflicting claims which far exceeded the complaints of New York City against its neighbors within greater New York.

To assess the historical role of the city, any definition or classification based solely upon figures will not do. A city is a unique corporate entity. Not unlike physical individuals, it lends itself to generalizations which can be quantified or reduced to formulae, but formulae are valid only within the context of one specific historical period and geographic home. Quantity does not adequately represent quality. There has been only one Athens, one Florence, one Paris. No agglomeration of the same size and density, with the same social composition and economic structure, even if it could be found, produced the same abnormal flora of genius in every field.

No doubt, it is important to note that in the time of Dante Florence had about 125,000 inhabitants, produced 75,000 pieces of cloth in a year, and was the home of the three greatest banks in Europe, whereas in the time of Leonardo da Vinci it had only 75,000 inhabitants, produced fewer than 50,000 pieces of cloth, and though it still boasted of the greatest bank of Europe, had suffered a drastic reduction in banking capital. This difference may help explain, for instance, why in the time of Dante the Florentines worked out the system of accounting we still use, double-entry bookkeeping, whereas two hundred years later, Leonardo da Vinci's amazing scientific discoveries remained buried in his notebooks, and their author emigrated in search of better opportunities. Again, the fact that Gutenberg's Mainz had only a few thousand inhabitants explains why the printing business had to move on to Venice to find a promising outlet, and the fact that Venice itself had no more than 200,000 inhabitants explains why even the best sellers sold so little. Still it had to be Venice, not just another city of that size, to provide a market both for the Latin classics in the admirable Aldine edition, and for the earliest printed manual of double-entry bookkeeping, written by a Friar who plagiarized an earlier handbook by a merchant.

To bring discipline in urban classification, some German scholars have suggested a division of agglomerations according to size: below 5,000 inhabitants there are only *Landstädte*—agrarian towns—then small, medium, large, and extra-large towns, respectively, above 5,000, 20,000, 100,000 and 1,000,000. By this token, medieval Paris and London did not rise above mediocrity, Calvin's Geneva was a small city, Charlemagne never knew anything but agrarian towns. All this is not without significance when we try to evaluate the influence of a city in technological innovation and economic development, but it does not tell the whole story. Fundamentally, what matters is whether or not the crossroads within the circle produced a quickening, a creativity that did not exist outside the circle. Bigger is not always better, progress may be stimulated by a deficiency as well as by abundance. It was the great demographic plunge of the early middle ages, the lack of manpower, that led men to look for labor-saving devices in agriculture and transportation, although the demographic growth and the urban development of the later middle ages were responsible for the diffusion of innovation and for the application of primary inventions, such as the watermill, to a growing number of industries as in a chain reaction.

The density of the agglomeration in my opinion is a still more misleading test. To be sure, Tacitus describes with unadmiring curiosity the fad of the Germans for scattered homes wherever they find a pleasant brook; a very unsocial habit when you wish to keep citizens milling around the public square. Bonvicino della Ripa, a thirteenth-century municipal patriot, takes pride in pointing out that in the perfectly circular area of Milan, houses are packed together tightly.

Suburban living, however, is not a modern invention. In the middle ages, some of the most important cities left a good proportion of their walled space unbuilt: they had market places, meeting places, churchyards, private orchards, and bushes. In the tenth century, Constantinople, then the largest and most industrious city in Europe, had in its center a valley planted with olive trees and vineyards. In Cordoba, the second largest city, the palace and patios of the Caliph occupied one third of the urban area.

Naturally, the growth of the population put some pressure on unoccupied lots, but more often than not it was met by expanding the walls. Sizes were not yet so large that distance from the center made a great difference, at least until the eighteenth century. Though Ricardo and Sombart have built interesting arguments on capital formation through the increasing value of urban soil, the fact remains that in the fourteenth century, three shops in one of the best business locations of Florence were rented for approximately the same amount, year after year, through boom and bust, demographic increase and decline. While it is true that in Lübeck the descendants of the founding fathers, who owned lots on the marketplace, remained prominent for centuries, one wonders whether the decisive inheritance was the lot or the commercial privileges the founders had reserved for their families.

"A city is a city is a city," one is almost tempted to say. Yet there are white and red roses, and there were different types of urban settlement, with different attitudes toward technology and economy. Four of them seem to stand out: the stockade city, the agrarian city, the market city, and the industrial city. These are not inflexible "stages" of urban development; complex types do not always grow out of simpler ones, nor do the simpler types always disappear when the complex ones mature. Above all, classification is oversimplification, a necessary evil in historical method.

The stockade city is so simple that it is easily confused with the village. It is the earliest urban form, perhaps as early as sedentary life, but it also plays a role in the early medieval West, and in any colonial frontier. The stockade encloses, besides a wide empty space, the control towers of an agricultural district: a temple, a fortress, a storehouse, often all in one building. In this permanent kernel very few people live—the political, religious and military leaders with their assistants. The whole population of the district, however, gathers in the empty space on festive occasions or when driven together by war, famine, and natural calamities; and there also may be pilgrims and merchants coming from afar. It does not matter that they come and go; even in our own cities, foreigners and commuters are essential elements. Brief though the gatherings may be, they serve for the exchange of wares and ideas, they create a crossroads within the wall. The keepers of the towers provide continuity and stimulate growth by putting the wares and the ideas to work. We must not look down upon the feeble, intermittent contribution of this primitive town; the first invention, the first capital are the hardest to get. Besides, the stockade city is not so primitive in its offspring, the fair.

When the landowners of the district come to live permanently in the stockade, an agrarian city is born. They come because they like the security, comfort, and prestige one enjoys within the wall, and because they have dependants to till the soil outside and to bring the harvest to the crossroads inside. Artisans and merchants also come, but they depend on the landowners for their food. Some of them may wax as rich as the landowners, or even richer; but usually the goal of the successful tradesman is to buy land and retire from trade. Until and unless he becomes a landowner, he is subject to some kind of discrimination: he does not qualify for public office, or, still worse, he is not fully a freeman, not quite a citizen. He may even find it so hard to rub shoulders with the true masters of the city that he will settle in a separate stockade outside and beneath the city wall. If he lives in the city, he clings to the market square; the public square, we may repeat with Aristotle, is for the landowning patricians.

No culture has identified itself with the city as thoroughly as that of classic Greece and Rome. The Latin urbane tradition still lingers in our own language, where "brute" is a synonym of "uncivilized," that is, etymologically, "not living in a city." Virtually the entire legacy of the classic world is to be credited to cities. Who can claim as much for the modern town? Still, all Greek and Roman towns, even the most industrious ones, belonged to the agrarian type. While a landed elite molded in dignified leisure the style of urban life, commerce was mainly in the hands of freedmen, often acting as straw men for landowners who did not wish to dirty their hands, and the crafts were mainly exercised by slaves. Cleon, the tanner or the leather manufacturer, the only businessman ever to attain a commanding role in the Athenian democracy, proved a successful politician and general, yet was unanimously denounced as disgraceful and vulgar by the best citizens and writers. In Rome, the trading class of "knights" shared the power with the landowners only when civil wars gripped the republic. Augustus put the "knights" back where they belonged, morally below the humblest free farmers.

This did not make technological innovation and economic development impossible. Money does not smell, as Vespasian used to say. Knowledge of any kind, even mechanical knowledge, was eagerly pursued by the polite urban society. But inordinate and limitless pursuit of gain was regarded as a sin against *aurea mediocritas*, the golden means; and the gap between the thinkers and the tinkers condemned to sterility some of the most promising scientific discoveries. The achievements of classic economy and techniques are famous enough. So is the fact that steam power, invented in Alexandria, was used only to make ingenious toys.

The mood of urban society radically changed when the merchant became the leader, that is, when the market city appeared. This urban type did not emerge at the same time as the market, for markets existed in the agrarian city as well and, intermittently, even in the stockade city. It appeared when market and public square became one thing, that is, when the superiority of the landowner was eliminated. This happened more than once and in more than one geographical area, but nowhere was the transformation as sweeping as in Western Europe, and most particularly in Italy between the tenth and the fourteenth century. In Belgium and in many other countries, the stockade or suburb of the merchants merged with the high city of the noblemen. In Italy, where merchants had always lived inside the town, the landowners themselves openly engaged in trade, associated as equals with ordinary merchants and other commoners, and sold their land to invest the proceeds in commerce. Those who failed to do so gradually sank into economic and political insignificance. Wealth rather than birth thus became the main basis of class distinction, the foundation of power and prestige. Limitless gain displaced golden mediocrity as the supreme goal of the citizen.

This picture does not agree with Henry Adams' description of the medieval cathedral town, or with Aquinas' plans for the Christian life of the merchant. But Aquinas was a philosopher, and tried not so much to explain the hard facts of business as to explain them away. His views, though not at all irrelevant, provide no more clues to the Commercial Revolution than Kierkegaard's views reflect the Industrial Revolution. As for cathedral towns, they existed and shone, but played no conspicuous role in the economic and technological development of their time. Or rather, Milan built her cathedral when she had money and manpower to spare, so that it did not interfere with her economic development; Beauvais built a taller church than she could afford and condemned herself to economic mediocrity.

Religious strictures notwithstanding, the self-governing market city of the later Middle Ages outstripped our industrial republic in the unabashed pursuit of gain. We do not officially proclaim that millionaires make the best presidents and senators, or that "what is good for General Motors is good for the country"; the most successful medieval Communes frankly were governments of businessmen, by businessmen, for businessmen. The merchant rulers expected supernatural bodies, such as the Pope, the Emperor, the King, to worry about ethical purposes, while they ran the city as a chamber of commerce. If they tended to despise noblemen and craftsmen, it was because the former had lost their wealth and the latter had little chance to acquire it. Nevertheless, they wished to see to it that "any man," again quoting Bonvicino della Ripa, "may earn his dignified living according to his station." Idleness alone found no mercy with them: Dante set apart the most dishonorable section of the Other World for "those who lived without infamy and without praise," and Paolo di Pace da Certaldo broadcast the following advice: "If you have money, do not stand still nor keep it at home dead, for it is better unprofitably to act than unprofitably to stand by. . . . Even if you gain nothing, you gain enough when you lose nothing of the capital and maintain your trade contacts."

The constant flow of immigrants for four centuries after 950 suggests that this restless, competitive life offered a sufficient reward in liberty and the pursuit of happiness. The freedom of the wall lured the serfs and the small tenants from the humble security of their villages to what might be, at worst, unskilled work for starvation wages, but, at best, apprenticeship and promotion in a craft. A craftsman ordinarily was better off than a peasant, but he, too, toiled with his hands aided by simple tools. After providing for sustenance, he seldom had a surplus for investment; the discipline of the guild limited his initiative in hiring more helpers, in changing his methods, or in trying out new tools. The freedom of the cross-roads, however, tempted him to forsake the modest tranquillity of his shop for the adventure of commerce, banking, and navigation. This was the way to power and prestige: even in the greatest centers of the textile industry, such as Ghent and Florence, leadership rested not with the weavers, but with those who bought wool, sold cloth, and lent the proceeds on interest.

The marginal utility of the merchant determined the scope of technological innovation and economic development in the market city. It was a very broad scope, but not an all-embracing one. The Commercial Revolution of the later middle ages stopped short of an industrial revolution. It gave water mills to the fuller, whose work was especially strenuous, and to the silk thrower, whose material was very expensive, but equipped the spinstress only with a spinning wheel, the weaver with a pedal loom. The pressure of demand was not sufficient to warrant a greater investment in labor-saving devices for all stages of production. As a matter of fact, the revolution had started in a milieu where the luxury demand of a few wealthy people offered far greater opportunities than the ordinary consumption of the masses. Although its tendency was to increase the latter and to transform yesterday's luxury into today's treat and tomorrow's necessity, it did not fully turn the mind of the merchant from a search for high profits from limited sales to a promotion of massive sales at a low profit. Minds change slowly: it took the economic slump of the Renaissance, the stern labor relations of the Reformation, the Midas complex of Mercantilism, and lastly, the great scientific and political revolutions of the eighteenth and nineteenth centuries to complete the switch and prepare the industrial city. The latter type belongs to the present as well as to the past, and cannot be adequately described in this paper.

Let us pause still another minute in contemplation of the market city. The "market galley," featured by the Genoese and Venetian state-controlled navigation companies of the early fourteenth century, was a graphic symbol of the ambivalent disposition of the merchant. She was the end product of centuries of experimentation to combine the advantages of fast but slim and expensive oarships with those of cheap and roomy, but clumsy, sailships. She could use the labor-saving propulsion of the wind, but she still utilized the muscles of free, if underpaid, oarsmen. She had some room for bulky cargoes, but needed a substantial complement of luxury wares to pay for her way. She represented the best imaginable compromise between quantity and quality.

After so many generalizations, I should like to present one concrete example: Genoa at her medieval peak, around 1300. I choose Genoa not only because I was born there and am still somewhat spellbound in her circle, not only because one of her citizens in 1492 played a significant role in technological and economic development, but also because Genoa was a typical, almost exasperated case of the market city. Her population of about 100,000 made her the fourth largest city in Italy; outside Italy, only Constantinople may have surpassed her, while Paris remained slightly behind. The returns of taxes derived from Genoese sea trade indicate a more than fourfold increase from 1274 to 1293; in the latter year, they postulate a taxable total of nearly four million Genoese pounds, roughly ten times the receipts of the French royal treasury for the preceding year. It was true that trade was subject to sharp fluctuations; Genoa had a capitalistic economy, complete with business cycles.

Capitalism meant, for example, that men and women of all ages and condition, from the archbishop to the bath attendant, from the aged widow to the orphans under wardship, were the clients of one or another of the two hundred notaries who keep records of credit transactions, drafting tens of thousands of contracts every year. The time factor was so important that each contract was dated not only by the day but also by the hour; it was so pressing that notaries worked long after dark and sometimes went on board ship to help merchants too busy to come ashore. Practically every Genoese had a stake in the ships, the trains of pack animals, the international fairs, the business offices in the West, and the colonies of the Levant, and an investment with the bankers, the shopkeepers, or the craftsmen in the city, be it a matter of many thousand pounds or only a few pence. The servant loaned to his master, the master to the servant. Those who had nothing to invest contributed their labor. No object was too humble, none too rare to be offered for sale in small or large lots. A hardware seller stocked up a hundred chamber pots, and a jeweller in one sale disposed of 111 precious rings, 169 sapphires and topazes, 348 hardstones, 59 pearls, and 132 cameos, one of which contained a piece of the Holy Cross.

Capitalism also meant that illiteracy was virtually unknown. Some tradesmen were amateur poets and others boasted of law degrees. Genoa was the earliest Western city known to have used Arabic numerals, the earliest to have equipped her seamen with navigation maps, the earliest and most successful in developing maritime insurance contracts, the earliest to strike gold coins, precisely at the moment when gold was cheapest. The government, though continuously shaken by party strife and rival pressure groups, was a paragon of mercantile efficiency. It kept accounts according to the latest principles of banking administration, and the consolidated public debt paid dividends so regularly that its shares, of one pound each, sold in the open market above par. Private business also was administered with the utmost care: "write down at once whatever you do," a Genoese rimester told his fellow citizens, for "whoever is slow in writing his records cannot live long without damage and error." City planning was geared to the needs of trade: the handsome arcades, some of which still grace the surroundings of the harbor, were built by private citizens in obedience to a municipal regulation, in order to provide shelter for prospective customers intent on window shopping. Public funds and private charity joined in the construction and maintenance of dockyards, lighthouses, bridges, hospitals, and highways. This was ceaseless work, but it passed through spurts of greater activity whenever a recession forced the administration to conjure up useful projects for the relief of unemployment.

Not all capitalists today vote Republican; not all medieval capitalists supported rugged individualism, unobtrusive administrations, and free competition at home and abroad. Venice, Genoa's greatest rival, inherited from Byzantium a tradition of class solidarity, government control, and protectionism. Not so Genoa: free enterprise and initiative bordered on anarchy; the state authorities had very little to say; commerce and immigration were as free as they could be in the most flexible medieval Communes. Restrictions in the trade of foreigners were gradually lifted; what little was left of them could easily be evaded if the stranger became naturalized. This he could do without any formality, as soon as he stated his intention of accepting all the duties of a citizen in return for all the privileges.

This policy was also adopted in the colonial empire Genoa acquired through war and still more through the commercial penetration of her private citizens. One did not have to be a Christian to enjoy full political and economic rights in most of the colonies; one did not always have to be on good terms with the Church to live peacefully in Genoa. The Albigensian heretics found toleration. There was no record, in the entire history of Genoa, of persecution of the Jews, although the Commune found a way to lighten the expenses for the illumination of the cathedral by requiring the Jews to pay their share.

This does not mean that Genoa was indifferent to religion. Every business contract begins with the invocation, *In nomine Domini amen,* and contained such pious inserts as "the profit which the Lord will give us," "the loss against which may the Lord guard us," "the voyage in which the Lord will guide us." But the laws of business were supreme in their own sphere and were not to be set aside for any principle of canon law. "Against those who pretend that contracts of exchange and of insurance are illegal and usurious . . . according to the Scriptures . . . and have recourse to ecclesiastical courts and magistrates in order to obtain delays of payment . . . since if these contracts were not honored . . . this would result in great loss and inconvenience to the citizens and merchants of Genoa . . . let any person bringing forward such cavils . . . be condemned in good justice to pay one half pound fine for every pound he will have refused to pay." Such were the words of a decree of the Genoese Commune in 1369.

Medieval Genoa had its faults. Dante, who always had a nice word to say about his neighbors, called the Genoese "shirkers of every tradition and ridden with every blemish." Among the charges most frequently made against the Genoese were: insatiable greed for money, addiction to conspicuous consumption, propensity to tax evasion, ruthless competition with weaker neighbors, bragging, loose morals.

All this has a familiar ring. Probably the larger cities tend to indulge in larger sins, but sins may be found in Peyton Place as well as in New York.

Believe it or not, in the thirteenth century, Paris was more sedate than Genoa. Although Parisian ladies already were setting the fashion for ribbons and hats throughout Europe, clergymen and clerks there were usually too impecunious to lead a very gay life. Yet Paris, too, had been slipping. Almost a thousand years ago, one Raoul Glaber complained that she was a nest of effeminate strangers in short gowns, pacifists, atheists, cheats, and thieves. "Were it not for God's great mercy delaying His wrath," he said, "Hell would devour these people with its frightful-roaring mouth!"

Today, in the midst of nuclear science and racial folly, cities are still leading in economics and technology, still lending themselves to severe charges. "Megalopolis" has again been denounced in the latest book of one of its most spirited citizens. But mercy has delayed wrath for a thousand years. Let us hope it will continue to do so, for another thousand years at least!

Bibliographic Orientation

On ancient cities, only incidentally discussed in the present paper, the following works supply brief accounts and references for further reading: R. E. Turner, *The Great Cultural Traditions* (2 vols., New York, 1941); A. H. M. Jones, *The Greek City from Alexander to Justinian* (Oxford, 1940); L. Homo, *Rome impériale et l'urbanisme dans l'antiquité* (Paris, 1951).

The multilingual symposium of the Centro Italiano di Studi sull'Alto Medioevo, *La Città nell'alto medioevo* (Spoleto, 1959), though devoted chiefly to the early middle ages, is the best and most recent general discussion of all problems concerning medieval cities in Europe. Another, larger symposium of the Société Jean Bodin, *La Ville* (2 vols., Brussels, 1955–56), deals with all urban history very unevenly, in papers of various types and quality ranging from excellent to below par. H. Pirenne, *Medieval Cities* (Princeton, N. J., 1925), bears the imprint of a superior mind, but is too short and outdated on many important points. M. V. Clarke, *The Medieval City State* (London, 1926), short and unimaginative, is helpful for constitutional developments. J. H. Mundy and P. Riesenberg, *The Medieval Town* (New York, 1958), includes a concise introduction and a few useful documents in translation. The three medieval volumes of *Cambridge Economic History* offer a good deal of bibliographic information and review many aspects of the economic life of the European towns, but are not directly concerned with urban history.

All told, it is inevitable to resort to regional studies, but the coverage is uneven. One book, J. Lestocquoy, *Les Villes de Flandre et d'Italie sous le gouvernement des patriciens* (Paris, 1952), attempts an interesting comparison between the leading classes of two countries.

Italy, the home of the most successful medieval cities, has virtually no general work on the urban problem: every city is a world in itself, and the sum of urban history is the largest component of the history of the country. The lectures of A. Frugoni, *Storia della città in Italia* (Rome, 1957), though highly perceptive, are no more than a program for a book. For the early middle ages, P. Brezzi, *I Comuni cittadini italiani, origine e primitiva costituzione* (Milan, 1940), supplies a good collection of untranslated documents with valuable introductions; another collection, not limited to Italy but stressing the economic aspects of its urban history, is R. S. Lopez and I. W. Raymond, *Medieval Trade in the Mediterranean World* (2nd ed., New York, 1961). For the period from 1200 to 1500, E. R. Labande, *L'Italie de la Renaissance* (Paris, 1954), offers an agreeable survey and bibliographic information. Still, there is no real substitute for the individual histories of the principal cities, too many to be listed here. On Genoa, used as an example in the present paper, see the references in R. S. Lopez, "Le Marchand génois, un profil collectif," *Annales* (*Economies, Sociétés, Civilisations*), XIII (1958).

Belgium, second only to Italy in urban development, presents the same problems. There has been no general work on urban history after the memorable, but partly outdated studies of H. Pirenne, *Les Villes et les institutions urbaines* (4th ed., Paris-Brussels, 1939). A suggestive, but very short essay of H. van Werveke, "Les villes belges," in the symposium *La Ville*, II (mentioned above), summarizes the results of more recent research. Excellent monographs on individual cities are still piling up: A. Joris, *La Ville de Huy au moyen âge* (Paris, 1959) is a recent example.

France as a whole is covered in a most erudite, but too rigidly legalistic volume of Ch. Petit-Dutaillis, *Les Communes françaises* (Paris, 1947): the author leaves Paris out, on the ground that it had no communal charter! A. Luchaire, *Les Communes françaises* (2nd ed., Paris, 1911), and P. Viollet, *Les Communes françaises au moyen âge* (Paris, 1900), are outdated but still useful on certain aspects. In spite of its modest title, the posthumous work of F. Lot, *Recherches sur la population et la superficie des cités remontant á la période gallo-romaine* (4 vols., Paris, 1945–54), is tantamount to an urban history of France in monographic form.

Spain is covered in several good regional studies, all of them cited in the most recent one: L. G. de Valdeavellano, *Sobre los Burgos y los burgueses de la España medieval* (Madrid, 1960). For Portugal one can use two monographs on special aspects, V. Rau, *Subsidio para o estudio das feiras medievais portuguesas* (Lisbon, 1943), and T. B. de Sousa Soares, *Apontamentos para o estudio da origem das istituçoēs municipais portuguesas* (Lisbon, 1931).

On English towns, there has been no general book after the scholarly debate between C. Stephenson, *Borough and Town* (Cambridge, Mass., 1933), and J. Tait, *The Medieval English Borough* (Manchester, 1936), but some general views are offered in the essays of H. Cam, *Liberties and Communities in Medieval England* (Cambridge, 1944), and in J. Clapham, *A Concise Economic History of Britain*, I (Cambridge, 1949).

For Germany, H. Planitz, *Die deutsche Stadt im Mittelalter* (Graz-Cologne, 1954), stresses Southern German towns and the early period; F. Rörig, *Die Europäische Stadt im Mittelalter* (Göttingen, 1955), stresses Northern German towns and the later period. On Scandinavian towns, in languages other than theirs, one can use the relevant parts of the excellent book by L. Musset, *Les Peuples scandinaves au moyen âge* (Paris, 1951), and the papers of F. Lindberg, "La Baltique et l'historiographie scandinave," *Annales (Economies, Sociétés, Civilisations)*, XVI (1961) and A. E. Christensen, "Scandinavia and the Advance of the Hanseatics," *Scandinavian Economic History Review*, V (1957).

On Russian towns, in the middle ages, M. N. Tikhomirov, *The Towns of Ancient Russia* (Moscow, 1959) is useful but unimaginative; shorter but crisper views may be obtained from the pamphlet of A. V. Artsikhovski, *Nouvelles Découvertes à Novgorod* (Moscow, 1955), issued for the Xth Congress of History in Rome, or from the relevant parts of G. Vernadsky, *Kievan Russia* (New Haven, 1948). A symposium, in Western European countries has appeared in the Polish magazine *Ergon*, III under the title: *L'artisanat et la vie urbaine en Pologne médiévale* (Warsaw, 1962). On Czech towns, see also F. G. Heymann, "The Role of the Towns in the Bohemia of the Later Middle Ages," *Journal of World History*, II (1954).

There is no good book on the Byzantine towns, but G. I. Bratianu, *Privilèges et franchises municipales dans l'empire byzantin* (Paris, Bucharest, 1934), explores one aspect of urban history. Some other aspects are briefly examined in L. Bréhier, *Le Monde byzantin* (3 vols., Paris 1948–50), II, 186–218 and III, 77–148, and in the essays by G. Ostrogorsky, P. Charanis, R. S. Lopez, J. L. Teall in *Dumbarton Oaks Papers*, XII (1959).

It has been unfortunately impossible to include in the paper even a fleeting discussion of urban civilizations outside the Christian world. Let the reader who wishes at least an introduction read the papers of G. E. von Grunebaum, "The Structure of the Muslim Town," in his *Islam, Essays*. (Chicago, 1955); S. D. Goitein, "The Rise of the Near Eastern Bourgeoisie," *Journal of World History*, III (1957); J. W. Hall, "The Castle Town and Japan's Modern Urbanization," *Far Eastern Quarterly*, XV (1955); A. F. Wright, "Life and Death of a Cosmopolis: Ch'ang-an" (at present, available only in mimeographed form).

Finally, is it necessary to point out that a good proportion of what happened in history occurred in towns, and hence there is hardly a work of medieval economic, social, intellectual, political, artistic history that is wholly irrelevant. Here are, at random, four examples of such works: R. Mols, *Introduction à la démographie historique des villes d'Europe du XIVe au XVIIIe siècle* (3 vols., Louvain, 1954–1956); L. Torres Balbas et al., *Resumen historico del urbanismo en Espana* (Madrid, 1954); Ph. Wolff, *Histoire générale du travail, Le Moyen Age* (Paris, 1961); S. Stelling-Michaud, report on medieval universities in *XIe Congrès International des Sciences Historiques,* I (Stockholm, 1960).

The Economic Significance of Cities

SHIGETO TSURU

Agglomeration of population beyond a certain degree of density per area,[1] that is to say, emergence of a city, comes about with a certain minimum rise of productivity based on the division of labor. The division of labor depends, as Adam Smith pointed out two centuries ago, upon the size of the market; and the size of the market, in turn, depends on productivity. Here is an instance of

[1] Of course, it is impossible, and also unnecessary, to draw a hard and fast line on demographic density in defining a city for all purposes. If some indication is required, we might refer to the arbitrary level chosen by the Indian Census of 1951, i.e. "not less than one thousand inhabitants to the square mile." This criterion will obviously fail in a country like Japan where farming is done so intensively that one square mile (256 hectares) of cultivable land often supports 320 farm families, or possibly 1440 inhabitants.

"circular causation" [2] which characterizes a large part of socio-economic phenomena, in particular the economic phenomena, in particular the economic aspect of urbanization. In a particular situation the progress in the division of labor may give impetus to the emergence of a city as a market place, or the pre-existing agglomeration of people (for whatever reason) may stimulate further progress in the division of labor. In either case, the relation becomes mutually reinforcing for very good economic reasons. The progress of productivity in transportation and communication, which initially may have been stimulated by the economic logic of a market place, in turn enables expansion of the size of the market and this makes possible a further proliferation of the division of labor and consequently, a rise in productivity.

The evolution of cities during the past three hundred years, which manifested clearly this mutually reinforcing character of their economic functions, had in its background the evolution of a socio-economic system which we call capitalism. Capitalism is essentially an order of atomistic units in which profit-and-loss accounting of each unit independently of any other provides a signal for action. Order on the social scale, or even on the international scale, is presumably maintained through the "Invisible Hand" of unfettered competition. The economic rationale of the growth of cities can best be described in terms of a conceptual framework which separates as "external economies" those positive contributions to the rise in productivity which cannot be directly attributed to the action of the individual accounting unit in the system, i.e., of the private individual firm. In other words, *the economic significance of cities lies in the external economies they provide.*

We must here clarify the concept of external economies and its counterpart, that of external diseconomies. The term "external economies," was originally used by Alfred Marshall [3] to refer to those economies arising from an increase in the scale of production "dependent on the general development of the industry" and not on "the resources of the individual houses of business engaged in it." His concern was mainly with analysis of "the economies arising

[2] See G. Myrdal, *Rich Lands and Poor*, 1957.
[3] See A. Marshall, *Principles of Economics* (Eighth ed.), 266.

from an increase in the scale of production," and furthermore was restricted to intra-industry economies. As the term came to be used more and more, its application widened to cover also inter-industry economies, the economies external to one industry due to the growth of other industries. It then became apparent that the economies involved were not necessarily the function of the enlarged scale only.[4] The factor of inter-industry complementarities has come to be recognized as equally, if not more, important. The term "external economies" therefore now covers all those interstitial economies, either technical or pecuniary,[5] which arise independently of the resources of atomistic firms. If a subway line is opened, the surface intersection at the station will suddenly become busy and retailing opportunities will be enhanced. The location in this case has a complementarity value in connecting the transportation system with an office area or a residential section; and we speak of the benefits enjoyed by retailers as "external economies."

As the example just offered enables us to see, external economies can be appropriated by a private economic unit. A corner drugstore at the subway stop will suddenly be able to expand its sales; and, within limits, the storekeeper has a choice of lowering mark-up profits on goods he sells and thus expanding the radius of his customer area, or of garnering a greater absolute volume of profit with prices unchanged. When he has such a choice, the site value of land also rises; and if there is a transfer of ownership, the appropriation of external economies takes place partly in the form of capital gains. This process is wholly predictable. Thus it is quite conceivable that a subway company intending to develop a line buys up strategic pieces of land in advance, reaping capital gains on the rise in value. This type of situation is called "the internalization of external economies."

Just as cases of external economies arise through complementarities of all kinds, so do external diseconomies through concurrence of incidents in a particular situation. Pigou's classic example refers to the nuisance suffered by housewives who attempt to dry laundries outdoors near a factory with an active smokestack. In this case, the households may be compensated for the inconvenience through a lower house rent. But external diseconomies which

[4] It must be stated that Marshall himself was aware of this. See *ibid.*, 441.
[5] If external economies enable a firm to reduce the real input per unit-output, they are "technical." If they enable a firm to reduce the cost of unit input, they are "pecuniary."

arise in a modern city are in fact so complex in their nexus of causation that the extent of compensatory accounting expected of private individual economic units is extremely limited. In other words, in a private enterprise economy, the problem of "internalization" has not been symmetrical as regards external economies and diseconomies. The following observation by Hirschman, although it refers mainly to the nineteenth-century capitalism, expresses this point eloquently:

From the point of view of investment incentives, the capitalist system, especially as it existed in the nineteenth century, is hard to beat: there was a minimum of internalization of external diseconomies and there was no limitation on the internalization of pecuniary external economies through acquisitions, combinations, or mergers with closely interdependent economic activities.[6]

From the social point of view, a certain combination of socioeconomic incidents may involve both external economies and diseconomies, and we may abstractly speak of net economies or diseconomies of external character. The contention of this paper is that:

1. In the early stage of capitalistic development, cities provided a large measure of external economies which could be privately appropriated, and thus they had a strong economic rationale.

2. With the development of modern technology, some of the erstwhile external economies were diluted while external diseconomies grew more and more substantial; and thus it is becoming increasingly uncertain whether there are still net external economies or not.

3. Society's concern with external diseconomies has become more and more heightened; and some degree of their internalization is now expected of private firms.

4. The very indivisibilities, which contribute to the peculiar complementarities and thus to the external economies, observed in cities, make it difficult for established cities to adjust themselves to the requirements of dynamic technological changes without incurring heavy cost. Thus planning for urban renewal today constitutes a particularly challenging field which calls for an integrated effort of several disciplines as well as a marriage of forward-looking vision with factual analysis.

[6] A. O. Hirschman, *The Strategy of Economic Development* (1958), 58.

The external economies commonly observed in the agglomeration of population in modern times are correlated to changing technological innovations and therefore differ in relative importance according to the various phases of capitalist development in which they exist. For general purposes we may enumerate the following aspects:

1. The city as a nerve center of commercial activities.
2. The city itself as a market.
3. The city as an industrial center.

As the division of labor progresses with the extension of the market, the act of commerce which is implied in this situation calls for a nerve center. The efficiency of such a nerve-center will depend economically upon the degree to which it can draw external economies from a convenient network of transportation and port facilities and of communications, from financial institutions, and from the proximity to those sources of information which affect the reliability of commercial decisions. The last item includes, among other things, nearness to a political and administrative center; and in some countries, it is of considerable significance. For example in Japan, the external economies emanating from this source are of sufficient value that practically every commercial firm with a seat of operation in Osaka finds it necessary to incur the cost of a significant branch office in Tokyo, four hundred miles away, for information-gathering purposes.

That the city itself constitutes a convenient market for consumers' goods is obvious. Not only the density of population but also a certain demonstration effect common in urban life creates special external economies for sellers of mass consumption goods. It is in services, however, that the city as a market provides unique external economies. Services are by nature nontransportable; the barber's service has to be accepted at the site and at the moment of its performance. Agglomeration of population makes possible the growth of various service industries. Especially since the city tends to become the residential site for the elite class, whose demand for various forms of services is generally high, it provides unique external economies for tertiary industry as a whole. This relation *ipso facto* reinforces the agglomeration and strengthens the city as a market. It is universally observed that the occupational composition of the urban labor force is highly slanted towards the tertiary industry.

External economies provided by the city in giving locational convenience for industrial establishments were of unique importance in the early stage of capitalist development. An industrial factory required the supply, in a fairly dense concentration, of wage laborers who were "free" not only in the sense of "free to enter into the wage contract with an employer," but also in the sense of "free from attachment to the means of production such as land property." The agglomeration of population which constituted a city provided such a supply, either as an antecedent condition for, or as a consequence of, the establishment of factories. After that, modern industrial establishments also needed easy access to the supply of qualified personnel, such as engineers and other staff members; and it was doubtless easier to recruit these people in the city because of its cultural, educational, and medical facilities about which they cared. Both of these external economies, however, may not be so important now as in the early days of capitalist development. Technological developments in transportation and communication, as well as the multiplication of external diseconomies in a large city, have contributed to an increasing trend of dispersion of industrial establishments. Nevertheless, it is still true that the external economy of transportation and communication facilities continues to be a controlling factor for industrial establishments today.

The external economies of cities become the object of "internalization" and thus enhance the profitability of private business situated in cities. They may also make place for what Schumpeter called "interference of income"[7] and help support varied categories of tertiary employment. Either development strengthens the economic rationale of cities.

This picture of cities prospering on external economies, however, is relevant largely to capitalist societies of a generation or more ago. Various technological developments, starting with the effective use of electric power and the mass use of automobiles,

[7] Where there is an opportunity to internalize external economies to yield large profit, such profit tends to be shared by intermediaries who "interfere" by claiming income to themselves on the basis of their specialized service. A pecuniarily important part of the function of real estate dealers partakes of the character of this phenomenon.

The Economic Significance of Cities / 49

have given rise to a new configuration of forces, working very often in a centrifugal manner in relation to erstwhile centers of population agglomeration. The current flowering of innovations, which are for good reason characterized as the "scientific-industrial revolution," no doubt has far-reaching implications for the external economies of cities. It appears certain that the classic types of external economies of cities will be further modified and that the city planning of this new era will call for special insight into the significance of the latest technological changes.

Social Cost Accounting of External Economies and Diseconomies of Cities

The essence of the private enterprise economy is that the cost accounting is self-contained with respect to each economic unit. Otherwise, the imputation of profit to atomistic units is not possible. External economies and diseconomies of cities imply both benefits and costs, which may or may not be internalized. In addition, beneficiaries of the former, generally speaking, are private firms, while those who suffer from the latter tend to be the general public; and the benefits and costs cannot be brought into confrontation with each other within a single accounting unit. Furthermore, municipalities, too, are not in the habit of making a balance sheet on them.

Take, for example, the cost implications of external economies. It has been suggested by some that a part of the historical explanation for the North-South economic disparity in Italy is the somewhat one-sided expenditure by the central government in the North for defense purposes. All the garrisons were in the North. Military roads were constructed in the North. Even the arsenal which used to be located in Naples was moved to the North because Naples was vulnerable to bombing from the sea. All these things helped generate external economies for industrial development in the North; but the cost was shared by the nation as a whole. In fact, the regressive character of the Italian tax system probably caused the South to pay more than its *pro rata* share in terms of its value-added production. Here, then, is a case of one region enjoying certain external economies, the cost for which was paid by another region.

There is, of course, nothing unusual about this situation. A large part of social overhead structures, which create external economies, is built or established by governmental bodies through the use of public funds. In most cases, even the direct beneficiaries of them are not expected to pay in strict accordance with the benefit they receive, let alone the indirect beneficiaries who enjoy external economies incidental to the existence of such structures.

It is noteworthy, however, that there has been a fairly well-marked evolution in capitalist societies in the attitudes toward the need for counteracting external diseconomies as well as toward the question of who is to bear the burden of cost for counteracting them. There was a time, as reported by Walter Quebedeaux, Jr.,[8] when a smoke-abatement law was strictly enforced in England, so much so that one violator of the law, which prohibited the use of coal as detrimental to health, was prosecuted, condemned, and executed. But this was in 1307, that is, some time before a modern capitalist society came into being. As capitalism evolved, it nurtured the philosophy of *laissez faire*, according to which atomistic economic units were to be left free to pursue the aim of maximizing their own respective profit untrammelled by controls or interference of the government. "The Invisible Hand" was to take care of the task of harmonizing conflicting interests for social welfare. At this stage of capitalism the characterization by Hirschman, "there was a minimum of internalization of external diseconomies," was relevant.

However, two forces have changed the picture substantially in recent decades. A series of technological developments have aggravated the external diseconomies of cities, and increasing public concern over such diseconomies has fostered the view that private firms should internalize some of these external diseconomies. These two forces combined have given rise to the secondary, but no less important, consequence of exodus from cities of upper income families and of some private concerns, thereby "increasing the complexities cities must cope with and decreasing the resources with which they must do the coping." [9]

Some of the external diseconomies have become more and more serious lately. Air pollution, of course, is at least as old as the first smoke-abatement law of England of 1273. But the degree of

[8] In a paper read before a session of the 54th Annual Meeting of the Air Pollution Control Association on June 12, 1961.
[9] Joseph S. Clark, "To Come to the Aid of Their Cities," *New York Times Magazine* (April 30, 1961), 11.

pollution today is incomparably more serious, especially as numerous automobiles emit fumes into the city air.[10] Water pollution, on the other hand, may be said to be less of a problem for most cities inasmuch as they now are equipped with hygienic systems for which necessary expenditures are not spared. However, here and there rapidly growing cities suffer from chronic water shortages with which they seem never to be able to catch up. The tapping of subterranean water in such circumstances has created a serious problem of ground-level subsidence in some cities. Next, the traffic problem looms as probably the most serious diseconomy of modern cities with high density of automobile use. Diseconomy here could be counteracted by the expenditure of sufficient money for multi-level intersection roads, tunnels, and underground parking lots. To that extent, the diseconomy can be translated into additional cost for users. Even then, the speed with which one can exit from the center of a city necessarily is affected by congestion;[11] and it is not easy to retain the beauty of city landscape when a structural monster of multi-level intersection intrudes in the interest of the traffic convenience. Less direct than the above in their logical connection with the agglomeration of population are such manifestations of external diseconomies as slum areas and juvenile delinquency; but these are nonetheless characteristic of modern cities along with varied forms of vice, notably the organized gambling which in many cities defies the law or, still worse, is in collusion with the agent of the law.

Even in a society where the private enterprise system is dominant, general awareness of external diseconomies has lately been heightened, and public opinion is favoring more and more either the direct internalization of external diseconomies by private enterprises, or the sharing by residents of cost incurred by municipalities in counteracting such diseconomies. The financial capability of geographically defined municipal governments, however, is becoming increasingly inadequate in coping with the problem; and advocates of federal assistance in this regard are rapidly increasing in

[10] It may be noted in this connection that New York City finally warned major automobile manufacturers on June 4, 1961, to install anti-fume devices on their new cars voluntarily or run the risk of being compelled to do so. Previous to this, the Automobile Manufacturers Association had rejected a request by the Secretary of Health, Education and Welfare that the industry install the anti-pollution device.

[11] Cf. *Fortune* (October 1957), 158–159.

number.[12] What is required now seems to be a new frame of reference in dealing with economic problems of cities such that their social cost accounting can be rationally spelled out in the light of latest technological developments which affect the configuration of a modern metropolis. When this is done, the old idea of local autonomy, as well as the capitalistic tenet of self-contained atomistic accounting, may be found somewhat obsolete.

Tasks for the Future

A speedway bypassing the downtown congestion would establish its usefulness only when it is completed over a sufficient distance. A railroad terminal in a city without the ancillary structures, such as side-tracks for freight, would be like a school building without classrooms. In other words, many of the structures which contribute to the complementarities which are observed in cities do so because of their indivisibilities or, in a more expressive terminology, of their lumpiness. Furthermore, such structures are generally durable, lasting several decades or more for economic use. When a structure which contributes to external economies of a city is by nature lumpy and is at the same time durable for good reason, the marginal type of adjustment to a new situation, characteristic of a large part of rational economic action, has to be ruled out. Once a structure is built and completed, we will have to put up with it for some time even when we find that it stands in the way of something newer and better. Since municipalities are not run on the basis of private profit-and-loss accounting, the principle of accelerated obsolescence has broad room for application here so long as they command sufficient financial resources. But here again, social cost accounting is in order; and the opportunity cost in social terms may be quite exorbitant.

This point explains why so many cities suffer from the backlog of tasks for urban renewal—despite structure and configurations obviously made obsolescent by technological and other developments which dilute the erstwhile external economies and aggravate or create external diseconomies. An additional reason, inherent in the system of private enterprise economy, for the difficulty of drastic, large-scale, adjustment stems from the fact that the existing

[12] Senator Joseph Clark's article, cited earlier, is an example of this trend.

complementarities create private vested interests in the form of opportunities for internalizing external economies—vested interests which are inextricably tied to the system of private ownership of land and structures. A large-scale urban renewal can easily shift the configuration of external economies and cause windfall profits to some and calamitous losses to others. Whenever a single act is capable of causing both, and the compensation of loss by profits cannot easily be arranged, a stalemate is likely to be the result.

What, then, should we conclude from these observations in mapping our tasks for the future as cities become more and more enmeshed in the multiplying complexities of technological innovations?

First, it is obvious that the problem of cities today awaits cooperation of experts in several disciplines on a level far higher and more integrated than has hitherto been the case. In particular, the economists must play a much greater role in this cooperative task than they have in the past.

Second, because of indivisibilities and durability of structures which form the basis of external economies of cities and because recurring technological innovations require a new configuration of structures in order for net external economies to be maximized, a special degree of foresight and boldness, coupled with flexibility, is needed in present-day city planning, and once a plan is decided on, its execution had better be steadfast and unflinching. A technologically advanced city in a technologically advanced country may not be able to avoid groping and fumbling, but others which follow should be able to learn from the lessons of the forerunner.

Third, it might be proposed that economists interested in these problems engage in empirical research on social cost accounting of external economies and diseconomies of modern cities. A comparative study of cities in capitalist, socialist societies which brought out the differing effects upon this problem of different modes of ownership of land and structural properties would be especially rewarding.

Fourth, as we focus more and more on the aspect of the problem which we call external economies and diseconomies, quite possibly we shall be led to question the rationality of atomistic cost accounting in the context of the present-day technological development. In fact, the very concept of *external* economies and diseconomies presupposes the dominant light in which we regard the atomistic cost accounting. Rethinking on the matter may well call for a new conceptual frame of reference in dealing with the cost-benefit implications of urban configuration. At the same time, self-contained accounting by a municipal unit with old boundaries may no longer be able to claim rationality. Instead of viewing federal assistance, for example, as an "encroachment" on local autonomy or at best as something abnormal or extraordinary, we would do better to recast our thinking in terms of national responsibilities for metropolitan affairs. The problem which taxes democratic societies today, and not solely in the sphere of urban problems, is how to harmonize the tenet of decentralized decision-making with the increasing need for social and national orientation.

City Economies—Then and Now

ALEXANDER GERSCHENKRON

The following remarks were intended as an introduction to a critical discussion of the papers by Messrs. Lopez and Tsuru. They should not be read independently of those two papers.

A specific difficulty in social sciences stems from the frequent desire of the scholar to elevate a species that appeals to him to the rank of a genus or a well-liked genus to that of a family. A zoologist may be very fond of tigers, but he still would hesitate to claim that they alone compose the cat family. Professor Lopez' reference to the Egyptian symbol for the city—the cross within a circle, the wall and the crossroads—is admirable both because it is so illuminating for some types of medieval towns and because it illustrates the urge to let a favored subcategory drop its prefix.

No one would want to quarrel with the appropriateness of the circle. No one will deny that the nature of some important medieval cities is very properly intimated by a symbol which stands for a market serving long-distance trade. But are we really sure that there were no other medieval cities for which other inscribed symbols may be much more suitable? Is it just the cross and always the cross we want to put inside the circle? It is not difficult to think of a few different symbols which could be placed within the circle very fittingly: a compass or a hammer; perhaps a chisel; or a weaver's shuttle or a tailor's needle. In other words, is it legitimate in discussing the medieval city to forget so completely the industrial development that took place within its walls and that determined decisively the character of many, though by no means all, towns in medieval Europe? To repeat: also in this connection, the circle was of crucial importance. The texture of the circumvallation was as much of the spirit as it was of stones and mortar. If the medieval city had not been pared out from its environment, both physically and spiritually, it never would have become a powerful engine of economic change, a landmark in the industrial history of Europe.

One might be tempted, perhaps, following Professor Tsuru, to discuss that change in terms of external economies which were created and effectively utilized in the city. To be sure, we are all masters of our own terms and we can call external economies whatever we please. This particular case, however, seems to be much too big for the concept and strains it beyond all the limits of reasonableness. The most striking innovation in medieval cities was the emergence of a new attitude toward manual labor. Perhaps for the first time in the history of Western civilization the stigma traditionally placed upon manual labor was obliterated. The work of the artisan became respectable, sometimes eminently so. In the process, that work became surrounded by a number of highly significant social attitudes. Nowadays, through a somewhat humorless misunderstanding of Max Weber's playful hypothesis, those attitudes are usually presented as effects of Protestantism upon the rise of capitalism. This is a regrettable historical distortion which works havoc with the chronology of the social history of Europe. For it was precisely within the institutional framework of the medieval cities, antedating by several centuries the emergence and the diffusion of Protestantism, that new attitudes toward labor, the product of labor, and the consumer of that product came into being. Like freedom, also thrift and steady industry seemed to come from the "city air." True, the individual artisan received them from the outside, "externally," as it were. But to relate them to external economies, to their impact upon the volume of inputs designed to produce a given output and/or upon the cost of given inputs, would not begin to do justice to the great transformation which was taking place and implied an altogether new concentration upon high quality outputs produced by a labor force informed by the instinct of workmanship.

To some extent, this process of change took place in all medieval cities in Western and Central Europe. Its full fruition was reached in those towns where, mostly in the course of the fourteenth century, the craft guilds succeeded in obtaining a considerable measure of influence upon the political life of the town. In important areas, such as the Flemish or the Italian cities, that influence remained small, but nothing can be gained by generalizing Antwerp or Florence into the paradigm of all medieval towns. That would excise from the industrial history of Europe a rich chapter whose contents reached far into the future. In the much more recent past, it made a good deal of difference whether a country did or did not go through that specific experience of medieval industrialization. It is a quite defensible proposition to say that at the turn of this century a country such as Russia found the road of industrialization ever so much more arduous precisely because she had never been through the training school of craft guilds in the medieval city. As a result, irregular work habits, carelessness and negligence, low time horizons, and frightening dishonesty remained endemic in Russia, constituting persistent handicaps to economic progress. Things which in Germany had been learned long before the advent of modern times, Russian entrepreneurs and workers, traders and artisans had to absorb painfully in belated haste in the midst of a rapid and costly spurt of industrial development.

It is, however, precisely the story of Russian industrialization and urbanization that strongly forces upon us the recognition that the concept of external economies is at best only one among a number of possible keys to the understanding of modern city development. The more backward countries on the European continent were plagued by exactly the same problem which other and more advanced regions had faced much earlier, that is, by the creation of the "city man." Much water had to go down under the arches of city bridges before the urban dweller was ready to strike roots in the city, to say farewell forever, not only to sunsets and roses, but also to the irregular, weather-determined pace of work, to accept the discipline of the factory, and to begin to find substitutes in the city newspaper and the technical and political pamphlets for the abandoned folklore, the song and the fairy tale, of the native village. Again, this transformation is to some extent expressible in terms of external economies; but it implies a broad dynamic view of urbanization which is very different from the abstract economy to which the tame textbook concepts of external economies—and diseconomies—are applicable, however useful those concepts may be in themselves.

On the other hand, if from the processes of city growth in relatively backward countries or areas we return to the fully developed modern countries, much of the economic advantages of the cities appear to be a story of yesteryear. The economic difference between the city and the countryside is no longer what it used to be. The external economies of the city have lost much of their charm. The result is a new process of change which takes the textile factories out of the traditional urban environment of Lowell and Lawrence, Lynn and Salem, and transposes them into the rural areas of South Carolina. The same change is visible everywhere. We can see it, for instance, in Vorarlberg, the westernmost province of Austria, where rural populations in the isolation of high Alpine valleys perform the job of industrial labor in factories that are enclosed in those valleys and perform it in the most efficient way with the help of most modern machinery.

We do not have to travel so far from Cambridge, Massachusetts, to see the new, the "unurban" way of doing things. All that is necessary is to move some sixty or seventy miles northwest into southern New Hampshire. As we do it we must cross the "electronic route," that is, Route 128, the circular artery which surrounds Greater Boston and is studded with electronic factories. These may still be considered as lying within the economic *Weichbild* of Boston. But in New Hampshire you see everywhere, amidst little towns with a population of some 1,500 people and in still smaller villages, factories representing the last word of modern technology. They produce electronic equipment, micro-ballbearings, and precision instruments, and are based altogether upon the indigenous labor of those villages.

Now what has made all that possible? The fact that the native of a New Hampshire hamlet does not require any change in his general philosophy nor any upgrading in his general education in order to become an efficient worker in the factory is only one of the factors involved. The difference between the rural man and the city man has all but vanished in most relevant respects. But surely no less important is the tremendous rise in incomes in what Professor Tsuru still persists in calling a capitalist society. (It would have been, incidentally, quite in order for him to consider that many things which are now regarded as diseconomies are only viewed as such because incomes have risen and men's wants have changed as a result.) Along with the rise in incomes there have been certain specific technological changes.

The locational pattern of a New Hampshire factory is very simple. The raw materials and the semifabricates are brought by the road. The finished materials leave the factory by the road, unless the daily output is taken each evening to the local post office and airmailed to the customers, as does, for instance, a micro-ballbearing factory whose annual sales go into many millions of dollars. The degree of fabrication per weight unit has become so high that cost of transportation would be a negligible item, even if the weight losses of raw materials were not so small. The factory can look for its labor force within a radius of some ten to fifteen miles. This is possible because every worker has a motor car at his or her disposal. At the same time, the high level of national income has not only created a superb road network, but also has enabled the states and the towns to set aside sufficient resources for maintaining the roads and keeping them open through the hardships and hazards of a New England winter. Finally, the availability of cheap electric power, reliably supplied, provides the last element in that highly decentralized pattern.

This, then, seems to be the modern trend. Professor Tsuru's presentation would have gained if he had paid more attention to it. On the other hand, I am somewhat dubious about his suggestion that comparisons between capitalist and socialist societies may be illuminating in the study of urban policies that may be pursued now. I am not sure at all that the nineteenth century dichotomy of capitalism and socialism still deserves any place in a serious scholarly discussion in the second half of the twentieth century. It may be time to forget about that head of Charles the First. If the rise in incomes and technological progress are the main ingredients of change, we may expect them to assert themselves whether the institutional framework be called socialist or capitalist.

To say this, however, is not to deny a specific point. I take it that when Professor Tsuru speaks of socialist countries he wishes to include Soviet Russia among them. If this be the case, I am willing to admit that the government system that exists in the Soviet Union constitutes an effective hindrance to an industrial flight from the city as I have described it in the foregoing paragraphs.

Let me digress for a moment. The industrial laborer in New Hampshire finds very modern shopping centers, which include large supermarkets, erected in the midst of forests and lakes. In addition, the factory, anxious to keep the labor force satisfied, maintains connections with discount houses in order to provide the workers, and that perforce means everybody living in the area, with durable consumers' goods at low wholesale prices, thus introducing a new and very efficient system of distribution. This is part and parcel of the decentralized locational pattern. Such a pattern is still largely impossible in Soviet Russia. It is impossible first of all because the supermarket and self-service systems presuppose a level of incomes which allows the individual family to own an automobile and a refrigerator. It is impossible, second, because out of a given per capita income in Russia a much larger share is devoted to investment and military expenditures at the expense of consumption. This is the effect of the Soviet government system to which a decentralized industrial pattern which includes decentralized living conditions of the labor force is hardly acceptable. A dictatorial government prefers to see people live in large city blocks, in apartments through the walls of which sound travels freely (as one knows from multifarious references in Soviet novels), and where appropriate supervision of the inmates can be exercised by the appropriate authorities. It is doubtful, therefore, that those interested in urban policies in the United States have anything to learn from Russia; it is equally doubtful that Soviet Russia can afford to learn anything from the recent developments in the United States.

It is true, of course, that these developments are still passing through their early stages. The dead hand of the past loosens its grip but slowly, and the conventional cities are going to be with us for a long time to come. Naturally, a great deal will depend upon the rate of economic growth in the United States. If we succeed in achieving and maintaining a high rate of growth, the process of decentralization will proceed at an accelerated pace because a growing portion of the accretions to output is likely to be produced in the new locational environment. In more than one sense, this process is the consummation of a chain of events which began some six or eight centuries ago in the medieval cities of Europe. The "circle" is no longer necessary. It is going to disappear, but it is unlikely to be forgotten. For it has served mankind well, and truly great things have been accomplished within its charmed circumference.

Innovation and the Industrialization of Philadelphia 1800–1850

SAM B. WARNER, JR.

Today urbanization, technological innovation, and economic development are inescapable trends, the prominence of which raises questions about the relationships among them. Both in backward and advanced countries economic and physical planners would like to know if there are any connections between cities in general, or cities of a particular type, and rates of innovation and development. Only a general theory of sociology and economics which could simultaneously comprehend the culture and the region, the city and the labor force, the firm and the individual could satisfactorily answer such questions. At present no such general theory exists and it does not seem likely that one will soon appear. Nevertheless, cities are building and choices between alternatives must be made.

In such a situation descriptions of past experience can at least protect planners from popular oversimplifications.

Philadelphia provides an excellent case for development study.[1] Since the late eighteenth century it has continued to be one of the world's large industrial cities and is, therefore, by definition, a successful industrial environment. Its experience during the first half of the nineteenth century suggests that a city may simultaneously fulfill many roles. During the years 1800–1850 Philadelphia provided for some industries a nourishing environment for technological innovation; for others it passively received new technology which had been introduced and demonstrated elsewhere; in still other industries the city successfully resisted change for several decades.

It is useful to divide the process of technological innovation into two parts, invention and the adoption of invention. The large cities of northeastern United States do not seem to have been major invention environments during the first half of the nineteenth century. Rather the functional area of invention was the Atlantic region. The least dimensions of this region were England and Scotland, New England, New York, and Pennsylvania. Inventors moved from place to place within this region. Although the points of concentration of a particular industry, Lowell and Lawrence, Massachusetts, Hartford, Connecticut, and Providence, Rhode Island stand out as centers, no grouping of small industrial cities would adequately encompass the inventions of the period. Every town in the region had its tinkerers; talented inventors sprang up everywhere; both amateurs and professionals. Multiple invention was frequent, and often as not the appearance of a particular inventor in a town marked the beginning of a new industry for that place. The extreme variety of circumstances which surrounded each inventor does not suggest any common ecological pattern beyond that of the culture of the Atlantic region.[2]

[1] Professor Garvan in discussing the influence of the American Revolution upon Penn's plan for Philadelphia raises the same questions of cultural scale as are dealt with in this paper. He demonstrates the necessity of dealing simultaneously with both the extra-urban forces and the city itself in any account of urban change. A similar conclusion is worked out in detail in John Coolidge's *Mill and Mansion, A Study of Architecture and Society in Lowell, Massachusetts, 1820–1865* (New York, 1942).

[2] The cases for this paper have been taken from the cotton and woolen goods, rug, boot and shoe, and foundry and machine industries. The history of each significant invention can be followed in: Samuel Webber, *Manual of Power for Machines, Shafts, and Belts with the History of Cotton Manufacture in the U. S.*

influence of Chicago and read intellectual history of Gilded Age — City of the Gilded Age & Speculation

(The history of the industrialization of Philadelphia during the first half of the nineteenth century thus becomes the history of a city responding to the general Atlantic culture of innovation. In 1800 the city appeared peculiarly well adapted to take advantage of either local or outside inventions.) Capital was plentiful; the city was and remained for most of the next fifty years the banking center of the nation. It was also America's scientific capital. The American Philosophical Society attracted papers from all over the nation and its interest in practical subjects led to many investigations of commercially useful topics. In 1824 a group of Philadelphia merchants and manufacturers created the Franklin Institute. Its exhibits, lectures, publications, and prizes attracted wide attention.

(The city was also the home of a number of important engineers and inventors.) In 1798 Benjamin Latrobe had erected the large Center Square steam pumps for the city's water works. In the 1780's, while John Fitch's steamboats travelled up and down the Delaware, Robert Fulton lived in Philadelphia making a living as a miniature painter. Oliver Evans came to the city in 1786 and for many years his shop turned out a steady stream of new machines. He especially made improvements in high pressure steam engines and flour milling and textile machinery.

(Finally, the mixed business and government climate of the city and state actively advanced the industrialization of the city.) Businessmen controlled the city government and had a strong voice in the legislature. From the late eighteenth century until the depression of 1842 the state and city aided and carried out a host of transportation improvements. Most immediately important for Philadelphia's manufactures was the Schuylkill River development. Begun in the eighteenth century and completed in the 1820's, this network of canals and dams provided power for suburban textile mills and anthracite for the city's foundries. Public subscriptions of businessmen had created and supported the United Company for Promoting American Manufactures, an organization which introduced

(New York, 1879), Pt. 2, 1–57; Arthur H. Cole, *The American Wool Manufacture* (Cambridge, 1926), I; Arthur H. Cole and Harold F. Williamson, *The American Carpet Manufacture* (Cambridge, 1941); Frederic A. Gannon, *A Short History of American Shoemaking* (Salem, 1912); Joseph W. Roe, *English and American Tool Builders* (New Haven, 1916). For a detailed description of the culture of invention, Sigfried Giedion, *Mechanization Takes Command* (Cambridge, 1948).

historian as lawyer: the TRUTH is not as important as how well you present your case; the accepted way.

carding machines and spinning jennies to the city in 1776. In the late eighteenth century, also, the state legislature gave financial aid and monopolies to inventors. Philadelphia was the home of Matthew Carey, the leader of the American movement for the protection of infant industries by tariffs. Although this business and government climate was not unique in America, its presence seemed to promise as favorable a situation for the acceptance of innovation as could be found in the country.[3]

The industrialization of the city in the next fifty years was neither uniform, orderly, nor peaceful. In 1850, as in 1800, the city was one of the largest manufacturing concentrations of the world. Outside the city there had grown up a modern, fully mechanized cotton industry. Within the city small machine spinning shops and thousands of hand weavers carried on an extensive woolen, satinet, and rug business. This pattern persisted in Philadelphia despite the mechanization of these lines in mills in New England, New York, Ohio, and Pittsburgh. The city's boot and shoe industry had been made over into an extensive national business. As in other American shoe regions, production remained entirely the hand work of contractors' shops and some domestic craftsmen. The ornament of the city was its machine and foundry trades. In this case a nice complementarity of shops of all sizes and specialties made Philadelphia into one efficient and productive iron works. The city's machine tool and locomotive plants were among the most advanced in the world. They generated innovations of their own and also were connected by personnel to the technological improvements going forward in the advanced shops of Vermont, Connecticut, Massachusetts, and Rhode Island.

The contrast between the vitality and rapid progress of Philadelphia's machine and foundry trades and its resistance to innovation in textiles can perhaps be explained by two factors: differences in business leadership and differences in the organization of the city's labor force. Philadelphia had the unaccountable good fortune

[3] Ellis P. Oberholtzer, Philadelphia (Philadelphia, c. 1910), I, 315–317, 406–408; II, 53–61. J. Thomas Scharf and Thompson Westcott, *History of Philadelphia* (Philadelphia, 1884), III, 2226–2236. Cole, *American Woolen Manufacture*, I, 63. Carter Goodrich, *Government Promotion of American Canals and Railroads 1800–1890* (New York, 1960), 60–74.

[4] James L. Bishop, *A History of American Manufactures* (Philadelphia, 1868), II, 148–168, and *passim;* III, 1–95. J. D. B. DeBow, *Statistical View of the United States* (Washington, 1854), 300–301. Edwin T. Freedley, *Philadelphia and Its Manufactures* (Philadelphia, 1868), espec. 239.

to be the place of work of a few great innovator-businessmen in the machine and foundry trades. Matthias Baldwin, manufacturer of locomotives, Henry Disston, saw and file maker, and William Sellers, machine tool manufacturer, were all unusually talented and forceful businessmen. Like some of the early managers of Lowell and Lawrence textile mills, or Smith and Skinner, rug manufacturers of Yonkers, N. Y., the presence and example of the Philadelphia machinists propelled the city's development along the lines of their specialties.[5]

Before the Civil War Philadelphia had no such outstanding textile innovator-businessmen. In 1815 Isaac Macaulay, an imaginative entrepreneur, set up a modern carpet factory with a complete machine yarn preparation department and hand looms of the latest design. In the next thirty years he neither found imitators nor continued innovating himself. In 1837 a power carpet loom was exhibited at the Franklin Institute by Alfred Jenks, a cotton machinery builder of nearby Bridesburg. Nothing came of Jenks' loom. In 1842 another power loom was exhibited by the Institute; it was tried by one manufacturer and abandoned. No further inventions were reported for the city. At the same time the amateur inventor Erastus Bigelow took his models to the Lowell Manufacturing Company, and by 1845 the Lowell Company and the Tariffville Company of Simsbury, Connecticut, had changed all their rug weaving to Bigelow's power looms. Philadelphia rug manufacturers did not convert to power weaving until after the Civil War.[6] *But were 'Philadelphia' rugs considered*

more desirable quality status tradition

The condition of the city's work force also contributed to the slow modernization of its textile manufactures. In the machine trades no established crafts were threatened by the innovations and expansion of Baldwin, Disston, or Sellers. Fully integrated and mechanized textile mills presented quite the opposite case. After the American Revolution large numbers of English and Irish weavers came to Philadelphia. Simultaneously new English techniques of machine carding and spinning wool and cotton were introduced to supply the weavers with thread. By 1811 there were said to be 4,000 hand loom weavers in the city making a wide range of cotton, woolen, and mixed goods for the northeastern United

[5] Scharf and Westcott, *History of Philadelphia*, III, 2255–2257, 2263–2265, 2267–2269. Roe, *Tool Builders*, 239–260.
[6] Cole and Williamson, *Carpet Manufacture*, 26, 53–58.

The Moral of the Story is:

institutionalization ~~&~~ redards and/or actively resists growth and innovation. The diff between the 18th & 20th is that the 19th C was innovative because there were not enough established

States market. For the next thirty or forty years one of the special characteristics of Philadelphia was its weavers' quarters. In the Kensington-Northern Liberties sections and in Moyamensing were concentrated the homes of the weavers and the small machine spinning shops.[7] Downtown jobbers handled the national marketing. They in turn were supplied by the spinning shops which gave out the thread and supervised the weavers' work. The scale and concentration of Philadelphia's urban textile industry undoubtedly made it more efficient than New England's prefactory rural hand weavers. This urban efficiency also enabled the rug and woolen satinet weavers to persist in their organization long after integrated factories had been introduced elsewhere. The power woolen looms of the 1830's were only two, or at most three, times faster than hand work, so by concentrating on low-count coarse goods in woolens, satinets, and rugs the city's hand weavers maintained themselves against the machine. In the 1840's with the shift in popular taste to fancy woolens and the introduction of the Crompton power loom to weave them, Philadelphia's woolen weavers were doomed.[8]

Integrated cotton spinning and weaving factories, like those of New England, grew up rapidly outside Philadelphia in the 1820's and 1830's. Cotton was inherently an easier material to clean, prepare, and spin than wool, and cotton thread took the tension of power looms better. As a result the hand weaver was more quickly put at a disadvantage by power weaving of cotton than wool. Nevertheless, the late arrival of cotton mills to the city proper, despite the cheap coal and steam power of Philadelphia, suggests that labor opposition kept the mills out of the city until after the Civil War. In Lowell, hand weavers of rugs were replaced immediately upon the invention of a power loom which could be tended by women. The sudden discharge of all the hand weavers and the lack of disturbance caused by the event suggests that the Lowell mill owners had a strong control over the local labor force. In Philadelphia however, the weavers were numerous and well

[7] For other purposes the author and Mrs. Diane V. Friebert did an analysis of residential patterns of Philadelphia during the 1830's. The evidence indicated that during this period the city had broken into large specialized quarters. The very concentration of industrial workers and small spinning shops undoubtedly made the introduction of modern factory methods more difficult than would have been the case if the shops and workers had been thinly scattered throughout the city and suburbs.

[8] Cole, *American Woolen Manufacture*, I, 305.

institutions to be threatened by innovation nor were the existant ones strong enough to resist. This is not the case in the 20th. KC was successful because its organized. From 1825 to 1850 a series of strikes, riots, and even a march on the suburban cotton mills, marked their efforts to defend their trade.[9]

(Although the rug, satinet, and woolen weavers of Philadelphia delayed the modernization of their industry and perhaps also kept the cotton factories in the suburbs, the equally well-organized cordwainers enjoyed no such success.) Despite unions and strikes they lost control over their product and over the pricing of their labor. The growth of a national market for shoes created the opportunity for merchant capitalists to organize shoemaking around wholesale distribution. Without the aid of new technology the shoe wholesalers accomplished their goal by underselling established retailers and by lowering the standards for shoe manufacture so that cheap labor could compete against the craftsmen. By 1850 the reorganization of Philadelphia's boot and shoe industry had been completed, and it waited only the invention of McKay's stitching machine to assume its modern form of large scale factory production.[10]

[margin handwriting:] M.C.'s had momentum & prevalent values, they embodied the Am Spirit and thus were able to achieve their goals w/out serious challenge

The varied responses of Philadelphia to technological innovation and economic change are helpful to today's doctrine. The city per se was not necessarily the place of invention or innovation. The presence of a large skilled labor force could or could not assist in the process of innovation. The presence of effective innovator-businessmen was unpredictable but vital to the rapid progress of an industry. One hesitates to draw inferences from the experience of one hundred years ago to guide today's decisions. Perhaps the history of early industrialization can, however, release the planner from simple theories of cause and effect and offer him the freedom to take his chances in terms of the goals he wishes to pursue.

[9] John R. Commons et al., *A Documentary History of American Industrial Society* (Cleveland, 1910), V, 325–328. Oberholtzer, *Philadelphia*, II, 272–299.
[10] Commons, *Industrial Society*, III, 1–51.

[handwritten note:] Shakers and movers happened to be locked into or plugged into the ascending technologies and made use of them (span bridge and RR).

The Economics of Urbanization

AARON FLEISHER

The definitive assay of the role of the city in economic development and technological innovation will comprise two parts. One will consider the problem in the context of the urban-rural dichotomy. The other will weigh urban qualities and characteristics, and sort cities by their effects on technology and the economy. Professor Tsuru has treated only the first. He argues that because cities were centers of commerce and industry and themselves markets, they constituted a locale where external economies could be appropriated for private purposes; that this was particularly true and an especial advantage in the early stages of the development of the capitalist economy; and that technological changes and a heightened public concern over private nuisances makes it uncertain now whether cities can, in the net balance, still provide external economies.

The availability of external economies is taken to be a characteristic of all cities. They are not considered to be available elsewhere; they are not measured and hardly specified. And since cities were not sorted by the qualities of their external economies, they remain entirely undifferentiated.

That procedure, however, does not help us to get on to the second part of the problem, and in particular to inquire whether a scale of external economies—or for that matter, any other urban parameter—can be devised to distinguish cities according to their influence on economic and technological development.

The problem is difficult. A first try might attempt to estimate some limits of influence. Are there circumstances in which the city might exercise none? Professor Handlin has stressed that the forces which shaped the city come initially from without. But the city may exert its influence on the second round of effects. That is one possibility. Changes, once started, can also be self-propagating. Technology and the economy appear to be of this nature, in which case the city itself becomes an after-effect. Manchester, for instance, began as a factory center and grew into a city. These obscurities make it easy to slip into a *post hoc* error.

Professor Brogan has cited some singular events that shaped the economy of cities. In the past economic or technological innovations were personal events. The massive organization of research and development is a recent phenomenon. Alongside the much larger currents of urban change, the specifics of innovation seem almost random ripples. To the innovator they are not random, but the history of a city is not written by summing the detailed biographies of its citizens. In this sense all history contains another random component in addition to the weather. Where innovation is involved, this component may be particularly large.

Cities have long existed where the technology was primitive and the economy depressed. Merely by reason of its existence the city therefore does not provide a sufficient condition for the development of technology and the economy. Might its existence be a necessary condition? The example of Manchester suggests that it is not. Necessary and sufficient conditions, however, are structural members discernible only in scholarly worlds that are clean, simple and unencumbered, such as the mathematician's. The vocabulary of historical studies much more frequently comprises influences and tendencies.

This quick look suggests that the role of cities in economic development and technological innovations need not be decisive. It need not even be important. And because it may be unimportant, which is to say, not critical, the range of its variation will be large. Then clinical studies of cities would seem an efficient tactic by which to examine the problem.

Required first is a list of the possible parameters by which the influence of the city can be measured. External economies has been suggested; let us start there. We shall want to measure external economies, and we must observe immediately that the phrase refers not to a particular quality, but to a large basket holding many different kinds of presumed advantages. Professor Tsuru has listed some. There are external economies that accrue from transportation facilities, communications networks, from location and markets, from a division of labor, and from proximities to exchanges, banks, universities, courts, and government offices. No purpose is served in attempting to list any more. They might, with difficulty, be measured provided specific circumstances were prescribed and a set of relative values specified. But even if the number of external economies were restricted, their possible permutations still appear to be too many for man or machine to manipulate—all this apart from the fact that one man's economies are another's diseconomies. It seems difficult to make external economies operational.

Some of the components taken separately may be more easily measurable—transportation and communications, for example. The rest must be treated by some form of "parameterization." The word comes from the physical sciences, and means characterizing a complicated system (for certain limited purposes) by one, or a few, quantities. The device is obviously an approximation that seeks to capture, cheaply, the effect of the complicated system. It does not always work.

I do not know how to parameterize the external economies of cities. I should like to suggest that size is worth trying. Size is most easily measured by population. However the discrepancy between the legal and functional boundaries of a city makes for an essential confusion. Disregard it for the moment and consider size. All the urban qualities which can be construed as providing external economies would seem in some measure to increase with size. The correspondence need not be the same. For example, the market will increase approximately as the population does, but a communications network will increase more rapidly because each additional person requires many more than just one additional link.

Tables of size and economic growth would be interesting. Perhaps they might also be sorted by the principal function of the city, but that seems more difficult to do. The rate of growth as a function of size appears particularly interesting. Cities, like biological systems, do not seem to respond continuously to a stimulus. They are likely to exhibit a threshold at the low end; a minimum size at which growth and/or economic development will occur; and a saturation level at the high where growth tapers off appreciably. These limits look like valuable data.

Cultural attitudes supply another possible parameter. Professor Lopez discussed four idealized urban patterns and their characteristic values. His time segment did not overlap the modern city, but the idea is still applicable. Technological innovation seems to be more difficult than economic development to parameterize. The distribution of patents by location and time is a possibility, but that device is limited to modern cities. Counting potential interactions may summarize the city's influence on technological change. Very few of these problems will be solved shortly, but continued exploration of them may point a way toward doing so.

The Organization
of Technological Innovation
in Urban Environments

RICHARD L. MEIER

The two central arguments that connect cities with innovation and economic growth may be restated as follows:

1. External economies (and diseconomies) associated with any enterprise are most available to its neighbors. The effect diminishes with distance as well as with the number and variety of adjacent enterprises which may absorb the resulting advantages or disadvantages. Government is called upon to legislate against the most visible diseconomies affecting others and to authorize arrangements for exploiting the economies. True *innovation* can be said to occur only when a new combination of resources may usefully be imitated in similar environments elsewhere and may generate the same

external economies. Thus, through replication or imitation, innovation acts as a trigger for economic growth.[1]

2. The flow of information, ideas, concepts, artifacts and their human carriers from one context to another can be accelerated under conditions of high accessibility. The city is not only a crossroads, a place for outsiders to meet and trade, it is a living repository for culture—high, low, and intermediate. In this context *innovation* represents the addition of a new concept to an existing public repertory so that it is shared by groups outside the immediate circle of the inventor. An important share of the novel concept will improve the efficiency with which labor and capital are employed, but many also satisfy esthetic and other values. Since each new concept must have a term to denote it in public communications, the additions to a dictionary of current usage would be indicative of the rate of innovation and the directions it was taking.

The market should be considered as much a cultural institution as the forum or the cathedral. The market feeds upon information about special situations in social organization—supply on one side and demand on the other—and links them together. It requires an environment of mutual trust, which is founded upon repeated face-to-face contacts, despite intense competition. All these institutions have been the locus for record-keeping or knowledge-preservation. Cities are designed physically to promote access, under conditions of relative security (thus the need for walls before the advent of heavy artillery), not only to people, artifacts, and services, but also to accumulated stores of information.

From the beginning of the industrial revolution until the 1930's the inventor-entrepreneur was the chief innovator.[2] He

[1] The categories of external economies due to proximity, which Isard rightly lumps together under the term "agglomeration economies," emphasize economies of scale, localization economies (when similar activities cluster together) and urbanization economies (the spatial coherence of complementary activities as in integrated industrial complexes). Walter Isard *et. al., Methods of Regional Analysis: an Introduction to Regional Science* (New York, 1960).

[2] The words *inventor, entrepreneur,* and *innovator* refer to roles and behaviors that are quite widely assigned to these terms. Scientists and inventors produce the requisite insights, while entrepreneurs match opportunity against human wants and work out methods whereby the increase in output obtainable could be funnelled back into the firm or institution responsible for exploiting the invention. A production innovation occurs only if the enterprise is the first of its kind and is subsequently widely imitated and improved upon. An economic evaluation of the transition from inventor-entrepreneur partnership to the present corporate organization of invention is provided by Fritz Machlup, "The Supply of Inventors

drew upon his schooling in natural science and experience in the applied arts, solved a technological problem, and then collaborated with, or sometimes even created, an organization to exploit the solution. Cities, if they were not already in existence there, grew up around the successful factory or establishment that developed from the founder's workshop. Since simultaneity of invention and the appearance of equally good alternative solutions were remarkably common, only a few graduated into a scale of operations that created a new round of opportunities.[3] An even smaller fraction were fortunate enough to withstand the rigors of competition, substitution, technological obsolescence, and senescence.

The surviving urban enterprises in the United States appear to have had on the average two or three predecessors that are now defunct; a good share of the ongoing firms have been constructed from the techniques and skills salvaged from those no longer in existence. Existing organizations often owe their technology to several independent inventor-entrepreneurs whose efforts were amalgamated. The location of the older facilities operated by such firms are often in the cities, sometimes even on the very sites, where the inventor-entrepreneurs worked.

Much has already been said about the milieu that encourages invention. More often than not inventiveness is associated with the availability of leisure, mercantilism, the Protestant ethic, an open society that rewards achievement, and the presence of acculturative contacts.[4] Technological innovation—the reduction to practice of an invention on a commercial scale—seems to be most closely associated with social environments that are experiencing economic growth, and the latter is consistently linked to the growth of cities, of manufacturing, and particularly of services. The facts are not at issue here; it is the mechanism that needs to be elucidated. We do not seek an explanation for the "spark of genius" that distinguishes

and Inventions," *Weltwirtschaftliches Archiv 85*, 1960, 210–251. A contemporary systematic assessment based upon feedback concepts is also provided by Edward Ames, "Research, Invention, Development, and Innovation," *American Economic Review 51*, 1961, 370–380.

[3] Many examples are provided by Sigfried Giedion, *Mechanization Takes Command* (London, 1948).

[4] These factors are discussed in terms of the Parsonian structural-functional approach in a recent historical evaluation of the beginnings of the Industrial Revolution by Neil J. Smelser, *Social Change in the Industrial Revolution* (Chicago, 1959), esp. 63–79.

the inventor from more common folk, but rather the process by which his idea is transformed into net social benefit.

In the past three decades invention has become scientized, and the corporations and the military services have opened up many new paths for applied research. The political, social, and economic returns from the organization of research and development, including the professionalization of the technical specialties, have been so phenomenal that this category of economic activity has been doubling in size every five to eight years. The various research departments and independent organizations have found their old locations too cramped and have sought new sites likely to maximize research output over the next decade or so and at the same time provide flexibility in coping with the unforeseen challenges of succeeding decades. The spatial pattern deduced from successful locations that are associated with this new growth is rather obscure because the primary channels of communication—the reports in the files, the journals that come in the mails, the telephone, the library, and the professional meetings—do not bulk as large on the landscape as railroads, roads, or barge lines. There are no maps of information flow equivalent to the maps of commodity flow. Therefore any attempt to discover spatial pattern brought about by research and development must be deduced from scattered topical studies and interviews at key points. The conclusions reported here are speculative, yet even portions of the argument have been persuasive enough to direct the location of millions of dollars of enterprise capital in the past few years.

Forced-draft technical innovation today in most fields besides medicine is best carried out in the urban region of Southern California. Most government departments and large corporations have recognized the potentials of the Los Angeles area and have either established permanent links with one or more organizations there or bought up a smaller enterprise and developed it as a subsidiary. The quality of the research and development is not extraordinary as compared to the rest of the country, but the flexibility and speed in assembling an organization capable of tackling a given technical problem is unparalleled. Why is this so and how does it come about?

The foremost consideration has been the scarcity of engineers, physicists, applied mathematicians, computer programmers, and related technicians. To minimize the likelihood of scandal, salary levels had to be held down to levels not too far exceeding civil service standards. Any research entrepreneur who wished to build an organization was forced to depend heavily upon "psychic income" as an attraction even more than upon pay scale. The high educational level, the opportunity to live in new communities suited to one's taste, the youth and informality, superimposed upon solid technical achievements in the aviation industry, together made Southern California exceedingly attractive to a college-educated post-war generation whose origins were in the Middle West and the South. Many Easterners were drawn by the "cosmopolitan" culture and year-round gardening. The immigrants came despite the fact that job security was relatively poor; all of them were gambling their careers on a rising research market.

The striking factor in Southern California is mobility.[5] Technical people here seem to change organizations every two or three years while elsewhere they make two or three shifts in a lifetime. The organizations themselves have fat years and lean years, depending upon their luck with research and development contracts. One sees, therefore, a population of perhaps 100,000 professionals and top technicians grouping and regrouping to process practical problems that are up for bid, mainly from Washington. Only a city based upon automobile transportation could combine the preferred living patterns of research personnel with the organizational mobility needed for processing the complex crash programs from the Pentagon and the National Aeronautics and Space Agency. Research engineers in the West Los Angeles and San Diego areas are always confident that jobs will be opening up within commuting distance as each contract draws to an end. They know that they will not be forced to pick up the family and move to a more convenient location. The Santa Barbara, East Los Angeles, and Phoenix (a satellite of Los Angeles for research and development purposes) areas may not yet have reached that critical mass. A similar accretion in the North (the Peninsula area south of the San Francisco airport including Palo Alto and San Jose) seems to have done so despite somewhat less hectic reshuffling of technical personnel.

[5] This mobility is evident in the whole subculture and provides the dominant theme in any description of the region. Cf. Arthur L. Grey, Jr., "Los Angeles: Urban Prototype," *Land Economics* 35 (1959), 232–242.

Residential moves are still quite common in this class, but a large share tend to reflect changes in status such as promotion to posts of greater responsibility or transitions between academic, industrial, and entrepreneurial spheres of activity. Urban form on the Peninsula is also automobile-oriented, but the region seems to maintain, in research as well as taste, a sophistication that is a notch or so higher than Southern California, due largely to the attempts of Stanford University to capture for itself some of the external economies associated with research-oriented universities.

The Stanford story is a classic example of the discovery and exploitation of hidden opportunities created by the growth of research-oriented technology. A land-rich, but endowment-poor, private university first started a research unit, the Stanford Research Institute, which quickly became the largest of the nonprofit applied research organizations in the country. By being alert to opportunities all over the world, catholic in its research interests, and able to draw upon repositories of knowledge, particularly libraries, and skill that had been patiently accumulated in a university community for decades, it broke down a long standing compartmentalization of effort and provided bases for growth in new directions, particularly business research and broad gauge technical assistance overseas.[6] The tract of unsalable land that had been reached by the growing fringe of the San Francisco metropolitan complex would inevitably have generated some significant values, but a sizable multiplier was obtained due to the presence of the faculty, the library, and alumni loyalty.

Boston, with its Route 128, has a comparable development although on a still larger scale. Here it was a notable combination between a technical entrepreneurial tradition maintained at the Massachusetts Institute of Technology, which respected a man even more highly if he went into business on the side and developed his own discoveries in the form of salable components, and a long tradition in investment banking that was not satisfied with run-of-the-mill propositions.[7] The amenities of the outer suburbs made it possible to attract technical personnel (particularly from California!) and the location of the Route made it possible to assemble a subprofessional labor force from the youngsters leaving the declin-

[6] Anon. "Non-Profit Labs Carve Big Niche," *Business Week*, September 12, 1959, 102–108.
[7] Freeman Lincoln, "After the Cabots—Jerry Blakeley," *Fortune 62* (November 1960), 171–184.

ing mill towns. Here, too, it was possible to build up a critical mass of professional personnel, but further growth is greatly hampered by the inability of technicians in the Boston area to go to night school and work their way into professional status. Boston is the only major metropolitan area where a break exists in the technical training programs that requires taking leave from the job or quitting.

New York research and development is much too complex to be treated in a thumbnail sketch.[8] On its fringes, in Nutley, Bound Brook, Summit, White Plains, New Rochelle, Hicksville, and Mineola, the equivalent of another Route 128 will be found. New York has almost a monopoly on investment research in the Wall Street complex and on marketing research in the Madison Avenue area; and only a few blocks away one finds the world's pre-eminent bio-medical research center. Publishing and documentation, the lifeblood of research, are also focussed in Manhattan. The traditional industrial supports for New York are disappearing, but the research and development capability is so diverse and huge that replacements of a still unanticipated character must be expected. The opportunities for the salvage and reuse of structures and institutions are too visible to the research-based entrepreneur to be missed.

Planners are expected to be trustees of the public in the matter of expected external economies. The profession defines its special expertise as that of forecasting interactions between activities and then, primarily through land use controls and the design of new facilities, of proposing a direction for new development that assures fair shares among the respective enterprises and individuals at the same time that the general public benefits. Since economists discourse at length about the concept of external economies, but rarely are able to measure them, planners are forced to resort to rough estimates and to judgments based upon interviews and analysis of locational relationships.

What does this experience with research and development as a focus for urban planning and economic development reveal?

[8] Edgar M. Hoover and Ray Vernon, *Anatomy of a Metropolis* (Cambridge, Mass., 1959), 47–49. The other books in this series rarely isolated the research and development component.

There is space here to pick up only one strand of the planning that originated in the nineteenth century with the *industrial estate* laid out beside a major railroad or a harbor, that evolved into the more carefully serviced *industrial district,* and finally was transformed with the onset of "conspicuous production" in the 1950's into the *industrial park.*[9] Now, over the past half dozen years, *research parks* are being designed to accommodate small-to-medium-sized organizations, while in the larger organizations much attention is being paid to optimization of location and structural design of major research facilities.

One of the earliest programs in the field was developed by the State of North Carolina to increase the supply of research scientists and engineers and to attract the modern industry. The promoters developed a "Research Triangle," whose points on the map were institutions of higher learning with a supply of students to be drawn upon as technicians and research assistants as well as recruits for full time staff, and faculty members who could be used as consultants. At the heart was a research park with computer service, and pleasant surroundings for residences.[10] It has become by far the most attractive location for industrial laboratories in the South, thus far specializing in polymers, fibers, and tobacco research. Industrial estates are being created nearby so that many of the new enterprises born of the research will find it convenient to settle down in the vicinity. The roads are mediocre, but they will no doubt be improved even before the need is felt. The airline connections are already better than for most university towns.

In Ann Arbor, Michigan, all the experience to date is being drawn upon. Advanced mechanization in the automobile industry, along with decentralization of production, has created massive unemployment in the Detroit area and threatens to turn one of the richest states into a permanently depressed area. An important component in the program to stimulate new growth in Michigan is the establishment of a development area equivalent in effect to the

[9] William Bredo, *Industrial Estates—Tool for Industrialization* (Glencoe, Illinois, 1960).
[10] *Industrial Development 129* (June 1960), 18–48. This is the most extensive description of the tie up between research and development promotion, education, industrialization, and economic development so far made available. For the official story see Luther H. Hodges, "The Research Triangle of North Carolina," *State Government 33* (1960), 17–22.

Peninsula region in Northern California and the periphery of Boston.[11]

The superimposition of certain special features seem to be helpful in attracting and holding the scientists, engineers, technicians, entrepreneurs, and their organizations. Many of the same conditions seem to add to their general productivity, however that may be measured. These features are worth listing and explaining:

1. *Immediate access to cultural and natural amenities.* The principal requirements are for good high schools, varied outdoor recreation, wooded building sites, and a rich music and fine arts program.

2. *Adjacency to a major research-oriented university or hospital.* This implies a relatively complete and well organized library, the availability of consultants, the presence of bookstores, stationers, wholesale electronics shops and other specialized suppliers, a supply of computer programmers and chemical analysts, etc.

3. *Proximity to large capital-intensive installations.* A large number of skilled, disciplined workers are to be found in such areas. This pool can be drawn upon to take advantage of the most productive opportunities that are to be exploited on a moderate scale (often these involve the building of prototypes which, should they go into mass production, would be manufactured at some other place, such as the South, where labor is less expensive).

4. *Professional class suburban environment.* The style of life affected by engineers and scientists is highly significant. It is quite compatible with that of lawyers, doctors, teachers, and managers. Neighborhood frictions arise immediately, however, with a portion of the business class, with much of the semiskilled labor types, the improvident element, and the centers of established wealth. Traffic is abhorred but still, surprisingly, tolerated by almost all.

5. *An exit on a metropolitan expressway.* This means that the headquarters are accessible over a wide area, deliveries are prompt, and the airport is accessible. An organization intent upon creating an image of itself in the mind of the public will wish to bring its function to the attention of passersby through the exposition of ultramodern architecture. Firms oriented toward the future exploit the view from the automobile with surprising forms and colors rather than with sales pitches over television.

[11] *The Michigan Yearbook 2* (December 1960). Robert R. White, "The Institute of Science and Technology," 69–74. Winston E. Koch, "Industrial Research in Depth," 78–87.

6. *The availability of cheap, general purpose structures.* When hatching an idea the jump from the laboratory to a long-term contract requires very often an intermediate stage that is carried out under conditions of capital scarcity, and therefore utilizes old factories, store fronts, or lofts which can be rented cheaply. Many technical ideas developed by consultants, academics, and smaller operators would be halted in the absence of what is referred to in the argot as "brooder" equipment.

Ann Arbor shows up remarkably well on all the counts as compared to any other place between the Alleghenies and the Rockies. There are, in effect, two research parks, on opposite sides of the University.[12] However, in choosing sites and promoting a facility, many facts and situations cannot be ascertained ahead of the commitment. An excellent idea with the wrong timing will trigger off no responses. If research and development all over the continent continue to grow at a decent rate, its prospects should be good. It is being imitated in Lafayette, Indiana, Chicago's Near South Side, points near the missile bases in Florida, and at the University of Alabama.

The kind of city that will result from these trends is still difficult to comprehend. If a fertile combination is found between the automotive organizations and multipurpose research capabilities, and a new burst of growth results, Ann Arbor may suffer from the same external diseconomies as those which affected Palo Alto in recent years—intense traffic congestion during rush hours and smog. The problem of finding a proper place for research and development within the metropolitan region, a breeding ground for innovation, is being considered by the planners for the first time. They need much data and some experience.

[12] See the brochure of the new Greater Ann Arbor Research Park, Chamber of Commerce, Ann Arbor, June 1961.

III

The City in the History of Ideas

Two Stages in the Critique of the American City

MORTON WHITE

It is a significant fact of our national life that our most distinguished and influential writers have felt and expressed an extraordinary amount of antipathy toward the American city.[1] To appreciate the extent and depth of this feeling one need only examine some of the writings of Jefferson, Emerson, Thoreau, Hawthorne, Poe, Melville, Henry Adams, Henry James, William Dean Howells, Theodore Dreiser, Frank Norris, Josiah Royce, George Santayana,

---

[1] This essay is a slightly revised version of Chapter XV in Morton and Lucia White, *The Intellectual and the City: From Thomas Jefferson to Frank Lloyd Wright*, (Harvard University Press and M. I. T. Press, 1962). Readers are referred to that work for documentation. See also Morton and Lucia White, "The American Intellectual versus the American City," *Daedalus* (Winter 1961), 166–179; reprinted in Lloyd Rodwin, ed., *The Future Metropolis* (New York, 1961), 214–232.

John Dewey, Jane Addams, Robert Park, Louis Sullivan and Frank Lloyd Wright. Of course these writers express different kinds and degrees of negative feeling toward the American city, and a distinction must be made between intellectuals who deplored urban life as such, and those who criticized it with the intention of improving and reforming it. Nevertheless, America's transcendent intellectual figures give the general impression of fear of the American city as they knew it. In some cases it was fear of what the American city was; in others, fear of what it might become.

Obviously, not all Americans nor all American writers felt this way. One cannot deny the existence of a vast literature of vulgar city boosting. But while our chambers of commerce echoed with shouts of approval for the rapidly growing city, an antiphonal dissent filled America's literary and philosophical pantheon. After the first great spurt of urbanization at the beginning of the nineteenth century, representatives of what Parrington called the main currents of American thought, however unlike each other they might have been and however divergent the currents they represented, looked at the post-Colonial American city with attitudes of distrust and dismay. This was true of Jefferson, the deist and child of the Enlightenment; of the transcendentalists, Emerson and Thoreau; and of Hawthorne, Poe, and Melville, who represented what has been called the power of blackness in American thought. It was also true of Henry Adams and Henry James, those fastidious critics of the American city after the Civil War, as well as of literary realists and naturalists like Howells, Norris, and Dreiser. It was even true of Jane Addams, the social worker who might be said to represent the power of whiteness in American thought; of Dewey, the pragmatist, of Josiah Royce, the idealist, and of the materialist, Santayana. The list would not be complete without the architectural functionalists, Sullivan and Wright.

How shall we explain this persistent distrust of the American city? Surely it is puzzling. First of all, because we think of the city as a place in which intellectuals congregate. Second, because we know that urbanization has been increasing constantly in America for the last one hundred and seventy-five years, and may wonder why our most celebrated writers have so often shown animus toward it, why representatives of some of our most distinctive intellectual movements have been so critical of one of our most distinctive social developments. And last, because the intellectual traditions of other western countries, for example, France, have not been as persistently antiurban in feeling and ideology. The fact of intellectual antipathy and ambivalence toward the city seems to cry for some kind of explanation on several counts. Why, we may reasonably ask, is there so much criticism of the American city in American thought from Jefferson to Wright?

When one asks this question, one often hears in reply that something called "romanticism" is responsible for the phenomenon. But this is a mistaken view. It is mistaken, not because it is wholly false, but because it is not wholly true. It offers too simple an explanation. The desire to explain the phenomenon in terms of espousal of one large, global "ism" is, of course standard among idealistic historians who are directly or indirectly influenced by Hegel, and who invariably seek to account for historical phenomena by referring to a spirit which dominates an age or country and which realizes or actualizes itself in the historical process. Yet such a mode of explanation is not offered only by official Hegelians. It is often proposed by those who would disavow any connection with the tradition of absolute idealism, perhaps without full recognition of the similarity between their approach and that of a philosopher from whom they might well wish to disassociate themselves. Such unconscious idealists, as they might be called, view our intellectual history as the perpetuation or working out of premises accepted in our early national life. Bertrand Russell once facetiously observed that Americans are given to the idea that their history is explained as the result of their being—in Lincoln's words —dedicated to a proposition. And while the prevalence of economic determinism in American historical thought of the twentieth century shows how inaccurate this is as an account of the habits of our professional historians, there is truth in the observation as applied to the effort to explain the persistent intellectual criticism of the American city simply as an expression of romanticism.

On such a model of explanation, we ask why certain intellectuals all shared a critical attitude toward the American city, and we answer by saying that they all subscribed to the same romantic *Weltanschauung*. But we cannot successfully explain intellectual antiurbanism in this monistic way. The American city has been so vast, so varied, and so much in flux that it has provided men either in fact or in their imaginations with a variety of things to dislike. The American city has been thought by American intellectuals to be: too big, too noisy, too dusky, too dirty, too smelly, too commercial, too crowded, too full of immigrants, too full of Jews, too full of Irishmen, Italians, Poles, too industrial, too pushing, too mobile, too fast, too artificial, destructive of conversation, destructive of communication, too greedy, too capitalistic, too full of automobiles, too full of smog, too full of dust, too heartless, too intellectual, too scientific, insufficiently poetic, too lacking in manners, too mechanical, destructive of family, tribal and patriotic feeling. And just because different intellectuals have disliked the city for so many different reasons, it is unlikely that one simple hypothesis will provide *the* explanation of why American thinkers have found the city objectionable. Nevertheless, the temptation to offer such simple hypotheses is great, for it is natural to seek in the various reasons given for disliking the city some central thread, some unifying ground for dislike. And so it is that a historian will often seize upon the concept of romanticism in an ultimately futile effort to subsume all the antiurban complaints under one broad belief or doctrine. But while such an explanation may often be correct in the case of a given intellectual, especially if he is Emerson or Thoreau, the difficulty begins when one goes further and argues that all criticism of the city may be explained in this way.

An examination of the various American writers who have expressed antipathy to the American city makes abundantly clear that we cannot string so many intellectual beads on even so powerful an intellectual cord. If by romanticism we understand at least an attachment to the wilderness, a love of spontaneity as against reason, of the heart as against the head, of poetry as against calculation, then it is simply not true to say that all American writers who have chosen to attack the main features of the American city have done so because they viewed it as inferior to the wilderness. Henry James and John Dewey are notable cases in point. James was disturbed by some of the distinctively urban features of New York, and Dewey expressed the gravest concern about the impact of American urbanization. But they were not led to adopt their attitudes by a preference for the American wilderness. If Henry James disliked New York, it was not because he loved the soil, but because New York lacked the society, the civilization, and the brilliance he admired so much. It lacked history, organic social relations, and most of all, elevated conversation. John Dewey's distaste for the American city in the 1920's was not that of a tiller, a sower, or a reaper. It was primarily the distaste of a man who valued social intelligence and face-to-face human relationships, and who was deeply committed to believing in the importance of scientifically grounded communication in the conduct of the good life.

It is true, of course, that the tenets and attitudes of romanticism have dominated a good deal of our literary practice and our esthetic theory. Having been instructed by the illuminating studies of Richard Chase, Harry Levin, the late F. O. Matthiessen, Perry Miller, and Henry Nash Smith, among others, we know that many of our American writers have been dreaming romancers more often than novelists in one sense of the latter word, and that they were deeply affected by the intellectual wave called romanticism. But that wave had been damped, as the physicists say, by the end of the nineteenth century. Therefore, reference to romanticism will help explain the opposition of only certain writers to the city, namely those who lived when the energy of the wave was at its highest and before it encountered certain powerful counterwaves in our intellectual history. The fact is that the heritage of romanticism is not inescapable in American life. Scratch an American writer and you won't always find a Natty Bumppo. It is wrong to suppose that resident in the American tradition there is one intellectual pull or impulse away from civilization that can explain *all* criticism of the city. That is why the study of the history of intellectual attitudes toward the city is not simply a chapter in the study of intellectual attitudes toward Nature. If the citation of John Dewey is not sufficient to make the point, and if Henry James be eliminated as a counterexample because he was an expatriate, then William Dean Howells may be cited as a stay-at-home artist whose opposition to the American city cannot be construed as the product of a romantic admiration for nature in the sense of the forest or the wilderness, nor the product of a resolution to be savagely natural. Howells wanted to "bang the babes of romance about" and yet he wrote in *A Traveler from Altruria* and *Through the Eye of the Needle*, two of the most antiurban tracts ever to be produced by an influential American literary man.

And what about Theodore Dreiser who, after a long career of excited literary concern with the city, came to think of the nation's metropolis as a sinister place? Surely Dreiser, like Howells, was not an agrarian or a romanticist. Nor was Henry Adams, who despised New York because he thought it gave more power to immigrant Jews than it did to him, "American of Americans, with Heaven knew how many Puritans and Patriots behind him." In his *Age of Reform* Richard Hofstadter rightly points out that the same distrust of the city that was conspicuous among the agrarian populists was also common among Henry Adams' class of solid and respectable gentlemen—his brother Brooks, Henry Cabot Lodge, Theodore Roosevelt, John Hay, and Albert J. Beveridge—who, as Hofstadter puts it, were "in all obvious respects the antithesis of the populists." These gentlemen did not imagine themselves to be doctrinaire partisans of the agrarian's soil, or of the forest as against the city.

It must be repeated that if one were to prepare a list of reasons why American intellectuals have in fact distrusted or disliked the city, it would be impossible to summarize or give the gist of the whole of it by the use of the magic word "romanticism." The concept of romanticism, at least in one of its many senses, will not be able to embrace all of the antiurban pejoratives. If one construes it as a revolt against civilization in the name of untouched nature, it is impossible to subsume under that rubric Henry James' complaint that New York was incapable of refined conversation. The point is that we cannot make out a case for an exclusively romantic theory of antiurbanism, if only because many objections to the American city have not been made—either explicitly or implicitly—in the name of nature's virtues as against those of civilization. Some of them have been made in the name of civilization itself. Therefore, we must conclude when we study the literature of antiurbanism that there are different reasons for the different expressions of antiurbanism, and that some of these reasons are in a sense opposed to each other. The American city has been criticized by writers who doubted or despised the values of civilization as well as by writers who were intensely dedicated to civilized life. In short, the American city has been caught in the crossfire of two powerful antagonists—primitivists and sophisticates; and no mechanical recitation of the misleading aphorism that like effects are produced by like causes can gainsay this fact. Indeed this fact makes it easier to see why antipathy to the American metropolis has been so persistent, why it even weathered the great change in intellectual climate that came with the Civil War. In spite of a rapid reversal of intellectual winds, the city continued to be buffeted by them.

It is undoubtedly true that many of our pre-Civil War intellectuals were critical of the city because of their affiliation with romanticism. Writers like Thoreau, Emerson, Hawthorne, Poe, and Melville used stock romantic arguments against the American city and voiced stock romantic feelings about its defects. But we cannot understand this phase of the story without bearing in mind certain social facts about the nation at that time. Just to the extent to which it was primarily nonurban in its way of life, literary and philosophical critics of the city could speak more plausibly of life in the wilderness as a viable alternative to life in the city. Hence a stereotyped romantic attack on the American city was retailable by Thoreau and Emerson as well as by lesser figures like Cooper, Simms, Bryant, and the painters Durand and Cole. The artistic defense of an undefiled nature against the encroachments of civilization made more sense in a period when there were fantastic amounts of undefiled nature to which a romantic writer and his readers could flee, than it could have made at a later date. We must recognize therefore that a fuller explanation of this pre-Civil War, romantic antiurbanism would take into account the fact that it reached its zenith in rural America. In a predominantly rural country, romantic criticism of the city acquired considerable plausibility. Emerson's highly metaphysical attack on urban life derived its popularity in part from the fact that it was published at a time when large numbers of people could abandon the city for vast tracts of untouched nature. This does not mean that traditional romanticism can be expressed only in a period which is preponderantly nonurban in its way of life, but it does suggest that it can flourish as the predominant intellectual style only under such circumstances.

After the Civil War, however, doctrinaire love of the wilderness was not a serious factor in the animadversions on American city life that we find in Henry Adams, Henry James, William Dean Howells, Theodore Dreiser, and John Dewey. Although a critic of the American city like Henry Adams disliked the city for reasons that coincided with some of those adduced by Emerson —they both despised commercialism—it would be absurd to speak of Adams as "to that extent" a romanticist in an effort to save the theory that romanticism is the explanation of antiurbanism. To attack the city on romantic grounds is to attack it in a stereotyped way, to bring to bear the full weight of romantic ideology. Some elements in that ideology, like the distrust of commerce, may turn up in other critiques, but these other critiques do not, merely by sharing something with the romantic critique, become romantic or even partly so. One might just as well say that anyone who ever took a political position that coincided with that of a Communist was "to that extent" a Communist. A similar level of absurdity might be reached if one were to call George Santayana a crypto-romantic because he fled Boston and hated New York, or if one were to speak similarly of T. S. Eliot because he thought of the modern city as a wasteland.

After the Civil War the American city was attacked by leading intellectuals on grounds that were, if anything, almost antiromantic. Even Frank Lloyd Wright said he opposed citification in the name of civilization. The American city was no longer abandoned for the forest by figures like Henry Adams, Henry James, William Dean Howells, and John Dewey. *If the American city was then found wanting, it was found wanting not because it was too civilized but rather because it was not civilized enough.* For the generation of post-Civil War intellectuals, for realists and pragmatists and naturalists, American city life was not deficient because it was artificial, rational, self-conscious or overrefined. On the contrary, it was too wild, too vulgar, too ostentatious, too uncontrolled, too gaudy, too full of things that disturbed the sensibility of the fastidious like Henry James and George Santayana, and too chaotic for scientifically oriented minds like Dewey who sought a planned social order.

It was this antiromanticism that may have helped to produce in American writers a more positive attitude toward the European city at the end of the nineteenth century than that which had predominated before the Civil War. In the early part of the century many romanticists preferred the American city on moral grounds to what they regarded as depraved European centers like Liverpool, London, Rome, and Paris, even when they preferred these European cities on esthetic grounds. But the American city in the Gilded Age was often fled by men of sensibility for what they regarded as the more refined, more sophisticated, and better-planned cities of Europe. The same forces that urbanized the country helped make literary and philosophical romanticism a less popular doctrine among major intellectuals after the Civil War, and helped replace it by criticism of the city that diverged sharply from Rousseauian or Thoreauvian romanticism. When Henry James and John Dewey lamented the decline of urban conversation and communication, and when Henry Adams found himself lost in New York, they were giving voice to their common feeling that the more advanced forms of human intelligence and sensibility were missing from New York; they were not lamenting the absence of the more primitive experiences that Thoreau missed in the city. The social workers who criticized the later nineteenth-century American city did not mean to praise it when they referred to "the city wilderness." Stephen Crane did not mean to praise the city in *Maggie* when he likened it to a jungle, nor did Upton Sinclair. Edith Wharton did not mean to praise upper-class New Yorkers when she said in *The Age of Innocence* that they resembled primitives in their ritualistic behavior. The critique of the city had shifted radically from the days when a romantic would have prayed for the city's transformation into a wilderness or a jungle. Even Lewis Mumford, that latter-day admirer of Emerson, complains that Megalopolis is too primitive and too barbaric.

The history of the critique of the American city, then, is divisible into two distinct and contrasting stages: one in which romanticism was employed in attacking the city for being over-civilized; and another stage in which the city was accused of being undercivilized by anti-, or at least nonromantics. The shift from a predominantly rural society to an urban one linked the promise and the possibilities of civilization with urbanization; and after the Civil War, intellectuals were more respectful of those possibilities. But they were not satisfied with mere possibilities. Urban intellectuals therefore turned upon the American city and criticized it for not living up to its possibilities and its promises; and as a result we find the growth of a city-based attack on the city itself, all in the name of the very things that a real romanticist would have scorned: science, sophistication, and order.

No doubt, a great deal of urban reform was prompted by a desire to recapture the spirit of earlier village life. But village life as conceived by John Dewey, Robert Park and Jane Addams was not purely impulsive, purely instinctual, purely of the heart. It was not part of untouched nature: it was not life in the forest or the wilderness. Santayana, a sharp critic of the American city, looked, not to the wilderness, but to the prebarbaric rural *city* as a place in which the life of reason could best be lived, and one of Howells' characters exclaimed: "Think of a city operated by science, as every city might be now, without one of the wretched animals tamed by savage man, and still perpetuated by the savage man for the awkward and imperfect uses of a barbarous society! A city without a horse, where electricity brought every man and everything silently to the door." The "capitals" in Howells' Altruria were also to be freed of the romantic horse in the same scientific spirit. In Howells' qualified nostalgia for the village one may find an ingredient of romanticism as conceived by some writers, without doubt. But we must avoid defining "romanticism" so broadly as to include under it any attitude which is critical of the city, for then, of course, every antiurbanist will be by definition a romanticist and the concept will become useless to us as an explanatory device. Romanticism was not the presiding spirit of antiurbanism after the Civil War, if we think of romanticism as antipathetic to science and technology, as celebrating nature after the fashion of Emerson when he said that he found something more dear and connate in the wilderness than in streets or villages. For romanticism in this sense was certainly not the spirit of Howells, who acknowledged his fear of loneliness in the country and his love of village streets. Nor was it the spirit in which Dewey, Henry James, Robert Park, Jane Addams, Theodore Dreiser, and Frank Lloyd Wright criticized the cities they knew.

Although the nation was stricken in its early history with a severe attack of Natty Bumppoism, by a serious case of intellectual hostility to the city in the name of nature, the fact that later varieties of antiurbanism were often motivated by opposed considerations indicates that romantic antiurbanism cannot be regarded as a permanent feature of the American mind. And once we see this, we are liberated from a mythical view of our intellectual past, and a stultifying view of our intellectual future. The tendency to see this country's mind as traditionally romantic is the product of a misguided philosophy of history and a failure to assess the facts of intellectual life after the Civil War. For at that time it became evident that romanticism was not a permanent affliction of the American intelligentsia. If distinguished writers continued to criticize the city sharply, it was primarily on other grounds. They recognized that at last America had developed complicated centers of culture and civilization but had not done enough to realize their potentialities. After the Civil War antiurbanism was therefore more rational, less metaphysical and less silly than meanderings about the supreme virtue of spontaneity, the heart, and the forest. We are not all heirs of Natty Bumppo, thank God, and we can escape that part of our so-called romantic heritage if we face the facts of history and the world about us.

The Idea of the City in European Thought: Voltaire to Spengler

CARL E. SCHORSKE

During two hectic centuries of social transformation, the problem of the city pressed relentlessly upon the consciousness of Europe's thinkers and artists. The response of the intellectuals to this pressure was infinitely varied; for social change brought in its train transformations in ideas and values more protean than the alterations in society itself. No man thinks of the city in hermetic isolation. He forms his image of it through a perceptual screen derived from inherited culture and transformed by personal experience. Hence the investigation of the intellectuals' idea of the city inevitably carries us outside its own frame into a myriad of concepts and values about the nature of man, society, and culture. To chart in its proper context the changing idea of the city since the eighteenth century far transcends the bounds of the possible in a brief paper. I can do no more than present a few major strands of thought on the city, in the hope that the resulting pattern may suggest further lines of investigation.

One may, I believe, discern three broad evaluations of the city in the past two hundred years: the city as virtue, the city as vice, and the city beyond good and evil. These attitudes appear among thinkers and artists in temporal succession. The eighteenth century developed out of its philosophy of Enlightenment the view of the city as virtue. Industrialism in the early nineteenth century brought to ascendancy an antithetical conception: the city as vice. Finally there emerged, in the context of a new subjectivist culture born in the mid-nineteenth century, an intellectual attitude which placed the city beyond good and evil. No new phase destroyed its predecessor. Each lived on into the phases which succeeded it, but with its vitality sapped, its glitter tarnished. Differences in national development, both social and intellectual, blur the clarity of the themes. Moreover, as the decades pass, strands of thought once seen as antithetical merge to form new points of departure for thought about the city. In the history of the idea of the city, as in other branches of history, the novel fructifies the old more often than destroys it.

Surely it was the unspoken assumption of the great middle class in the nineteenth century that the city was the productive center of man's most valued activities: industry and higher culture. This assumption was an inheritance from the preceding century, an inheritance so powerful that we must devote some attention to its character. Three influential children of the Enlightenment—Voltaire, Adam Smith, and Fichte—had formulated the view of the city as civilized virtue in terms congenial to their respective national cultures.

Voltaire sang his first lauds of the city not to Paris, but to London. London was the Athens of modern Europe; its virtues were freedom, commerce, and art. These three values—political, economic, and cultural—spring from a single source: the respect of the city for talent.

> Rival of Athens, London, blest indeed
>   That with thy tyrants had the wit to chase
> The prejudices civil factions breed.

> Men speak their thoughts and worth can win its place.
> In London, who has talent, he is great.[1]

London was for Voltaire the fostering mother of social mobility against the fixed hierarchical society.

The virtues he found in London, Voltaire soon generalized to the modern city as such. His views of the city form a belated chapter in the Battle of the Books, of Ancients versus Moderns. Voltaire wielded his rapier smartly against the defenders of a vanished past, of the golden age of Greece and the Christian garden of Eden. Why should mankind exalt the poverty-stricken Greeks?—or Adam and Eve with their matted hair and broken fingernails? "They lacked industry and pleasure: Is this virtue? No, pure ignorance." [2]

Industry and pleasure: these two pursuits distinguished urban life for Voltaire; together they produced "civilization." The urban contrast between rich and poor, far from holding terrors for the *philosophe*, provided the very basis of progress. Voltaire modelled his rich man not on the captain of industry, but on the spendthrift aristocrat pursuing a life of ease in the city, a true child of the pleasure principle. Voltaire described his *mondain's* luxurious rococo *hôtel*, with its exterior "ornamented by the striking industry of a thousand hands." [3] He savoured the rich man's daily rounds, his life of refined sensuality: the *mondain* rides in a handsome gilded carriage across imposing city squares to an assignation with an actress, then to the opera and a lavish meal. Through his sybaritic mode of existence, this squandering *bonvivant* creates work for countless artisans. He not only provides employment for the poor, but becomes a model to emulate. Aspiring to the life of civilized ease led by their betters, the poor are encouraged to industry and parsimony, and thus improve their state. Thanks to this happy symbiosis of rich and poor, elegant ease and thrifty industry, the city stimulates progress in reason and taste and thus perfects the arts of civilization.[4]

[1] Verses on the Death of Adrienne Lecouvreur, as translated by H. N. Brailsford in his *Voltaire* (Oxford, 1947), 54.

[2] Voltaire, "Le Mondain" (1736), *Oeuvres complètes* (Paris, 1877), X, 84.

[3] *Ibid.*, 83.

[4] *Ibid.*, 83–86. Voltaire here secularizes the traditional medieval view of the division of function between rich and poor in the social economy of salvation. In the medieval view, the rich or "noble" were saved by their generosity, the poor by their sufferings. Each was necessary to activate the virtues of the other. Voltaire introduced into this static symbiosis the dynamic of social mobility. (Cf., for a

Despite his rather bourgeois stress on the city as a force for social mobility, Voltaire regarded the aristocracy as the crucial agency in the progress of manners. The removal of the nobles to the city, especially in the reign of Louis XIV, brought a "sweeter life" to the uncouth townsman. The gracious wives of noblemen formed "schools of *pôlitesse*," which drew the urban young people away from the life of the pothouse, and introduced good conversation and reading.[5] Voltaire thus viewed the culture of the new city somewhat as, in our day, Lewis Mumford and others have seen the planning concepts which inspired it: as an extension of the palace. But where Mumford found baroque despotism—a strange combination of "power and pleasure, a dry abstract order and an effulgent sensuality," coupled with a deterioration of life for the masses—Voltaire saw social progress.[6] Not the destruction of community, but the diffusion of reason and taste to individuals of all classes: such was the function of the city for Voltaire.

Like Voltaire, Adam Smith attributed the origin of the city to the work of monarchs. In a wild and barbarous feudal age, the cities, needed by the kings, were established as centers of freedom and order. The city thus laid the foundations for progress in both industry and culture: ". . . When [men] are secure of enjoying the fruits of their industry," Smith wrote, "they naturally exert it to better their condition and to acquire not only the necessaries, but the conveniences and elegancies of life."[7] For Voltaire, the advent of the nobility civilized the towns; for Smith, the town civilized the rural nobility and at the same time destroyed feudal lordship. The nobles, "having sold their birthright not like Esau for a mess of pottage in time of hunger and necessity, but in the wantonness of plenty for trinkets and baubles . . . , became as insignificant as any substantial burgher or tradesman in the city."[8] The city levelled nobles down and burghers up, to produce a nation orderly, prosperous, and free.

The dynamic of civilization thus lay in the city for Smith no

Baroque statement of the traditional view, the ideas of Abraham a Santa Clara analyzed by Robert A. Kann, *A Study in Austrian Intellectual History* [New York, 1960], esp. 70–73.)
   [5] Voltaire, *Le siècle de Louis XIV* (2 vols., Paris, 1934), ch. III, 43–44.
   [6] Lewis Mumford, *The Culture of Cities* (New York, 1938), 108–113, 129–135. For a more differentiated analysis of the development of the modern city, see Martin Leinert, *Die Sozialgeschichte der Grossstadt* (Hamburg, 1925), III, *passim*.
   [7] Adam Smith, *The Wealth of Nations* (New York, 1937), 379.
   [8] *Ibid.*, 390–391.

less than for Voltaire. Yet both as economist and as moralist, Smith committed himself less fully to urbanism than Voltaire did. He defended the city only in its relationship to the country. The exchange between raw material and manufacture, between country and town, formed for him the backbone of prosperity. "The gains of both are mutual and reciprocal." But Smith regarded mobile capital as essentially unstable and, from the point of view of any given society, untrustworthy. ". . . [A] very trifling disgust," wrote Smith, "will make [the merchant or manufacturer] remove his capital and . . . all the industry which it supports from one country to another. No part of it can be said to belong to any particular country, till it has been spread over the face of that country, either in buildings, or in the lasting improvements of lands."[9] The urban capitalist is thus a rather unpatriotic nomad. Although the city improves the countryside by providing a market and manufactured goods, although it enriches mankind by making possible the transcendence of animal needs, its enterprising denizens are socially unreliable, labile.

Other vices of a subtler sort accompany the urban virtues: "unnaturalness and dependence." Smith maintained that "to culti- vate the ground was the natural destination of man." Both by in- terest and by sentiment, man tended to return to the land. Labor and capital gravitated naturally to the relatively risk-free country- side. But above all, the psychic satisfactions of the planter surpassed those of the urban merchant or manufacturer. Here Adam Smith showed himself an English preromantic: "The beauty of the coun- try, . . . the pleasures of the country life, the tranquility of mind which it promises and, wherever the injustice of human laws does not disturb it, the independency which it really affords, have charms that more or less attract everybody. . . ."[10] The city stimulated, the country fulfilled.

Smith pressed his psychological prejudices even at the expense of his economic logic when he argued that the farmer considered himself an independent man, a master, while the urban artificer felt always dependent on his customer, and thus unfree.[11] If the virtue of the city was that of the stimulus to economic and cultural

[9] *Ibid.*, 395.
[10] *Ibid.*, 358.
[11] *Ibid.*, 359. The farmer likewise depends, in Smith's theory, on his customer, for only the sale of his surplus enables him to purchase city-made necessities. In a free market economy all are interdependent.

progress, it did not afford the sense of security and personal free-dom of the farmer's life. Adam Smith's model for the "natural" return of men and capital to the land was North America, where primogeniture restricted neither personal freedom nor economic progress.[12] Here alone city and country stood in their proper re-lationship. The city stimulated thrift, wealth, and craft; it thus provided the artificer with the wherewithal to return to the land and to fulfill himself ultimately as an independent planter. Thus even this great champion of *laissez faire* and of the city's historic role, expressed that nostalgia for the rural life which was to charac-terize so much of England's thought on the city during the nine-teenth century.

The intellectuals of Germany took little interest in the city until the early nineteenth century. Their indifference was under-standable. Germany had no dominant capital in the eighteenth century to correspond to London or Paris. Her cities fell into two basic classes: on the one hand, there were surviving medieval towns, such as Lübeck or Frankfurt, still centers of economic life but with a rather sleepy traditional bourgeois culture; on the other hand, there were new baroque political centers, the so-called *Residenzstäde*, such as Berlin or Karlsruhe. Paris and London had concentrated political, economic, and cultural power in their hands, reducing the other cities of France and England to provincial status. In divided Germany, the many political capitals coincided only infrequently with the many economic or cultural centers. German urban life was at the same time more sluggish and more variegated than that of England and France.

The generation of great intellectuals which arose at the end of the eighteenth century in Germany elaborated its ideas of free-dom against the arbitrary power of the princes and the stultifying conventionality of the old burgher class. In neither dimension was the role of the city as an active element of progress of central con-cern to them. Against the atomizing and dehumanizing impact of despotic state power, the radical German humanists exalted the communitarian ideal of the Greek city-state.

During the Napoleonic Wars, Johann Gottlieb Fichte broke with the retrospective classical ideal to formulate a view of the city which governed much of German thought in the nineteenth

[12] *Ibid.*, 392–393.

century. Fichte adopted from western thinkers the notion of the city as the culture-forming agent *par excellence*. But where both Voltaire and Smith attributed the development of the city to the freedom and protection granted it by the prince, Fichte interpreted the German city as a pure creation of the *Volk*. The Germanic tribes which fell under the sway of Rome became victims of western *raison d'état*. Those which remained untouched in Germany perfected their primitive virtues—"loyalty, uprightness (*Bieder-keit*), honor and simplicity"—in medieval cities. "In these [cities]," Fichte wrote, "every branch of cultural life quickly developed into the fairest bloom." [13] To the branches of culture recorded positively by Voltaire and Smith—commerce, art and free institutions—, Fichte added yet another: communitarian morality. Precisely in the last, the German folk soul expressed itself. The burghers, in Fichte's eyes, produced "everything which is still worthy of honor among the Germans." They were neither made civilized by aristocrats and enlightened monarchs as in the view of Voltaire, nor motivated by self-interest as in the view of Smith. Inspired by piety, modesty, honor and, above all, by a sense of community, they were "alike in sacrifice for the common weal." The German burghers had shown for centuries that, alone among the European nations, Germany was "capable of enduring a republican constitution." Fichte called the age of the German medieval city "the nation's youthful dream of its future deeds, . . . the prophecy of what it would be once it had perfected its strength." [14]

In his glorification of the city as civilizing agent, Fichte thus added several new dimensions. The city in his vision became both democratic and communitarian in spirit. The medieval city took on the sociocultural characteristics assigned by other German thinkers—Schiller, Hölderlin, and the young Hegel—to the Greek polis. Fichte thus fortified the self-consciousness of the German bourgeoisie in its struggle for nationalism and democracy with a concrete model from its own history, a lost paradise of its own creation to regain. And with it, enemies to combat: the princes and the immoral state. The bloom of the city had been "destroyed by the tyranny and avarice of the princes, . . . its freedom trodden under foot" until Germany had sunk to its lowest ebb in Fichte's

[13] J. G. Fichte, *Reden an die deutsche Nation* (Berlin, 1912 [?]), 125–126.
[14] *Ibid.*, 127, 128.

age, when the nation suffered the imposition of the Napoleonic yoke.[15] While he did not devaluate the role of the city in commerce, he rejected Smith's "swindling theories about . . . manufacturing for the world market" as an instrument of foreign power and corruption.[16] Fichte had neither Voltaire's appreciation of the role of aristocratic luxury in urban culture-building, nor Smith's fear of the city entrepreneur's rootlessness. By extolling the burgher-city as a model ethical community, Fichte introduced ideal standards for the later critique of the nineteenth century city as a center of capitalist individualism.

The stronger medieval survivals in German society permitted Fichte to develop notions which transcended in their historical import the ideas of the city held by his French and English predecessors. For Voltaire and Smith, the city possessed virtues making for social progress; for Fichte, the city as community incarnated virtue in a social form.

Even while the idea of the city as virtue was being elaborated during the eighteenth century, a counter-current began to make itself felt: the idea of the city as vice. The city as seat of iniquity had, to be sure, been fair game for religious prophets and moralists since Sodom and Gomorrah. But in the eighteenth century, secular intellectuals began to raise new kinds of criticisms. Oliver Goldsmith deplored the destruction of England's peasantry as mobile capital extended its sway over the countryside. Unlike Adam Smith, he saw accumulating wealth produce decaying men. The French Physiocrats, whose notions of economic well-being centered upon maximizing agricultural production, eyed the city with suspicion. One of their leaders, Mercier de la Rivière, presented what seems like a deliberate transformation of Voltaire's urban gentleman riding gaily to his assignation: "The threatening wheels of the overbearing rich drive as rapidly as ever over stones stained with the blood of their unhappy victims." [17] Social concern for the prosperity of the peasant freeholder brought anti-urbanism in its wake, no less surely in Mercier's Europe than in Jefferson's America. Other intellectual currents only reenforced developing doubts

[15] *Ibid.*, 126.
[16] *Ibid.*, 251.
[17] Quoted from Mercier de la Rivière's *Tableau de Paris* in Lewis Mumford, *The Culture of Cities* (New York, 1938), 97.

about the city as "civilizing" agent: the preromantic cult of nature as a substitute for a personal God, and the sense of alienation which spread among the intellectuals as traditional social loyalties atrophied.

By the end of the eighteenth century, the spendthrift rich and the industrious artisans of Voltaire and Smith became transformed into Wordsworth's getters and spenders, equally wasting their powers, equally alienated from nature.[18] The rationality of the planned city, so prized by Voltaire, could appear to William Blake to impose "mind-forged manacles" on both nature and man. How different is Blake's poem, *London*, from Voltaire's earlier paean of praise:

> I wander thro' each charter'd street,
> Near where the charter'd Thames does flow,
> And mark in every face I meet
> Marks of weakness, marks of woe.[19]

Before the full consequences of industrialization were made manifest in the city, the intellectuals had already begun that revaluation of the urban environment which has not yet run its course. The reputation of the city had become entangled with concern over the transformation of agrarian society, with the fear of "mammonism," the cult of nature, and the revolt against mechanistic rationalism.

To this emergent view of the city as vice, the spread of industrialism in the first decades of the nineteenth century gave a powerful new impetus. As the promise of the beneficent operations of natural law in economic life became transformed into the findings of the "dismal science," so the hopeful mutual identity of interest of rich and poor, town and country turned into the warfare between Disraeli's "two nations," between the insouciant wealthy and the depraved slum dwellers.

What the romantic poets had discovered, the prose writers of the English social realist school in the 1840's described in its specific urban setting. The city symbolized in brick and grime and squalor the social crime of the age, the crime which more than any other

[18] William Wordsworth, "The World," in *Oxford Book of English Verse* (Oxford, 1931), 609.
[19] William Blake, "London," in *The Portable Blake* (ed. Alfred Kazin, New York, 1946), 112.

preoccupied the intelligentsia of Europe. The *cri de cœur* first raised in Britain spread eastward with industrialism until, a hundred years after Blake, it found voice in the Russia of Maxim Gorki.

Were poverty, squalor, and upper class hardheartedness *novae* in the urban universe? Assuredly not. Two developments account for the fact that the city in the early nineteenth century became the stigmatic symbol of these social vices. First, the dramatic increase in the rate of urbanization and the establishment of the jerry-built industrial town dramatized urban conditions which had hitherto passed unnoticed. Second, this negative transformation of the social landscape came against the background of Enlightenment expectations, of optimistic thinking about the progress of wealth and civilization through the city such as we have seen in Voltaire, Smith and Fichte. The city as symbol was caught in the psychological trammels of disappointed hopes. Without the dazzling picture of the city as virtue, inherited from the Enlightenment, the image of the city as vice could hardly have achieved so firm a grip on the European mind.

The critical responses to the industrial urban scene may be loosely distinguished between archaistic and futuristic. The archaists would abandon the city; the futurists, reform it. The archaists, such as Coleridge, Ruskin, the Pre-Raphaelites, Gustav Freytag in Germany, Dostoievsky and Tolstoy, firmly rejected the machine age and its modern megalopolis. In their respective ways, all sought a return to agrarian or small-town society. The utopian socialists in France, such as Fourier with his phalansteries, and even the syndicalists showed similar antiurban traits. For the archaists, the good life simply could not be lived in the modern city. They revived the communitarian past to criticize the grinding competitive present. Their vision of the future involved, to a greater or lesser degree, the recapture of a preurban past.

It is my impression that the failure of nineteenth-century urban architecture to develop an autonomous style reflected the strength of the archaistic current even among the urban bourgeoisie. Why, if railway bridges and factories could be built in a new utilitarian style, were both domestic and representational buildings conceived exclusively in architectural idioms antedating the eighteenth century? In London even the railway stations struck archaic poses: Euston Station sought in its façade escape to ancient

Greece, St. Pancras to the Middle Ages, and Paddington to the Renaissance. This Victorian historicism expressed the incapacity of city dwellers either to accept the present or to conceive the future except as a resurrection of the past. The new city builders, fearing to face the reality of their own creation, found no aesthetic forms to state it. This was almost as true for Napoleon III's Paris, with its strong tradition of controlled architectural continuity, as for Wilhelmian Berlin and Victorian London with their more flamboyant historical ecclecticism. Mammon sought to redeem himself by donning the mask of a preindustrial past that was not his own.

Ironically, the true archaistic rebels against the city, whether esthetic or ethical, found the medieval styles they advocated caricatured in the façades of the metropolis. Both John Ruskin and William Morris bore this cross. Both turned from an archaistic estheticism to socialism, from the classes to the masses, in the search for a more promising solution to the problems of industrial urban man. As they did so, they became somewhat more reconciled to modern industrialism and to the city. They passed from archaism to futurism.

The futuristic critics of the city were largely social reformers or socialists. Children of the Enlightenment, they found their faith in the city as civilizing agent severely strained by the spectacle of urban misery, but their melioristic thrust carried them over the chasm of doubt. The thought of Marx and Engels shows in its most complex form the intellectual adaptation of the progressive outlook to the era of industrial urbanization. Both revealed in their early writings a Fichtean nostalgia for the medieval artisan, owner of his means of production and creator of his entire product. The young Engels, in his *Condition of the Working Classes in England* (1845), described the plight of the urban poor in terms little different from those employed by the English middleclass urban reformers, social novelists and parliamentary commissioners of the 1840's. Engels described the industrial city realistically and indicted it ethically, yet offered no serious solution to its problems. Neither he nor Marx, however, suggested that the clock be turned back; nor did either support the "model community" solutions so favored by the nineteenth century utopians.

After nearly three decades of silence on the urban problem, Engels once again turned his attention to it in 1872, treating it now in the context of matured Marxian theory.[20] While still rejecting the industrial city existentially, he now affirmed it historically. Where the domestic worker who owned his home was chained to a given spot as victim of his exploiters, Engels argued, the urban industrial worker was free—even though his freedom was that of a "free outlaw." Engels scorned the "tearful Proudhonist's" looking backward to rural small-scale industry, "which produced only servile souls. . . . The English proletarian of 1872 is on an infinitely higher level than the rural weaver of 1772 with his 'hearth and home.'" The driving of the workers from "hearth and home" by capitalist industry and agriculture was not, in Engels' view, retrogression, but rather "the very first condition of their intellectual emancipation." "Only the proletariat . . . herded together in the big cities is in a position to accomplish the great social transformation which will put an end to all class exploitation and all class rule."[21]

Engels' attitude toward the modern city paralleled exactly Marx's attitude toward capitalism; both were equally dialectic. Marx rejected capitalism ethically for its exploitation of the worker and affirmed it historically for socializing the modes of production. Similarly, Engels excoriated the industrial city as the scene of labor's oppression, yet affirmed it historically as the theater *par excellence* of proletarian liberation. As in the struggle between big capital and small entrepreneurship Marx espoused the former as the "necessary" and "progressive" force, so in the struggle between urban and rural production, Engels favored the industrial city as the purgatory of the fallen peasant or small-town artisan, where both were to be cleansed of servility and both were to develop their proletarian consciousness.

What place would the city occupy in the socialist future? Engels shied away from concrete blueprints. Yet he was convinced that a start must be made toward "abolishing the contrast between town and country, which has been brought to its extreme point by present-day capitalist society."[22] Late in life, Engels resurrected in his discussion of the city of the future the antimegalopolitan outlook of the utopian socialists. He saw in the model communities of Owen and Fourier the synthesis of town and country—and lauded

[20] "The Housing Question," in Karl Marx and Friedrich Engels, *Selected Works* (2 vols., Moscow, 1958), I, 546–635.
[21] *Ibid.*, 563–564.
[22] *Ibid.*, 588.

this synthesis as suggesting the social essence, though not the form, of the living-unit of the future. Engels' anti-megalopolitan stance was clear: "To want to solve the housing question while at the same time desiring to maintain the modern big cities is an absurdity. The modern big cities, however, will be abolished only by the abolition of the capitalist mode of production." [23] Under socialism, the "intimate connection between industrial and agricultural production," and "as uniform distribution as possible of the population over the whole country . . . will . . . deliver the rural population from isolation and stupor" and bring the blessings of nature into city life.[24] Engels refused to specify his ideas of population-centers more precisely, but his whole argument suggested a strong affinity to the small-city ideal common to urban reformers since the close of the nineteenth century.

Where Adam Smith, on the basis of a theory of reciprocal urban and rural development, had seen the city man's fulfillment in a return to the land as an individual, Engels envisaged socialism as uniting the blessings of town and country by bringing the city to the country as a social entity; and conversely, nature to the city. In the course of three decades, his thought had passed from ethical rejection of the modern city, through historical affirmation of its liberating function, to a transcendence of the urban-rural debate in a utopian perspective: the synthesis of urban *Kultur* and rural *Natur* in the town of the socialist future. Though bitterly critical of the contemporary city, Engels rescued the idea of the city by integrating its very vices into his economy of social salvation.

A new generation of continental writers in the 1890's expressed views not far removed from Engels'. Unlike the English social novelists of the 1840's, they thought neither of pre-industrial life as bliss nor of Christian-ethical solutions to modern urbanism as viable. Emile Zola, in his trilogy *Trois villes*, painted Paris as a sink of iniquity. The Christian message was too weak and corrupted to regenerate modern society; neither Lourdes nor Rome could help. The cures must be found where the disease centered: in the modern metropolis. Here, out of degradation itself, would arise the humanistic moral and scientific spirit to build a new society. Emile Verhaeren, an active socialist as well as an avant-garde poet, showed the modern *Villes tentaculaires* sucking the life's blood out

[23] *Ibid.*, 589
[24] *Ibid.*, 627–628.

of the countryside. Verhaeren shared with the archaists a strong feeling for earlier village and town life, but the horrendous vitality of the city had turned the archaistic dream into the modern nightmare-actuality of bigotry and emptiness which ruled in rural life. The last cycle in his poetic tetralogy, entitled *Dawn*, showed that the industrial energies which, for a hundred years, had dragged man into oppression and ugliness, were also the key to redemption. The red light of the industrial mills betokened the dawn of the regenerated man. The red revolution of the masses would work the transformation.[25]

Were the archaists then dead by the end of the century? No. But they flowered in more fateful blooms, the *fleurs du mal* of totalitarian nationalism: Léon Daudet and Maurice Barrès in France, the proto-Nazi litterateurs in Germany. Condemners of the city all, they assaulted not the city as vice, but its people as vicious. The liberal urban rich were at best the allies of the Jew; the urban poor were the depraved and rootless masses, supporters of Jewish materialistic socialism. Back to the provinces, the true France, cried the neo-rightist French! Back to the soil where blood runs clear, cried the racist Germans! The German proto-Nazis—Langbehn, Lagarde, Lange—joined to their cult of peasant virtue the idealization of Fichte's medieval burg. But where Fichte used his archaic model to democratize German political life, his successors employed it for a revolution of rancor against liberalism, democracy and socialism. Fichte spoke for a middle class on the way up; his proto-Nazi successors, for a petty bourgeoisie which felt itself on the way down, crushed between big capital and big labor. Fichte exalted the communitarian city against the despotic *Residenzstadt;* his successors, against the modern metropolis. In short, where Fichte wrote in hope as a communitarian rationalist, the proto-Nazis wrote in frustration as blood-and-soil irrationalists.

The second wave of archaism may be most easily distinguished from the first by its lack of sympathy for the city man as victim. The sympathetic attitude had passed by 1900 largely to the futurists, the social reformers or revolutionaries who accepted the city as a social challenge and hoped to capitalize its energies. The remaining archaists viewed the city and its people not with tears of pity but with bitter hatred.

[25] Cf. Eugenia W. Herbert, *The Artist and Social Reform* (New Haven, 1961), 136–139.

How does the idea of the city as vice in 1900 compare with that of the city as virtue a century before? For the futurists of 1900, the city possessed vices, as for Voltaire and Smith it had possessed virtues. But those vices, the futurists believed, could be overcome by the social energies born of the city itself. The neo-archaists, in contrast, had fully inverted Fichte's values: for him the city had incarnated virtue in a social form to be emulated; for them it incarnated vice, and was to be destroyed.

Somewhere about 1850, there emerged in France a new mode of thought and feeling which has slowly but forcefully extended its sway over the consciousness of the West. No agreement yet exists on the nature of the great sea-change in our culture ushered in by Baudelaire and the French Impressionists, and given philosophical formulation by Nietzsche. We know only that the pioneers of this change explicitly challenged the validity of traditional morality, social thought, and art. The primacy of reason in man, the rational structure of nature and the meaningfulness of history, were all brought before the bar of personal psychological experience for judgment. This great revaluation inevitably drew the idea of the city into its train. As virtue and vice, progress and regression lost their clarity of meaning, the city was placed beyond Good and Evil.

"What is modern?" The intellectual transvaluators gave a new centrality to the question. They asked not, "What is good and bad about modern life?" but, "What *is* it? What true, what false?" Among the truths they found was the city, with all its glories and horrors, its beauties and its ugliness, as the essential ground of modern existence. Not to judge it ethically, but to experience it fully in one's own person became the aim of the *novi homines* of modern culture.

Perhaps we can most readily distinguish the new attitude from older ones by examining the city's place in relation to the ordinance of time. Earlier urban thinking had placed the modern city in phased history: between a benighted past and a rosy future (the Enlightenment view) or as a betrayal of a golden past (the anti-industrial view). For the new culture, by contrast, the city had no structured temporal locus between past and future, but rather a temporal quality. The modern city offered an eternal *hic et nunc*, whose content was transience, but whose transience was permanent. The city presented a succession of variegated, fleeting moments, each to be savoured in its passage from nonexistence to oblivion. To this view the experience of the crowd was basic: all its individuals uprooted, each unique, all conjoined for a moment before the parting of the ways.

Baudelaire, by affirming his own deracination, pressed the city into the service of a poetic of this modern life-attitude. He opened vistas to the city dweller which neither lamenting archaist nor reforming futurist had yet disclosed. "Multitude and solitude: [these are] terms that an active and fertile poet can make equal and interchangeable," he wrote.[26] He did so. Baudelaire lost his identity, as the city-man does, but he gained a world of vastly enlarged experience. He developed the special art he called "bathing himself in the crowd." [27] The city provided a "drunken spree of vitality," "feverish joys that will always be barred to the egoist." Baudelaire regarded the poetic city dweller as cousin to the prostitute—no longer an object of moralistic scorn. The poet, like the prostitute, identified himself with "all the professions, rejoicings, miseries that circumstances bring before him." "What men call love is a very small, restricted and weak thing compared with this ineffable orgy, this holy prostitution of a soul that gives itself utterly, with all its poetry and charity, to the unexpectedly emergent, to the passing unknown." [28]

For Baudelaire and the *fin de siècle* esthetes and decadents who followed him, the city made possible what Walter Pater called "the quickened, multiplied consciousness." This enrichment of personal sensibility, however, was bought at a terrible price: detachment from the psychological comforts of tradition and from any sense of participation in an integrated social whole. The modern city had, in the view of the new urbanite artists, destroyed the validity of all inherited integrating creeds. Such creeds had been preserved only hypocritically as masks of bourgeois reality. To the artist fell the duty of striking off the masks in order to show modern man his true face. The esthetic, sensuous—and sensual—appreciation of modern life became in this context only a kind of compensation for the lack of anchorage, of social or credal integra-

[26] Baudelaire, "Short Poems in Prose," *The Essence of Laughter* (ed. by Peter Quennell, New York, 1956), 139.
[27] Cf. Martin Turnell, *Baudelaire, a Study of his Poetry* (London, 1953), 193.
[28] Baudelaire, *Essence of Laughter*, 139, 140.

tion. Baudelaire expressed this tragically compensatory quality of the esthetic acceptance of urban life in desperate words: ". . . The intoxication of Art is the best thing of all for veiling the terrors of the Pit; . . . genius can play a part at the edge of the tomb with a joy that prevents it from seeing the tomb." [29]

To live for the fleeting moments of which modern urban life was composed, to jettison both the archaistic and the futuristic illusions, could produce not only reconciliation but also the wracking pain of loneliness and anxiety. The affirmation of the city by most of the decadents had the character not of an evaluation, but of an *amor fati*. Rainer Maria Rilke represented a variant of this attitude; for while he conceded the city's fatality, he evaluated the city negatively. His *Book of Hours* showed that, if art could veil the terrors of the pit, it could disclose them too. Rilke felt imprisoned in "the cities' guilt," whose psychological horrors he described with all the passion of a frustrated reformer:

> But cities seek their own, not others' good;
> they drag all with them in their headlong haste.
> They smash up animals like hollow wood
> and countless nations they burn up for waste.

He felt himself pinioned in the stone grip of the city, and the result was anguish, "the anguish deep of cities monstrous grown." The city here, though surely not beyond good and evil, was a collective fatality which could know only personal solutions, not social ones. Rilke sought his salvation in a poetic neo-Franciscanism, which negated in spirit the empty fate—the "spirally gyration"—which urban man called progress.[30] Despite his clear social protest, Rilke belonged rather to the new fatalists than to the archaists or futurists; for his solution was psychological and meta-historical, not socially redemptive.

Let us not fall into the error of some critics of the modern city by ignoring the genuine *joie de vivre* which the esthetic acceptance of the metropolis could generate. In reading the sophisticated urbanites of the *fin de siècle* one cannot but sense a certain affinity to Voltaire. For example, take Richard Le Gallienne's "London":

[29] *Ibid.*, 147–148.
[30] Rainer Maria Rilke, *The Book of Hours* (trans. by A. L. Peck, London, 1961), 117–135.

London, London, our delight,
Great flower that opens but at night,
Great city of the midnight sun,
Whose day begins when day is done.

Lamp after lamp against the sky
Opens a sudden beaming eye,
Leaping a light on either hand,
The iron lilies of the Strand.[31]

Le Gallienne expressed the same delight in the vital gleaming city as Voltaire. To be sure, the source of radiance was different: sunlight bathed Voltaire's Paris; nature glorified the work of man. Le Gallienne's city, in contrast, defied nature with mock-bucolic iron lilies and gaslit midnight suns. Not art but artificiality was celebrated here. Pleasure-seeking nocturnal London blotted out its grimy day. The Blakean meter of Le Gallienne's poem—was it intentional?—recalled Blake's workaday London, the gray historical transition from Voltaire's brilliant daylight to Le Gallienne's garish night-light. The night-bloom of London—as Le Gallienne showed he knew in other poems—was a flower of evil. But in an urban world become fatality, a flower's still a flower. Why should a man not pluck it? Voltaire's pleasure principle still had life in the *fin de siècle*, though its moral force was spent.

However marked their differences in personal response, the subjectivist transvaluators were at one in accepting megalopolis with its terrors and its joys as the given, the undeniable ground of modern existence. They banished both memory and hope, both the past and the future. To endow their feelings with esthetic form became the substitute for social values. Although social criticism sometimes remained strong, as it did in Rilke, all sense of social mastery atrophied. The aesthetic power of the individual replaced social vision as the source of succor in the face of fate. Where the social futurists looked to the redemption of the city through historical action, the fatalists redeemed it daily by revealing the beauty in urban degradation itself. What they saw as unalterable, they made endurable in a stance strangely compounded of stoicism, hedonism and despair.

Baudelaire and his successors unquestionably contributed to a new appreciation of the city as a scene of human life. Their esthetic revelation has converged with the social thought of the futur-

[31] Quoted in Holbrook Jackson, *The Eighteen Nineties* (London, 1950), 105.

ists to issue in richer and more constructive thinking about the city in our century. Since this form of thought is generally familiar, I shall close instead on another more somber intellectual synthesis, one which drove to its ultimate extreme the idea I have been discussing: the city beyond good and evil. This idea—with its historistic equivalent, the city as fatality—achieved its fullest theoretical formulation in the thought of Oswald Spengler, and its practical realization at the hands of the German National Socialists.

In his conspectus of civilization, Spengler brought together in the most sophisticated way many of the ideas of the city we have traced here. The city was for him the central civilizing agency. Like Fichte, he viewed it as an original creation of the folk. Like Voltaire, he called it the perfector of rational civilization. Like Verhaeren, he observed it suck the life out of the countryside. Accepting the psychological analyses of Baudelaire, Rilke, and Le Gallienne, he regarded modern urban humanity as neo-nomadic, dependent upon the spectacle of the ever-changing urban scene to fill the void of a desocialized consciousness. With all these affinities to his predecessors, Spengler differed from them in the most crucial area: he transformed all their affirmations into negations. This most brilliant of all historians of the city hated his subject with the bitter passion of the *fin de siècle* neo-archaists, the frustrated anti-democratic rightists of the lower middle class. Though he presented the city as fatality, he clearly welcomed its demise.

The German National Socialists shared the attitudes of Spengler—though surely not his richness of learning. The example of their urban policies illuminates the consequences of the fusion of two of the strands we have discussed: neo-archaist values with the notion of the city as a fatality beyond good and evil.

Translating neo-archaist notions into public policy, the Nazis began their rule with an active policy of returning the urban population to the holy German soil. They tried both permanent resettlement of urban workers on the land, and the education of urban youth in rural labor service.[32] Their antiurbanism did not, however, extend to Fichte's cherished medieval cities. Although the Nazi movement originated in a *Residenzstadt,* Munich, it chose medieval Nuremberg as the appropriate site for its annual party congress. The demands of the modern industrial state, however, could only

[32] Frieda Wunderlich, *Farm Labor in Germany, 1810–1945* (Princeton, 1961), 159–202, *passim.*

The Idea of the City in European Thought / 113

be fulfilled in an urban setting. The Nazis, while excoriating the "pavement literature" of the 1920's, and branding urban art as decadent, brought out in their city-building all the elements which the urban critics had almost strongly condemned. Was the city responsible for the mechanization of life? The Nazis slashed down the trees of Berlin's Tiergarten to build the widest, most monotonously mechanical street in the world: the *Achse*, where rurally regenerated youth could ride their roaring motorcycles in black-uniformed formation. Was the city the scene of the lonely crowd? The Nazis built huge squares in which the crowd could intoxicate itself. Had the city-man become deracinated and atomized? The Nazis made him a cog in a huge machine. The hyper-rationality which the neo-archaists deplored reappeared in the Nazi parade, the Nazi demonstration, the organization of every aspect of life. Thus the whole cult of rural virtue and the medieval, communitarian city revealed itself as ideological veneer, while the reality of antiurban prejudice brought the vices of the city to an undreamt-of fulfillment: mechanization, deracination, spectacle and—untouched behind the great squares of men on the march one knew not where—the still-festering slums. Truly the city had here become a fatality for man, beyond good and evil. The antiurbanites had brought to fruition the very features of the city they had most condemned. For they were themselves children of the unreformed city of the nineteenth century, victims of an Enlightenment dream gone wrong.

Boosters, Intellectuals, and the American City

FRANK FREIDEL

Did the favorable attitudes toward the city relatively prevalent in Europe during the Enlightenment and even up into the nineteenth century have their counterparts in the United States? Among many intellectuals they did not; one need go no further than to cite Jefferson, the great American exponent of the Enlightenment. But by digging a bit lower in the strata of intellectual levels, one can find some eighteenth century Americans who, like the Europeans of the Enlightenment, also saw the city as embodying the dynamisms for the spread of culture and capital. Dr. Franklin's contributions to the urbanization of Philadelphia are too well known to require repetition, and in addition he shared the enthusiasm of many of his contemporaries for life in the great cities of

Europe. Franklin came to feel so comfortable in London during the two decades he lived there that he was planning to retire to that city permanently when the alarms of the American Revolution forced him instead into his famous love affair with Paris.

In the intellectual stratum below Franklin, promoters of cities were legion. A Baltimore gentleman, writing in 1773, thus urged a friend in the Maryland Assembly to foster legislation that would be favorable to his city. Law and subordination, the gentleman pointed out, had evolved in the cities of the late Middle Ages. Furthermore: "Liberty, science, and commerce, the great friends of men, are sister adventurers. They are intimately, indeed inseparably connected together, and always take up their chief residence in the cities. Thither the greatest geniuses of the age generally resort, and incited by emulation or fired by ambition, they stimulate each other to successful exertions of native talents; which might have otherwise lain dormant, and forever deprived mankind of much useful instruction. To them repair the patriots, the men of letters, and the merchants, who become the guardians of the people's rights, the protectors of learning, the supporters of their country's trade. Thus free cities, considered in this light, are the repositories, preservatives, and nurseries of commerce, liberty, and knowledge."

These influences were at work, the gentleman argued, not only in the great cities of Europe but in the New World as well: "Even in this new, and as yet uninformed American world, a Boston, a New York, and a Philadelphia add lustre and dignity to the colonies to which they belong, and are advancing with rapidity toward perfection in arts and sciences, commerce and mechanics." As for Maryland, its lack of a similar "commercial capital" was the reason for the colony's lag in development.[1]

In this statement one finds compressed a large number of the arguments that contemporary Europeans were advancing in favor of the city. It is most noteworthy because it was made not by a leading intellectual, but by a practical minded city booster, someone who was trying to lobby urban development bills through a reluctant legislature. And so it has been throughout American history, that though some intellectuals have been hostile to the city, others of their company—admittedly for the most part lesser lights —have expressed enthusiasm for urban growth. Two of the most

---

[1] Quoted in Carl Bridenbaugh, *Cities in Revolt: Urban Life in America, 1743–1776* (New York, 1955), 215.

famous Southern editors during the decades after the Civil War, Henry Grady of Atlanta, and "Marse" Henry Watterson of Louisville, were, above all, city boosters. In 1896, the Emporia, Kansas editor, William Allen White, achieved instant national fame when, in a sarcastic diatribe against the Populists he extolled urbanism: "We don't need population, we don't need well-dressed men on the streets; . . . we don't need cities on these fertile prairies; you bet we don't. . . . Because we have become poorer and ornrier and meaner than a spavined, distempered mule, we the people of Kansas, propose to kick; we don't care to build up, we wish to tear down." [2]

White above all was in the civic booster tradition. This spirit, upheld by Benjamin Franklin in the maxims of "Poor Richard" almost as a doctrine of American faith, but scathingly satirized by Sinclair Lewis in his *Babbitt*, has seldom been approved by American intellectuals. Yet one wonders if the intellectuals did not feel some ambivalence toward the city: seeing in it much that was good as well as much that was unpleasant or evil. Did they not view different cities at different times in different ways? Raw, noisy, dusty, fly-ridden, prostitute-plagued Washington of the Civil War period evoked different responses from the Washington of broad malls and stately white buildings of the Coolidge era. Certainly attitudes toward Washington changed sharply during this span of six decades, even though the aged Civil War veteran returning in the 1920's would have found the alleyways noisomely familiar.

The attitude of American intellectuals toward their own cities as contrasted with their attitude toward European cities was subject to similar variation. In addition, the American intellectuals differed from their European counterparts in their attitudes toward the city, in part because the traditions of the two groups of intellectuals were different. Morton White makes a notable contribution when he attacks the usual explanation for the difference (that Americans grew up in a romantic, agrarian tradition) as being too monistic and intellectualistic, since Natty Bumppos are still among us—teaching United States history. The agrarian tradition was indeed important and of marked effect, but it has been too often oversimplified. It is too easy to explain that American intellectuals grew up in a society which attributed all good, all virtue, and all democracy to

[2] "What's the Matter with Kansas?" originally published in the *Emporia Gazette*, August 16, 1896.

the country; and that Europeans contrariwise, were reared in a society which attributed so much good to their cities. Yet, with countless ramifications, the agrarian tradition is a factor, to which could be applied, as an amendment to an oversimplified view, Oscar Handlin's suggestion that the sprawling towns that quickly came into existence in colonial America, towns that provided every man his own garden space behind his house, developed in America a suburban tradition in contrast to the urban tradition of Europe that dates back to the crowded, walled city. To this day, the larger part of American intellectuals live in their own homes surrounded by their own yards; the larger part of the Europeans still live in their apartments.

In the views and activities of one leading early American, John Adams, who was essentially antiurban, one can find some of the antiurban themes that have been basic among intellectuals ever since. There may well have been some ambivalence on Adams's part. Was he not expecting America to become urban when he penned his famous remark, "It has ever been my hobby-horse to see rising in America an empire of liberty, and a prospect of two or three hundred millions of freemen, without one noble or one king among them?" [3] Perhaps not. Perhaps he was visualizing a vast agrarian population like that of India or China, for he also wrote: "In the present state of society and manners in America, with a people living chiefly by agriculture, in small numbers, sprinkled over large tracts of land, they are not subject to those panics and transports, those contagions of madness and folly, which are seen in countries where large numbers live in small places, in daily fear of perishing for want." [4]

Here, Adams expressed one of the basic fears held by intellectuals in their opposition to the city—political fear. Even in his days, when city governments were still largely controlled by gentlemen, there was a fear of the propertyless element, the volatile urban mob, and of the wily agitators who incited this part of the population. Although Adams was a patriot, he defended Captain Preston and his men, and obtained their acquittal, against the charges brought against them because of their part in the Boston Massacre of 1770. Adams thus viewed the Massacre: "Endeavors had been systemati-

[3] Adrienne Koch and William Peden, eds., *The Selected Writings of John and John Quincy Adams* (New York, 1946), 75.
[4] *Ibid.*, 105.

cally pursued for many months, by certain busy characters, to excite quarrels, encounters, and combats, single or compound, in the night, between the inhabitants of the lower class and the soldiers, and at all risks to enkindle an immortal hatred between them. I suspected that this was the explosion which had been intentionally wrought up by designing men, who knew what they were aiming at better than the instruments employed." [5] Fear of the mob continued, and was heightened during the decades that followed by the frightening example of the Parisian mobs of 1789, 1820, 1848, and later. (As immigrants poured into American cities and became organized into political machines, gentlemen lost control of urban governments, and merged their political fears into religious and ethnic animus.)

A second great fear was intellectual and aesthetic, and here Adams's views illustrate interesting ambivalences. As a young man he had inquired: "Who can study in Boston streets? I am unable to observe the various objects that I meet, with sufficient precision. My eyes are so diverted with chimney sweepers, sawyers of wood, merchants, ladies, priests, carts, horses, oxen, coaches, market-men and women, soldiers, sailors; and my ears with the rattle-gabble of them all, that I cannot think long enough in the street upon any one thing, to start and pursue a thought." [6] On the other hand, Adams recognized that cities did nurture culture, and that the United States, when it became independent and sufficiently rich, must turn to the arts. Writing to his wife, Abigail, from Paris, in 1780, he expressed his regret that he lacked the time to describe to her the splendid gardens and striking statuary at the Tuileries. "I must study politics and war," he explained, "that my sons may have liberty to study mathematics and philosophy." His sons in turn should study mathematics and philosophy and the arts of commerce, "in order to give their children a right to study painting, poetry, music, architecture, statuary, tapestry, and porcelain." And so they did. [7]

The Boston of John Quincy Adams and Charles Francis Adams witnessed the growth of slums and the violence of mobs beyond John Adams's worst fears. As the earlier balance was threatened, a howling Protestant mob burned down a Catholic convent

[5] *Ibid.*, 28–29.
[6] Bridenbaugh, *op.cit.*, 35–36.
[7] Koch and Peden, *op.cit.*, 65–66.

in Charlestown; some decades later, Catholic immigrants took over the city government of Boston. The intellectual gentlemen of Beacon Hill and Back Bay were not entirely negative in their reaction to the changes; they built parks and playgrounds, beautified the Charles River Basin, established a symphony orchestra, promoted education, founded a great museum of fine arts, and engaged in a multitude of charitable enterprises to better the lot of slum-dwellers. John Adams's great-grandson, Henry, an observer of most of these city developments, both the bad and the good, became a virulent city hater. But while the earlier Adamses had lived in the country or in a suburb, Henry Adams built a mansion in the heart of Washington.

These illustrations may demonstrate how a few of the anti-urban and prourban factors were viewed by one man and one family. Obviously in any lengthier comments it would be necessary to examine the thought of various levels of writers from the mere civic booster to the most abstract thinkers. Also, one should study the physical changes that occurred in cities from decade to decade and correlate these changes with the prevailing attitudes of intellectuals. An articulate, educated person living in New York City about 1870 might praise its comforts and culture, and at the same time protest against the Tweed Ring, the hoodlums on the streets at night, the inches-deep, tarry filth on the pavements, the forest of telephone poles and maze of overhead wires, and the unpleasant taste of the drinking water. Later generations might not make these particular complaints, but could compile comparable objections.

Thus the way is open to fruitful study in a variety of areas. Out of this research and analysis should come some clear idea of the way in which varying attitudes toward the city grew out of concrete conditions as well as out of long-nurtured traditions. This knowledge could help point to directions for the building of future cities that intellectuals and nonintellectuals alike would find more congenial.

The City as the Idea of Social Order

SYLVIA L. THRUPP

Talk about cities is ordinarily of how they strike the eye, of whether life in them is pleasant, and of what makes one more important than another. Writing about them, too, is either of their design and fabric or of the social interaction that goes on against this background; histories of cities touch on both to enliven the story of how power—political, economic or religious—came to be centered in them and how their populations grew. The premise of this paper, that cities are the focal points of a civilization in its aspect of social order, is taken for granted and left implicit. We are as conscious as any people of the visual esthetic order, or lack of it, in our cities; indeed, air travel, especially when night blots out the countryside and leaves only the patterns of street lighting, makes us conscious in a new way of the beauty or defects of their ground plan. Yet few are aware of the part that the esthetic character of the city has played in developing and maintaining the sense of order out of which civilization grew and on which it depends.

Historians have written of its connection with the sense of order in this broader sense only fragmentarily. Yet the theme is a great one. It gives the city moral and intellectual dignity as an idea, but is not to be dismissed to the realm of symbolism. It concerns the practical life and history of every city, the more so when these are regarded, not as insular affairs, but in their relations with the countryside or trading territory out of which a city grew. A brief paper can do no more than try to link together, along the Western historical thread, the disparate ways in which the theme has so far been treated.

The sense of order has a resonance as old as culture; it antedates the city. Culture required continuity and could have it only by inventing the idea of order. Initially this took form in the mind's eye as a spatially structured cosmos with different levels in it for gods and men, connected by a hollow central shaft. The religious leaders of primitive communities persuaded their fellows that the proper location for a settlement was directly beneath the means of access to the home of the supreme gods, that is, at the centre of the universe. At the same time these thinkers devised a simple plan for linking any living-space, even a nomad camp, with this "sacred space," the procedure which Mircea Eliade describes as the "cosmicizing" of an area. A common example was the grouping of village huts about a cultic building embellished with features that made it represent the heavens and the means of access to them.[1] The village was then safe. The first cities in the ancient Near East were planned on a similar system, improved only by the greater impressiveness of the temples at their heart, which were true models of the universe and lent safety to a larger area. These cities, in short, were the supreme living expositions in their time of the idea of cosmological order. The idea was abstract yet visible and tangible in their design. In cosmological thinking there could be many such models; there was no inconsistency in multiplying centres of the universe, no monopoly of right location. For an enemy to destroy

[1] See *City Invincible* (ed. C. Kraeling *et al.*, Chicago, 1960), 363–66; also *Le symbolisme cosmique des monuments religieux* (Rome: Istituto Italiano per il medio ed estremo oriente, XIV, 1957), *passim*, especially Mircea Eliade's "Centre du monde, temple, maison," 57–82.

one's sacred centre would make defeat the more dangerous, but the centre could be rebuilt. There were not contending orders.

As the ancient cities became the seats of monarchy, consciousness of order rapidly matured in a second form, that of social order, consisting in the deliberate regulation of human relationships through custom corrected by law and by the royal power over a territory that had limits. With empire, the king's capital city stood preeminently for social order over the whole conquered territory. There were also lesser cities, the nodal points of the royal administration.[2] These provincial cities are the places where officials reside, where military levies must report and taxes be deposited. Like the capital city, though to a lesser degree, they are the backdrop for the public ceremonial which makes the idea of social order visible and comprehensible to the illiterate. The distinction between the provincial cities and the smaller places which we would call towns and villages, like the difference between capital and provincial city, is one of status gradient. Although the cities are more closely identified with the idea of social order and with the power that directs it, they are not thereby in logical opposition to rurality. They are simply to a superior degree the source of the order that covers urban and rural areas alike. The only logical opposition is the desolation of barren land where no man lives, not even shepherds or nomads, but only wild beasts, owls and demons—the fate that the prophet Isaiah willed for Babylon.[3] As between rival empires, however, there are now different and contending social orders.

The ancient world bequeathed also the identification of the city with a third form of order, perfect order. In its dialectic this is simply a rational combination of cosmological order conceived as proper formal relations between men and the gods, and social order conceived as authoritatively ordered relations among men. In the heavenly Jerusalem God will make men one with himself and with each other. In Plato's Republic God's place is taken by the idea of justice.

The idea of perfect order was born in the same atmosphere of ferment that gave birth to the idea of moral order. Yet the two are sharply distinct for many centuries. Moral order, as Eric Voegelin traces its emergence in his epic *Order and History*, is essentially subjective, dependent on a sustained conflict within man, and

[2] See *City Invincible, passim.*
[3] *Isaiah* 13: 20–22.

deriving, in his view of the West, from the Greek conception of man as engaged in a struggle against fate.[4] Perfect order on the contrary is by definition static, the creation of divine authority, and must have required a spatial location.

The city has therefore never been identified with moral order, and the birth of the latter as an idea to some extent jeopardizes the moral worth of the city's identification with social order. For it brings opposition now not only from without, from a rival empire with a different social order, but from critics within. In the Greek as in the Judaic tradition moral thinkers took a highly derogatory attitude toward the city both as an actual community and as claiming high status over other places through standing in a superior degree for social order, because in both capacities it necessarily embodied what they perceived to be evil as well as good. As a community the city concentrated in itself the best professional skill of the day regardless of the moral level of the profession—star prostitutes and confidence men as well as high priests and the best lawyers. As the idea of social order it justified the rule of the rich over the poor which the prophets denounced. Like many of the authors of the Jewish scriptures, Plato himself believed the pre-urban condition of men to have been morally better.[5] He placed his vision of perfect order in a city not because this form of community was more disposed than others to moral excellence but because of its high place in the status gradient. To have placed perfect order in a village, a camp-site or a farmyard would have been ridiculous.

The cities of the ancient world helped to produce another of the distinctive elements of the Western intellectual tradition, the application of the idea of evolution or progress to societies. The Graeco-Romans limited that criterion to a backward-looking perspective, for they saw their cities as the peak of human evolution. But with the aid of a condescending tolerance for the lower degrees of social order which were all that purely agrarian peoples or nomadic peoples could boast, these other societies could be seen as having at least a potential future. Nomads might become settled cultivators and cultivators might learn to build cities as well as villages. In the Mediterranean world this view passed on from Rome

[4] Eric Voegelin, *Order and History* (3 vols., Baton Rouge, Louisiana, 1956–   ).
[5] For the view that he also thought earlier types of city, Cretan and Spartan, better than Athens, see G. R. Morrow, *Plato's Cretan City: a historical interpretation of the Laws* (Princeton, 1960).

to the men of the medieval world as a way of viewing the course of history and by the late twelfth century was a commonplace among educated men even in northern Europe. Gerald of Wales applies it interestingly in his writings on the ethmology and history of the Welsh and the Irish.[6]

The idea of the city as standing for social order had thus survived the ages of barbarism and early feudalism. In spite of the obvious decline of urban life during these centuries cities had remained architecturally by far the most impressive visible groupings, and through the bishops' powers had remained the most important administrative centres. Moreover, they were indispensable as dramatic and sacred background to the political and religious ceremonial through which kingship retained its hold on men's loyalty. Even in the legendary history that was popularized in the twelfth century a king was unthinkable without a city: Arthur had to have a Camelot.

As they recover economic vitality the medieval cities come to be more and more the dominant expression of civilized order. At the extreme, in Italy, they again govern the countryside and uproot and urbanize the rural nobility. North of the Alps they become the instruments of advancing royal power and the means, along with castle towns and planned market towns, of holding newly conquered and colonized territory. In Germany, owing to the collapse of royal power and the crystallization of urban communities around exclusively commercial interests or in the miniscule towns around petty bourgeois routine, most of the nobility continued to prefer the old-fashioned life of family surrounded by servitors and dependents in castle and hunting lodge. Yet where outside cultural influence penetrated most deeply, as in southern Germany, territorial lords took to ensconcing themselves in strategically located dwarf administrative capitals whose architecture and planning were lucid translations of the ideas of power and social dominance and remained so throughout the age of Baroque rebuilding.

The city's hold on the imagination in the early modern centuries was substantially reinforced not only by the physical expansion of political capitals and centres of economic power but by speculative thought and by art. Speculative thought played with new patterns of perfect order that had little of the heavenly Jeru-

[6] *Opera Giraldi Cambrensis* (ed. J. F. Dimock, Rolls Series, 1867), 151.

salem about them—although in millennial thought Jerusalem shines on—but that under cover of Utopianism advanced a great deal of indirect incitement to social and economic reform. Baroque art completes as it were the counterpoint of the age. The princely capital designed in the geometrical symmetry of the circle or of some other form recognized as perfect is the benevolent despot's reply to the discontented: "See, all is well!"

The thinkers through whom the idea of moral order evolved were incapable of shaking the acceptance of the city as the idea of social order because they too accepted it. Medieval attacks on Paris and Rome as concentrating in themselves carnal temptation, new-fangled professional ambition and the avarice of lawyers were motivated by varying mixtures of conservative revulsion against the development of bureaucracy and of fear that loose women and lawyers were heralds of Anti-Christ. A chorus of criticism leaned on Apocalyptic thought to stigmatize Rome as Babylon while offering no alternative plan by which the Church could be governed without Rome.[7] St. Bernard pleading with Paris students to flee this Babylon and enter his austerely reformed monasteries was in effect urging them to flee the social order. The purpose of the monastic rule as he saw it was to maintain a disciplined meditation on the sufferings of Christ throughout the monk's every waking moment, in order the better to prepare him for the hereafter.

With the Enlightenment the career of the city as the idea of social order entered a new phase. Gradually, through recognition of the changing role of cities in the economic order, they are worked into the new scheme of thought in which the idea of progress is forward-looking. Montesquieu strikes a new note in characterizing modern cities as radically different from ancient Rome. Rome, he asserts, grew out of the same type of barbarian fort that could have been found in the Crimea, a retreat for raiders living by pillage. She never really reformed her ways; the fate of the Empire was determined by the pickings of pillage. The modern city, on the contrary, is part of a productive economic order.[8] Voltaire traced the origins of this order to medieval urban industry. Despite his detestation of the middle ages, he saw its craftsmen humbly and obscurely preparing the foundations of a new civilization. His

[7] See John A. Yunck, "Economic Conservatism, Papal Finance, and the Medieval Satires on Rome," *Mediaeval Studies,* XXIII (1961), 334–51.

[8] *Esprit des lois,* chap. 12.

praise of the cities he knew and delighted in as the home of pleasure reflects only one aspect of the city's ancient role of meeting esthetic needs, although aristocratic pleasure was taking on new refinements. His remarks are not very penetrating. A Babylonian or an ancient Roman could also have discoursed on aristocratic city pleasures. What is extraordinary, in a Frenchman, is his infatuation for London, which was already darkening the air with coal smoke. The reason for this enthusiasm was his perception that of all the countries of Europe the England of his day was the only one ideally fitted to become the home of deism.[9] London, for Voltaire, stood for England, for the English social order.

The idea of progress had to contend with as many enemies as the armies of Napoleon, the most lethal being the readiness with which its optimism could be twisted into the pessimism of the cyclic view of history. Adam Smith himself, the apostle of economic progress, was uncertain whether men could become enlightened enough to avert the ultimate decay that had overtaken in succession every civilization of the ancient past; Playfair assumed that they could not; and Ricardo buttressed that assumption by his system of economic reasoning. Economic pessimism sharpened the anxiety with which moralists now watched the disturbing growth of British cities. What little was generally known of the failure of the ancient civilizations was connected through Biblical reading with the moral weakness of their city people. If urban industry was now to add a new cause of breakdown and decay the outlook was poor. Socialists were optimistic because they hoped to take over the cities and reshape the whole institutional context of industry. No one in Western Europe could envisage a social order devoid of cities. Even the Fourierites and the Owenites in their attempts to make a fresh start on the organization of production were simply making a fresh start in small-scale urban development. The anarchists were more radical in their belief that the status gradient between city, town, and village could be levelled out by means of new cooperative devices that would eliminate social injustices. Only in Russia, under the joint influence of nationalist and populist sentiment, could agrarian socialists think of employing village institutions as the model and nexus of a better social order.

At the start of the nineteenth century moralists on the Con-

[9] See Franco Venturi, "L'illuminismo nel settecento Europo," *Rapports, XIth Congress of Historical Sciences* (Stockholm, 1960), vol. IV.

tinent could still hope to forestall excessive urban growth by attacking Adam Smith's doctrines of free enterprise as calculated to destroy traditional culture. Fichte appealed to the small-town German burghers in this vein.[10] Equally characteristic was the call of the cameralist economist Adam Müller, in the post-Jena crisis, for national leadership from officialdom and the Junkers. The bitterness and eloquence of his attack on every figure connected with urban credit or money power from the merchants even of the medieval cities through Adam Smith to the bankers of his own day are astounding.[11] Müller advocated strong paternalistic government to restrain free enterprise. In Germany, as he wished to see it, the dominant cities would obviously have been those housing bureaucrats and soldiers, with only such trade and industry as would be needed to serve these. Such cities would have been visible embodiments of the principle of authority. Through the Junkers this same principle would have extended over the villages, where it would somehow be supported by a traditional spirit of community.

Fichte and Müller agreed in desiring more rational use of authority to obstruct the growth of world-market cities. Disciples of Adam Smith wished authority to be used discreetly to the opposite end, to free the way for enterprise. In short, all who took any stand on the kinds of progress that the early phases of nineteenth century industrialism brought, socialists included and anarchists the only group excepted, alike wanted to back by authority some form of organization that they advocated as rational. The one rugged individualist who opposed this trust in rational organization, William Blake, was jeered at by his contemporaries as mad.

To Blake the one issue that mattered was whether life in society left room for individual creativity and spontaneity of feeling. When people lived by a rationally constrained morality, conceived of society as based on rational contract, and in looking at the stars could think only of a mechanism, how could they find joy? He blamed three men—Voltaire, Locke, and Newton—for having pushed life into these loveless habits, and he never tired of railing at them. At the same time he could place true freedom only in the golden age of myth. As to the future, he was not optimistic. Some degree of constraint inhered in the nature of society. Nothing could

[10] See Carl E. Schorske in this volume.

[11] Müller is discussed further, with references, in my "The Role of Comparison in the Development of Economic History," *The Journal of Economic History*, XVII (1957), 560–561.

be done with the social order beyond trying to persuade people to be more tolerant of spontaneity.

Having these convictions Blake was content to accept the conventional connections of the city with social order and with perfect order. London, for which he had the affection of a native, and where as artist-craftstman he found more scope for his talents than provincial cities offered, was to him England, an England whose order had even in ancient times included other cities as well as villages. His "dark Satanic mills," which to the unwary reader conjure up factory walls, were any constructs stemming from the influence of Voltaire, Locke and Newton, and the "marks of woe" he saw in London faces are merely the stamp of the same demonic trinity. His own thought is embedded in the ponderous allegory which makes his long poem *Jerusalem* virtually unreadable. Babylon is a popular woman he beholds "in the opening streets of London"; a few lines further on he explained that she was "Rational Morality." Beside her another woman named Jerusalem wandered the same streets "in ruins." She is the emanation of spiritual man, destined with the awakening of nations in the seventh age of the world to become his resplendent bride in the character of the city of perfect order. She is also the potentiality of London as the city of "Universal Humanity," for it is here in the foggy streets of London that Blake calls for the light of Jerusalem to descend. His scheme demanded also that he furnish even the terrestrial Paradise with a city, which again is London-Jerusalem. By this token his readers were to know that perfect order as an idea had eternal existence and meaning. Yet muffled as it was in Druidic myth, Blake's meaning reached very few.[12] The pre-Raphaelite response came late and loaded with pseudo-medievalism.

But the city never lost vitality as an idea. After the middle of the nineteenth century, when economic pessimism had subsided, poets and novelists of extraordinary sensitivity explored the city-dweller's life as aesthetic experience. This brought the great capitals rather than industrial cities to the fore. Seen in historical perspective, the adventure of city-literature from Baudelaire to the anti-novelists of today has been to carry the early romantic philosophy

[12] Northrop Frye, *Fearful Symmetry, A Study of William Blake* (Princeton, 1947) is a study of his allegory; see especially Part II and Chapter 11. See also Ruthven Todd, "William Blake and the Eighteenth Century Mythologists," *Tracks in the Snow* (New York, 1947). My quotations from Blake are from his *Jerusalem*, stanza 74

of individuation through a sequence of new phases. The individual has been dissolved successively into sensation, into fleeting personal relationships, into ignominy and fear. Yet the artist's pursuit of self-awareness has not weakened but has strengthened the idea of the individual in a society avowedly based more and more upon it. The striking contrast between this city-literature and that produced under totalitarian control of the artist brings out very clearly the differing nature of the city as an idea in different social orders.

Following the lead of literature, and of criminologists, sociology also turned to the exploration of great cities, at first mainly in regard to matters of concern to social reformers. The bias of this approach caused "the city" to be conceived as something pathological, the more so as small communities tended to be idealized as healthy. Robert Park's leadership in American urban sociology brought more realistic concepts through precise analysis both of processes of social disorganization and of the complexity inherent in the structure of city occupations, with its inevitable juxtaposition of the reputable and the disreputable. More objective analysis of rural communities and small towns and of the conditions under which they too may present features of disorganization then became possible.

The onrush of industrialism is today fast making any urban-rural dichotomy patently unrealistic. This very fact, however, is likely to refix it in nostalgic views of the past, a new urban romanticism taking the place of the older, agrarian romanticism. The scholar's task is not so much to attack either one or the other but to reconsider the historical validity of the dichotomy. It is preferable to treat all types of community in relation to the intensity of their engagement in the maintenance of the common social order to which they belong. Their degree of engagement is manifest in their share in concentrations of power and of cultural creativeness. It is manifest also in the esthetic sense of order shown in their spatial form and architecture which, in towers, spires, skyscrapers, and domed roofing, still bear traces of their origin in the sense of cosmological order. Although even in a contemporary society the gradations of engagement can never be precisely measured as on a scale, the historian can become aware of changes in the angle of the gradient. For example, in Renaissance Italy the gradient as between city and village grew steeper. Why this was so is still not fully explained, for city society and intercity affairs have virtually monopolized research attention to the neglect of the countryside. American history displays an opposite trend, the peculiar vigor of American democracy having always tended to level the gradient. The truculent criticism of cities as being too civilized in early nineteenth-century American writing is unthinkable in the Europe of that time.[13]

An urban-rural dichotomy can find only tenuous support in moral condemnation of cities, although the record of this in prophecy, sermons and stereotyped images in other literature may perhaps, if it is searched, yield some theories of decadence, some attempts to analyze the processes, apart from the military contingencies, by which city-based empires decayed. More likely, such research will yield only the pervasive influence of the millennial dream. Those who, like early and reformist monks in Buddhist and Christian cultures, and like Thoreau in New England, retired to meditate in rural peace did so not because they believed rural life to be ultimately satisfying but because they believed nothing on this earth could be satisfying except through the miracle of a new age. Their dreams were of the golden age that lies at the heart of all varieties of millennial thought and that flickers even in the most orthodox Heaven. They were not seeking a viable basis for social order in rurality but rejecting the social order as worthless. It is true that the myth of the terrestrial Paradise did more to make a social order of rurality. But early religious efforts along these lines in Hispanic America foundered to the extent that the myth may have played some part in the Westward push in North America, it may indirectly through the disillusionments of the frontier have promoted urbanization. A. K. Moore has argued with cogency that disillusionment arose, not merely from hardship, but from the disorder that plagued the frontier, disorder with which settlers found themselves unprepared to deal because they had brought with them no clear conception of how order should be organized in the Paradise they were seeking.[14] Many pioneers may have remigrated for this season to the small towns that grew up behind the frontier, their children in turn migrating in search of more cultural nourishment to cities, and often not finding enough even there. This sequence of expectations and disappointments may go

[13] See Morton White in this volume.
[14] A. K. Moore, *The Frontier Mind: a cultural analysis of the Kentucky Frontiersman* (Lexington, Kentucky, 1957).

far to explain the changes in attitudes to city life of which Morton White has written.

There are vast gaps in our knowledge of city history. Yet regional study has gone far to establish the radius of European cities' economic influence at different times and has been examining their social and cultural relations with the countryside. To find planners and sociologists interested may encourage such work and spur comparative study.[15] The chief difficulty at present, if the historian is asked how any given division of economic and cultural functions between different types of community worked, in a given region, is the fact that even when a pattern of this kind might appear to remain fixed, the people involved in it might have been moving from place to place in a highly variable fashion through time. Population has for centuries been more mobile than is generally realized; its migrations are a largely unstudied aspect of any of the older social orders. Today's planner cannot wait for the long labor that historians have before them on such questions. History can tell him only what he knows already, that his problem is a philosophical one.

[15] See John Friedmann, "Cities in Social Transformation," *Comparative Studies in Society and History*, IV: 1 (Nov. 1961), 86–103.

IV

History and the Contemporary Urban World

The Death of the City:
A Frightened Look at Postcivilization

KENNETH E. BOULDING

Civilization, it is clear from the Latin meaning of the word, is what goes on in cities—conversely, a city is a peculiar product of the state of man known as civilization. The traditional view of civilization is that it represents a higher state of mankind than the precivilized or savage society which preceded it and that it is indeed a state of mankind which has never been fully realized. When there are elements in modern society of which we sharply disapprove, we are apt to reprove them by calling them "uncivilized." The traditional view of the history of man, therefore, is that of a general spread of cities and of civilization over the world from its origins in Egypt, Sumeria, and the Indus, and a gradual refinement and "urbanity" of life and manners as a result.

Even in civilized man, however, there is a deep ambivalence about the city. The city is not only Zion, the city of God; it is Babylon, the scarlet woman. On the one hand, we have the opposition of urbane splendor and culture with rural cloddishness and savagery; on the other hand, we have the opposition of urban vice, corruption and cruelty, as against rural virtue and purity. The Bible, to take but one instance, furnishes us with innumerable examples of this deep ambivalence towards the city. It is at once the house of God and the house of iniquity. Amos, the herdsman, denounces it; Jeremiah weeps over it; Christ is crucified in it. One of the great threads through the Bible is the destruction and re-building of the city—a pattern which is wholly characteristic of the age of civilization.

Before considering the death of the city we must consider its birth. We must ask, that is, what is it in the social system that we call civilization that produces dense agglomerations of mankind rather than the relatively even distribution of population that is characteristic of precivilized societies. The answer seems to be that there are two different types of cities; the political and the economic. Economic cities may be further classified as trade cities, production cities and extraction cities, according to the proportion of these activities which takes place in them.

The political city is probably the earliest of all cities. All civilization is a by-product of agriculture; that is, of the domestication of crops and animals and the resultant food surplus from the food producer. Such a food surplus is a necessary, but not a sufficient condition for the development of civilization and the establishment of cities. There are many examples of primitive peoples which have enjoyed food surpluses for substantial periods of time and which have "wasted" these in elaborate rituals or in the sheer enjoyment of life. The city arises first when political means are devised to channel these food surpluses into the hands of a ruler. The first organization is an army which can extract the food surpluses from the food producer by means of coercion and hence can feed itself. If there is something left over from the consumption of the army, there will be food available to feed priests, kings, and artisans and so the possibility arises of erecting temples and palaces. Because military organizations tend to produce other military organizations as their enemies, the palaces and temples usually have to be surrounded by a wall. So the institution of war which is also highly characteristic of the age of civilization begins.

The agglomeration of the city here serves mainly defensive purposes. If we ask why the products of the food surplus are not distributed fairly evenly over the countryside, the answer is that if they were so distributed, they could not be defended. The characteristic obverse of the defense city, therefore, is a poor and miserable countryside in which the food producers produce more than they can eat themselves but have their surplus taken away from them without being given much in return. With this food surplus, the rulers feed their armies, their priests, their servants and their artisans. They build pyramids and palaces, Parthenons, and cathedrals. These artifacts, however, are concentrated in the cities, partly because it is convenient for a ruler to have a court, that is, an entourage around him and to keep his army where he can oversee it. Partly also, the city arises because the citizens can build a wall around it and keep their possessions temporarily safe. The defense city, however, is unstable—no matter how high the walls they will eventually be breached. I do not believe anyone has ever calculated the expectation of life of a defense city, but it must be fairly small; I would be surprised if it were more than two or three hundred years. The inevitable pattern of a defense city is the pattern of rise and fall. Jerusalem, Nineveh, Babylon, Carthage, and Rome all followed the same grim rhythm.

Trade and manufacture often begin in the political city, for the first traders and artisans gather under the shadow of the fortification. Nevertheless, economics is different from politics; an economic city is different from the political city. The economic city begins when man discovers that under some circumstances it may be cheaper to produce and to trade than to coerce. In the pure defense society, the ruler has to feed the soldiers that coerce the food producers to extract the food surplus. The subsistence of the soldiers may be considered as a cost of the food surplus extracted. Under some circumstances, this may be so large as to eat up almost the whole of the food surplus. It may then be cheaper for the city to produce something and to trade it with the food producers for the food surplus. Instead of feeding soldiers, we now feed artisans and merchants, and with the product of the artisans and the services of the merchants we extract the food surplus from the food producers by offering them something in exchange. Trade and production, we observe, go hand in hand. Without production there would be nothing to trade; without trade there would be no point in production.

It is the combination of production, trade, and defense that produces the great civilizations. Defense must go beyond the cities to establish a reign of law over the whole countryside. This it can only do if the food producers are not hopelessly exploited. That is, it is trade and production that make the establishment of widespread law possible. Only if there are widespread law and security, however, are widespread trade and production possible. These two aspects of the great civilization, therefore, reinforce each other. There seems to be a profound historical tendency, however, for defense to encroach upon the production and trade aspects of society to the point where the society becomes unstable. The costs of defense become cumulatively greater and the society less able to support them until the civilization crumbles.

We still need to ask ourselves why trade and production should produce concentrations of men into cities. The question here is why, in the absence of any necessity for defense, do not the economic activities of trade and production spread themselves evenly over the geographical field? There seem to be two answers to this question. One is to be found in the mere existence of the cost of transport. Lösch[1] has shown in his brilliant work on the location of industry that even if we started off with economic activity uniformly distributed over a homogeneous plain, the existence of costs of transport alone would result in a geographical structuring of the economic activity simply under the impact of the principle of profit maximization. The lines of transport will develop a roughly hexagonal pattern and at the nodes where the lines of transport come together, concentrations of economic activity, that is, cities, will develop.

The second cause of urban concentrations of economic activity is the heterogeneity of what might be called economic space. We see this in its simplest form in the extractive city such as a mining city. This obviously has to be where the mine is. Such a city is usually short-lived and has something of the air of a camp, but if the mine is rich it can afford an opera house and it will temporarily have many of the marks of a classical city. Fishing, we may

[1] Lösch, August, *The Economics of Location* (New Haven, 1954).

note, which is a permanent form of sea mining, produces villages rather than cities, because the "mine" is not rich enough to support a large population.

A society where the agricultural surplus is extracted by trade will produce market towns in the middle of farming country. These can become cities of a kind, especially if they are allied with a cathedral which makes it a spiritual, political city. The great trading cities, however, generally have established themselves at points where there was a sharp break in the cost of transport; that is, at the ports. The importance of this factor is reflected in the number of cities of more than one-half-million people in many parts of the world located at a point of discontinuity between water and land transportation. The location of mankind is dominated by two facts about cost of transport. The first is that, by and large, water transportation is cheaper by almost an order of magnitude than land transportation, although this differential has been diminishing in the course of the last two hundred years. The second is that the transshipment from water to land transportation is also extremely costly. I have frequently, and so far without success, urged that the geographers draw a really significant map of the world in which the distances would be in proportion to cost of transport. A general projection of this kind is, of course, impossible, but it would be possible to do this in a polar projection based upon a particular point, such as for instance, New York City. That is, we could draw a map of the world in which the position of each point was determined by its direction from New York and in which its distance from New York was proportionate to the cost of transport from New York. We could do this fairly easily for a particular commodity such as wheat. Such a map would be almost totally unrecognizable and yet it would represent a much truer picture than the usual projections. The oceans would shrink to a little puddle in the middle of the map with small extensions up great rivers. Around this puddle would spread the world port city, and we would see New York, Boston, Philadelphia, Baltimore, London, Hamburg, Calcutta, Bombay, Tokyo, Sydney, and so on, clustered around the puddle of the oceans and forming an almost continuous world city. This would even include St. Louis, Minneapolis, Cleveland, Detroit, Chicago, and Duluth. Away from the world port city would stretch the great land hinterlands, and even the points of transshipment themselves would bulk large. If we impose the

Lösch hexagons on a projection of this kind, we get a pretty fair explanation, I suspect, of the distribution of world's population.

We finally come to the production or manufacturing city which is the result of a certain heterogeneity in pure economic space. This takes two forms; the existence of economies of scale in the production of a single commodity, and the existence of what the economist calls external economies; that is, economies in one line of production as a result of the existence of neighboring producing operations. Large automobile plants are generally more efficient than small. This fact alone will lead to the concentration of production of automobiles in a few plants, and therefore in a few places, and the population of automobile workers will be concentrated there as well. The presence of one automobile plant in a city, however, may make it cheaper to put another one there for various subtle reasons. It is not surprising, therefore, to find specialized manufacturing cities like Pittsburgh, Manchester, and Detroit.

So much then for the birth of the city and the reasons that have given rise to it. What gave rise to the city, however, is the same set of causes that gave rise to civilization. The crux of my argument now is that civilization is passing away and that the city will pass away with it.

We are now passing through a period of transition in the state of man quite as large and as far reaching as the transition from precivilized to civilized society. I call this the transition from civilization to postcivilization. This idea is shocking to many people who still think that what is going on in the world today is a simple extension of the movement from precivilized to civilized society. In fact, however, I think we have to recognize that we are moving towards a state of man which is as different from civilization as civilization itself was from the precivilized societies which preceded it. This is what we mean by the innocent term "economic development." There is something ironic in the reflection that just at the moment when civilization has, in effect, extended itself over the whole world and when precivilized societies exist only in rapidly declining pockets, postcivilization is stalking on the heels of civilization itself and is creating the same kind of disruption and disturbance in civilized societies that civilization produces on precivilized societies.

Just as civilization is a product of the food surplus which

proceeds from agriculture, which represents a higher level of organization of food production than primitive hunting and food gathering, so postcivilization is a product of science, that is, of a higher level of organization of human knowledge and the organization of this knowledge into know-how. The result of this is an increase in the productivity of human labor, especially in the production of commodities, which is quantitatively so large as to create a qualitatively different kind of society. The food surplus upon which classical civilization rested was extremely meager. In the Roman Empire at its height, for instance, it is doubtful whether more than twenty or twenty-five per cent of the total population were in nonfood-producing occupations. That is, it took about seventy-five per cent of the total population to feed the hundred per cent, and only twenty or twenty-five per cent could be spared to fight wars, to establish states, and to build the great monuments of civilization, both of architecture and of literature.

In the United States at the moment, which is the part of the world furthest advanced toward postcivilization, we can now produce all our food requirements with about ten per cent of the population and still have an embarrassing agricultural surplus. This is a change in an order of magnitude. We can now devote ninety per cent of the population to nonagricultural pursuits. In the production of many other commodities, the increase in the productivity of labor is even more spectacular and with the coming of automation, we may find even another order of magnitude change in this quantity. By contrast there are many occupations, notably the service trades, in which there has been very little technical change over the past few thousand years. In such occupations as hair-cutting, teaching, and personal services generally, the productivity of labor has shown little change. As a result of these differential changes in the productivity of labor, there has been an enormous revolution in the relative price structure. The prices of those commodities in the production of which technical improvement has occurred have fallen drastically relative to those commodities and services the production of which has been technologically stagnant. Furthermore, no end is at present in sight for this process. It is doubtful whether we have even reached the mid-point of this enormous process of change. We devote increasing resources to technological improvement and to the advance of knowledge and up to now there seems to be little in the way of diminishing returns to this activity.

I do not believe this to be an infinite process and I have a strong conviction that all processes, even this one, eventually reach something like an equilibrium. The equilibrium level of knowledge and technology which the present process of scientific and technological development implies, however, is still a very long way in the future, and most certainly is beyond the level of our present imaginations. It is by no means impossible to suppose a world at the end of this process in which we can produce our whole food supply with one per cent of the population, in which we can produce all basic commodities such as clothing, housing, and so on with perhaps another two or three per cent or perhaps even at most ten per cent, and in which, therefore, economic life revolves very largely around the organization of personal services. We have not yet begun to think out the details of such an economy. It is clear that many of its institutions and forms of organization will be very different from what is now familiar to us.

In the meantime the rise of postcivilization is presenting an enormous crisis to the institutions of civilizations, whether these are the lingering institutions of civilization in the postcivilized countries or whether these are what might be thought of as the civilized, that is, the poor countries. The nature of the present crisis may be dramatically reflected in the observation that Indonesia, which we think of as one of the poorest countries in the world in desperate need of economic development, has in fact about the same population and per capita income as the Roman Empire at its height. Jakarta is a city at least as large as ancient Rome, if perhaps not quite as splendid. In many ways the level of life and civilization in Indonesia goes beyond that of Augustan Rome. Yet, this is a country which is desperately unhappy with its present state and very anxious to rise out of it.

Just as civilization almost always produces a disastrous impact upon the precivilized societies with which it comes into contact—witness for instance the sad history of the American Indians—it also seems all too probable that the impact of postcivilized on civilized societies will be equally disastrous. There are three major aspects of this breakdown of the institutions of civilization. The first is the breakdown of the system of national defense. I have elaborated elsewhere on this phenomenon[2] so that I need not develop the proposition here. The breakdown is the result partly of a

[2] *Conflict and Defense* (New York, 1961).

dimunition in the cost of transport of violence which, coupled with the increase in the range of the deadly missile, has shattered what might be called the classical system of unconditional national security. These two phenomenan have destroyed what I call "unconditional viability" even for the largest nations, and in particular have rendered the cities of the world pitilessly vulnerable.

The second symptom of the disintegration of civilization is the population explosion in the civilized countries, and even in the incipient postcivilized countries. Classical civilization maintained whatever equilibrium it had because its high birthrates were offset by high death rates. In the ideal type of civilized society, we might suppose a birth and death rate of about forty with an expectation of life at birth of twenty-five. In postcivilized society, the expectation of life at birth rises to seventy. An equilibrium of population under these circumstances requires birth and death rates of about fourteen per thousand. The first impact of postcivilized techniques, however, on civilized society is frequently a dramatic reduction in the death rate. In many tropical countries, for instance, in the last twenty years, death rates have been reduced from twenty-five or thirty per thousand to about ten per thousand simply as a result of the introduction of DDT and relatively primitive measures of public health. The birth rate, however, stays up at forty with the result that these societies are now suffering a three per cent per annum population increase. This puts a burden on them in the current investment in human resources which may be more than they can bear, and it may therefore prevent them from making the transition into postcivilization. Postcivilized society requires as one of its conditions a large investment in human resources, that is, education. A poor, civilized society may prove to be incapable of devoting enough resources to education in the face of the three per cent per annum increase and in the face of its enormous numbers of children. Under these circumstances, it can easily regress towards even lower levels of civilization until the death rate rises once again or until some methods of population control are adopted. There are many parts of the world today in which we may be repeating the history of Ireland from 1700 to 1846—a gloomy prospect indeed.

It is the third aspect of the disintegration of civilization with which we are mainly concerned here, however. This is the disintegration of what might be called the classical city. The classical city is a well-integrated social organization. It has clearly defined boundaries and limits and it earns its living by a judicious combination of politics (that is, exploitation), production, and trade. It is unsanitary, so that its death rate is high; it almost certainly does not reproduce itself and it continually renews itself by drawing on the excess population as well as on the excess food supply of the country. There is a sharp differentiation between the culture of the city and of the country. The city is also a focus of loyalty and even the national state is frequently only an extension—or a colony—of the capital city.

In postcivilization all the conditions which gave rise to the classical city have gone. The parameters of the great equations of society have changed to the point where the classical city is no longer included as one of the solutions. The things which give rise to the need for concentrations all disappear. The city is now, for instance, utterly defenseless; it is a sitting duck for the H-bomb, and so called civil defense in the cities becomes little more than an obscene attempt to persuade the civilian population that they are thoroughly expendable in a modern war. The diminution in the cost of transport both of commodities and of communications has greatly diminished the value of concentrations of population for the purposes of trade and human intercourse. The classical city is based fundamentally on the necessity for face-to-face communication. For many purposes even today this necessity remains. The telephone, for instance, is not an adequate substitute for a personal conversation simply because it uses so restricted a channel that much of the nuances of communication which are transmitted, for instance, through gesture are lost. The possibility of communication by means of modulated light beams, however, has opened up an enormous number of long-distance channels, and it may well be that in the not-too-distant future we shall each sit in our own studies and conduct long-distance televised conferences with people all over the world. We are very far from having exhausted the implications, both political and economic, of the communications revolution in which we are living. Stock markets and legislative assemblies, for instance, in a physical sense are civilized rather than postcivilized institutions, and one doubts whether they will survive another fifty or one hundred years with the present type of development.

The impact of the automobile on the city is one stage in its disintegration, and this has been well-documented. We are all familiar, I am sure, with the notion of Los Angeles as the first post-civilized urban agglomeration—an agglomeration created by and poisoned by the automobile. Under no circumstances could Los Angeles be called a city in the classical sense of the word. We must now recognize, indeed, I think, that California has become the first example of what I would call the "state city," that is, an urban agglomeration state-wide in its extent. Even the Shasta Dam has become a weekend playground for people from Los Angeles, and of course, the tentacles of the Los Angeles water system tend to engulf the whole West!

Another symptom of the disintegration of the city is the enormous rise in this country of part-time farming. The number of part-time farms is now close to, if it does not already exceed, the number of full-time farms. This represents in effect a dramatic explosion of the city over the countryside. Many of these part-time farmers commute forty or fifty miles to work in a city factory. The notion of the United States as consisting essentially of three or four loose, sprawling megalopolises separated by small stretches of largely empty countryside is by no means remote.

We can almost say that the city is destroyed by its own success. The paradox here is that by the time ninety per cent of the population are urban, the city has really ceased to have any meaning in itself. The converse of this phenomenon is the disappearance of rural life as a distinctive and peculiar sub-culture within the society. Over large parts of the United States this has already happened. The Iowa farmer has an occupational subculture but he does not have a rural subculture. He is merely an ex-urbanite who happens to be living on a farm, and he earns his living by thoroughly urban methods. He is, furthermore, a professional, usually with a college degree, and he is far more remote, say, from the European peasant than he is from the American factory engineer.

We may very well ask ourselves, therefore, whether we visualize a period in the not very distant future when in postcivilized societies, the city will really have disappeared altogether as an entity. We can even visualize a society in which the population is spread very evenly over the world in almost self-sufficient households, each circulating and processing everlastingly its own water supply through its own algae, each deriving all the power it needs from its own solar batteries, each in communication with anybody it wants to communicate with through its personalized television, each with immediate access to all the cultural resources of the world through channels of communications to libraries and other cultural repositories, each basking in the security of an invisible and cybernetic world state in which each man shall live under his vine and his own fig tree and none shall make him afraid. There may be a few radioactive holes to mark the sites of the older cities and a few interesting ruins that have escaped destruction. This vision is, of course, pure science fiction, but in these days one must not despise science fiction as a way of keeping up with the news.

Some modifications of this rather idyllic picture have to be made even in postcivilization, I suspect. A high level postcivilized stable technology would almost have to be based on the oceans for sources for its basic raw materials, as the mines and the fossil fuels will very soon be gone. There will, therefore, be some manufacturing concentrations around the shores of the world. We may even see a revival of the form of the classical city for pure pleasure where people can enjoy the luxury of walking and of face-to-face communication. Inequality of income in such a society is likely to be reflected in the fact that the poor will drive vehicles and the rich will walk. We are already, I think, beginning to see this movement in the movement of the rich into the city centers and the development of the mall. These cities, however, will be stage sets —they will arise out of the very freedom and luxury of the society rather than out of its necessities.

Just as we are deeply ambivalent toward the classical city and towards civilizations, so we are likely to be equally ambivalent towards postcivilization and we are likely to find a deep nostalgia for the city. Even in the new Jerusalem (the mile-cube city, we may observe perhaps only just around the corner as being the only practical way of having twenty million people living together) there will be nostalgia for the old Jerusalem and for Athens. We may well find a new race of prophets extolling the virtues of civilization—its purity, honesty, and simplicity, its closeness to nature, and its closeness to God by contrast with the even deadlier vices of postcivilized society. The only real hope for the classical city, however, is that nothing ever really passes away! Man has evolved in the great process of evolution but he has not displaced the amoeba; he has had to learn to coexist with, and indeed be symbiotic with, all the previous orders of life, even though many particular species have passed away. Similarly, in social evolution I suspect that higher forms do not necessarily displace the older and presumably "lower" forms. In the great ecosystem of the new society we may find a certain coexistence between postcivilized, civilized, and even pre-civilized social forms. Every evolutionary development has its price, and there may always be those who do not wish to pay it. My elegy of the city, therefore, may be premature and we may find for a long time to come the new Jerusalem and the old living side by side even on this tiny spaceship of a planet.

Implications of Modern City Growth

DENIS W. BROGAN

Nearly forty years ago, as an innocent young man on the eve of going up to Oxford, I spent four or five months in Rome, learning Italian. It was "anno primo" of the newborn Fascist regime. A new empire was being founded, but I was more impressed with the ruins of the old. For in that remote time, modern Rome did not fill all the space within the Aurelian wall of the third century. The ancient city still overshadowed the modern. The grass and trees and ruins round San Sebastiano recalled the lesson of Ozymandias and, immediately outside the wall, the Campagna stretched, not quite boundless but nearly bare of human relics later than those of the imperial city. As I had been born in Glasgow, just within the

Empire, I was impressed by this vision of past greatness and confirmed in my youthful historical pessimism.

But to go back to Rome now is to get another lesson. The city has long flowed round and over the walls. At least half of modern Rome is outside the imperial area, and the once lonely and majestic landscape of the empty Campagna has, today, all the charm of the approach to downtown Chicago from Midway airport. Cities, like suns, arise and have their setting, but Rome (and Athens) have shown what power, what monstrous power of recovery the city has, have forced us to contemplate again the problem of the place of the city in history, its past and future, and to consider the possibilities of human life in the megalopolis.

We begin with the possibility, as Professor Boulding has pointed out, that the city—the "strong place" which could withstand, behind its wall, the invaders, the raiders, the rivals—may now be a death trap. The great urban aggregates cannot be defended from the bomb delivered by rocket or plane. In an age of cities of totally unprecedented size, the target area is greater than ever, the possibility of defense smaller than ever. Only a highly advanced but sparsely populated country like Sweden, or a densely populated but not highly advanced state like China can contemplate atomic war with even a remote approach to equanimity. Only the Swedes are technically and economically prepared to do something serious about defense; only the rulers of China, with a vast surplus population and a tradition of ruthlessness in the matter of human life that recalls the bloody history of Paraguay, can even pretend to believe that they can survive atomic war. From being a stronghold,[1] the city has become a death trap.

At the time that the city has become a possible funerary monument to the ingenuity of the human spirit, it has begun to dissolve for reasons that Professor Boulding has expounded brilliantly. The old idea of a city set on a hill or bounded by its walls, secure on its insular site, sited like the *cité* of Carcassonne above the plain whence came food and foes, hardly fits our modern "urban aggregate." True, the phenomenon is not totally new. The Roman walls that I saw nearly forty years ago were built when the Empire was in visible decline, when it was not impossible that immortal Rome

[1] To show that it is not merely a matter of weapons that determines the ferocity of war, it should be remembered that the war that Paraguay fought against Brazil, Argentina, and Uruguay was the bloodiest in modern history.

might be seized by barbarians as it had been seized by the Gauls five hundred years before. At the height of its power and glory, Rome needed no walls; no more did eighteenth-century Paris or London. It was significant of the change in the French position that Paris was refortified in the middle nineteenth century, to be besieged in turn by the Germans and the French. It was significant of the shallow optimism of the interwar period (an optimism which I shared) that the old Paris fortifications were pulled down, the defenses pushed east to the Maginot Wall and that Paris fell, for the first time in its history, in the summer of 1940 without anyone firing a shot in its defense.

The Paris that fell in 1940 was the typical city that had replaced the "stronghold." Vienna, Cologne, Brussels had lost their walls. Berlin, in a real sense had never had them, nor had modern Moscow or Leningrad. But the siege of Leningrad, the bitter defense of Vienna and, then, of Berlin, showed that the old military role of the city had not disappeared. Despite all the brave talk of a fortress in the Alps, the Third Reich died when Berlin fell. And if we cannot (and we cannot) envision the positive role of the great cities in a future atomic war, we can be confident of their negative role at the receiving end. They will be the favorite targets as they were when "the Assyrian came down like the wolf on the fold."

But the city is threatened with more than the destruction from the air that has been a commonplace threat since the prophetic novels of H. G. Wells. We know now, as we knew fifty years ago, that if mankind acquired the technical power to commit suicide, the survivors, if any, would be the country dwellers, the "pagans" who survived the fall of Babylon and of Rome. If survival in numbers be the criterion of political success, the countries with large, technically backward, rural populations will inherit the earth—if anything is left of it.

But to turn away from these gloomy platitudes to my main theme. It is true, I think, to say that we know far more about urban life in the past and present than we do about rural life. There is no rural Aristophanes or Juvenal. Most great writers have been by birth or adoption, city men. Falstaff might babble of green fields but his spiritual and physical home was on the South Bank of the Thames, not very far from the Old Vic. The examples could be repeated. An astonishing number of great French writers were born in Paris and nearly all were Parisians by adoption. Even the great French painters tended to cluster in Paris or in its surroundings, and the great Tuscan painters crowded around Florence or Siena. So we tend to see the countryside, as apart from the city-side (if I may be allowed to coin a word), as something inspected from the city, recorded by city men. There is, of course Arcadia, but Arcadia is notoriously a city man's view of the countryside. And without having any knowledge of the background of Chinese painting, I suspect that the Emperors who paid for the pictures (or even executed them) were, like the painters, city men by taste and habit, not in the least ready to submit to the servitudes of real rural life. We know much more about the city than we do about the country, and we know a lot of what we know about the country because city men by birth, or by adoption, have taken the trouble to give us more or less veracious accounts of the country, accounts less abundant and less convincing than the accounts we have from city men about city life, from the comic or satirical poets, from the chroniclers, from the writers of more or less scandalous narratives, above all from the modern dramatists and novelists.

And yet we do not know nearly enough about the history of the city. Mr. Mumford in his recent book[2] is forced again and again to say "probably" or "possibly" where we should like him to be able to say "certainly." We don't know enough about Rome or Athens, not nearly enough about Antioch or Alexandria. We don't know enough about London, the most remarkable city in history, metropolitically speaking (note I do not say "city state"). We know that it was one of the greatest cities in the northern half of the Roman Empire. We know more about it than we knew twenty years ago (thanks in great part to the blitz which has done so much for archaeology), but we do not know enough. We don't know what happened to it in the dark fifth and sixth centuries; we do not really know when it recovered the position it has never since lost, of being the heart of England and one of the great cities of Europe. There are, of course, many valuable studies of areas of London produced under governmental or academic auspices. But handy and scholarly histories and descriptions of London are sadly missing. Professor Rasmussen's book[3] has many great merits indeed. especially its handling of some interesting problems in London

[2] Lewis Mumford, *The City in History* (New York, 1961).
[3] Steen Eiler Rasmussen, *London: The Unique City* (New York, 1937).

architectural history. But even as an architectural history it is badly lacking. It ignores whole categories of London buildings, the churches and public buildings. More serious, it disregards a large part of the technical infrastructure which has accounted for the growth of London, that is, the history of the port, of the water supply, and to a great extent, of urban transportation.

Paris is better off, but not enough so, and it must be said that the last history of Paris that I read, lavishly and admirably illustrated, was outrageously bad as to historical treatment of the theme.

But it is not this defect in our archaeological knowledge that puzzles and depresses me in my capacity as an historian. I am much more perplexed by the absence of adequate knowledge of the modern history of cities. I want to know why London began to expand in the early seventeenth century, then, on a much greater scale, in the eighteenth century. I want to know what the small scale of German urban life did to German political development in the seventeenth and eighteenth centuries. I want to know more about the role of "made" cities, Petersburg, Karlsruhe; in a sense, of the magnificent new capital of a dying state, eighteenth-century Warsaw. I want to know how much of the growth of Paris was due simply to its being the capital of a more and more centralized state and how much to its intrinsically good geographical position. Have we, that is to say, to explain the rise of Paris by the fact that it was the King's city or explain the success of the Counts of Paris in becoming Kings by the fact that they had Paris as their base? I can't answer all or many of these questions, and I shall return to the questions that I can pose more exactly or even, greatly daring, profess to answer.

There is surely something odd about the neglect of the city as a subject of research. Of course, it has been written about by many people. We know from Boswell that there was a history of Birmingham extant in the eighteenth century which Dr. Johnson found himself reduced to reading, and there are scores of sociological studies of given urban areas from *Yankee City* to the great studies of London life begun by Charles Booth. London, in one way, is well off. You can study many of its parishes, street by street. You can study it in Sir John Summerson's books (so useful to thrifty people in dealing with unscrupulous real estate dealers). But there is a gap. Perhaps it is due to the ambivalence in our attitude to the city that Professor Boulding has called our attention to.

We see the city both as the center of civilization and as the center of vice, degradation, moral poisoning. Johnson, the most devoted of Londoners, wrote a celebrated imitation of Juvenal in which he took nearly as gloomy a view of London as Juvenal had done of Rome. His friend and protégé, Goldsmith, devoted Irishman, and, like so many devoted Irishmen, unwilling to live for a day more than he could help in Ireland, lamented the fate of the country-side, the decline of

> a bold peasantry, a country's pride
> Which once destroyed can never be supplied.

Meantime he lived on contentedly enough, if moralistically depre-cating, in London. Civilization was seen, is seen, by the moralists of Fairfield County, of Bucks County as dazzling and corrupting. The farmer is reminded of the felicity of his lot, especially taxwise, in terms that recall Virgil's famous apostrophe:

> O fortunatos nimium sua bona norint
> Agricolas.

New York pays its homage to the now not conspicuous moral-izing character of the declining *polis* by having a statue to Civic Virtue. A statue, the modern denigrators of the city suggest, is all that we can afford today. The thing is beyond our powers, perhaps beyond our desires. Yet we live in cities or in the children of cities, suburbia and exurbia. In all the western world, the urban majority of the population is growing; the number of people needed to feed the urban majority is falling; urban habits of life are, as Professor Boulding has pointed out, as deeply rooted in what we call rural Iowa as in the cities or their dependent areas. If (as all the world agrees) the way of progress is toward the new industrial society (the whole world may be wrong, but that is another story), then we have to come to grips with the problem of city life. Is it self-destructive? Is the life of virtue impossible in urban society? Are the cities, if not the wider urban areas, committing suicide or being murdered?

I shall begin by asking your pardon for devoting so much space and time to my own country. My excuse is simple. I know much more about it and I have been interested in the problems of the growth of cities since I was a small boy. In my school days in Scotland, more than fifty years ago, our school geography books listed the twenty or so biggest cities in the world. I was born in one of them, Glasgow. How long it is since Glasgow passed from the front rank in mere size! It is no longer even the second biggest city in Britain, having been passed by Birmingham. And the problem of the slowing down of the growth of Glasgow or the unnatural growth of other cities brings me to the first of my questions. What makes cities grow? In 1870, Glasgow, Chicago, Berlin were all about the same size. But one of the three bounded ahead. It was not Chicago, it was Berlin. Berlin bounded ahead because of the growth of the Prussian state. (It had the chance for other reasons, but that it did bound ahead was due to political and military factors.) I would suggest that it is true that political factors often account for the rise of cities and give one city predominance over another. It is easy to draw up lists of favorable geographical factors that account for the growth of cities. Many of us will recall the French anecdote of the eloquent priest who stressed, as an example of divine providence, the fact that nearly all great cities had a river running through them. And I would be the last to oppose the idea that the point where land and water transport meet is often the point where cities grow. This can be illustrated from American history, from the cities situated like Richmond, Virginia, on the fall line, or like Albany, New York, or Hartford, Connecticut. It can be illustrated from the two largest, old, established cities in northern Europe, London and Paris; one is a great sea and river port, the other, a great river port. (It is Paris that has a ship for its emblem, not London.) But this is not the only occasion for the growth of a great city. In Britain, three out of the four biggest cities, outside London, were not at the beginning of their greatness, ports or transshipment points. Liverpool is a genuine port city, but Manchester and Glasgow made themselves ports after they had become big cities, and Birmingham, now the "second city," has not been and is not in any serious sense, a port or transportation center. I think that in every case it is possible to explain *why* one city grew while another with apparently equal or superior physical advantages languished. (Were not the founders of Chalcedon called "the blind" because they overlooked the superior advantages of Byzantium and, yet, did not that city with its incomparable site languish until Constantine made the political decision to refound it and make it the new Rome?)

I think that there are two factors apart from the ideal geographical situation to be considered when we ask ourselves why a city has grown or decayed, questions that may be highly relevant to some modern problems. One is a pretty recent but very important condition of success, that the site is usable by the new methods of transportation, first of all by the railroad, then by bus, truck, plane. We have to consider the "railway city" (which I suggest is what Chicago is, despite its lakefront and its river and canal connection with the Mississippi). Manifestly it is the case of Berlin (about which there is more to be said). Sir John Clapham has shown us how revolutionary the railroad was for the industrial and urban growth of the Ruhr. The railroad policy of a country, of big business, may determine the greatness of a city, and the decision which results in growth may be pretty arbitrary. Thus it is as certain as such things can be, that there would have been a great Australian city on Sydney Harbour but not quite certain that the largest of Australian cities should until recently have been on the not divinely appointed site of Melbourne. In every case, it is as well to look for the role of accident, of personal decision, of the first appearance of a new technique, of the personal taste or loyalties of an inventor or entrepreneur. I could give several examples from my own country, such as the location of the cotton thread industry in Paisley because of the decision of local entrepreneurs who succeeded in creating a monopoly position that, had the case been altered, might have concentrated the industry in Preston. But the most remarkable example is the near concentration of the French rubber industry at Clermont-Ferrand, in the very center of France, remote from ports, from coal, from river or canal transportation. The great Michelin plant is there because a British officer, who was connected with the pioneer Macintosh family of Manchester, married into a local family. And not only did this, in a generation or two, mean that Clermont was, and is, the head of the French rubber industry, but that in Clermont there are several rival though minor rubber companies. Odder still, when Dunlop decided to fight Michelin in France, they put their plant, not indeed, at Clermont, but at Montluçon, forty miles away and no better suited by nature to be an industrial city than Clermont is. I think if we get down to cases, we would find that many flourishing economic complexes have an accidental origin and that, today, the location of industry may not follow any pattern that can be set out to cover all cases. And from that what follows? That what can be done by accident or personal preference can be done by decision, by planning, that it is never safe to say that an area *can't* support an industry. Perhaps it can't. Perhaps urban growth in North Dakota is unlikely or impossible as well as undesirable, but the impossibility has got to be proved.

More important than the accident of personal preference, of marriage, of a happy technical discovery by a local boy,[4] is the action of the state. There are very few countries in the world in which the capital is not the biggest city. Often, the city became the capital because it was already the biggest city. Such was the destiny of London. The kings might prefer Winchester, but the nature of things preferred London. The case of Paris is not quite so clear. Its geographical situation is so excellent, however, that it is hard to believe that even if, by an historical accident, a feudal dynasty other than the Capetians had become Kings of the Franks, "France" would not have grown up around Paris.

More common is the case in which, as far as we can see, the capital city becomes the largest city because it is the capital. Once the government is established there, the political prestige and the economic expenditure of the central government push the city into the stage of "take off," and once that stage is reached, the capital continues to grow, if you like, absurdly. Such a city is Madrid. No one would make it the economic center of Spain, the biggest city, on any of the calculations of the economic geographers. It owes its resented predominance to the arbitrary and, if you like, foolish choice of Charles V (to placate the pedantic, I note that he was in Spain, Charles I.). The case of Berlin is not quite the same. If Berlin was the second city in Germany in the eighteenth century, that was purely due to the rising power of the Prussian state, to the garrisoning of a great part of the swollen Prussian army in the capital, to the forced draft economy of Frederick the Great. In the nineteenth century, the case was not so simple. Prussian leadership in the Zollverein, the acquisition of the Rhineland and the Ruhr aided the growth of Berlin but, as I have said, it was one of the great modern railroad cities. There was bound to be such a city in northern

[4] Thus James Watt could see the kettle boil in his home town of Greenock; he could develop the idea of the separate condenser on Glasgow Green and perfect his engine in the precincts of the University of Glasgow under the patronage of Professor Adam Smith, but he could not market his discovery at Carron. He had to go to Birmingham where there were workers skilled enough to make his engines with the fine tolerances he needed. And Birmingham owed some of its early predominance to the political fact that it was not an incorporated borough and so not limited by guild custom.

Germany but it was not bound to be Berlin. What made it Berlin was the power and prestige of the Prussian state. Not quite the same arguments can be used to explain the prodigious growth of the largest city in the world, Tokyo. Sir George Sansome and others have shown the ancient importance of the plain on which Yedo, now Tokyo, lies. Control of that plain has been one of the prizes of Japanese internal war. But can we doubt that the centralization of power under the Tokugawa Shoguns in Yedo gave what was to be Tokyo its decisive push on the way to greatness or, at any rate, to size? An even clearer manifestation of state power is the creation of Petersburg. Built on a marsh, blocked by ice in its long winter, cut off from the most fertile parts of Russia, Petersburg, Petrograd, Leningrad, has until recently, defied geography thanks to the power of the Russian state.

It would be absurd to pretend that the contemporary megalopolises owe their swollen growth merely to their situation as political capitals. Not all are political capitals. New York and, possibly, Milan are impressive examples of great urban aggregates which do not owe their position to strictly political forces. But they, like the great capital cities, London, Paris, and Tokyo, maximize certain real advantages of mere size although at a very great cost to themselves and the countries of which they are the economic centers. The increasing rapidity of transportation, the practically simultaneous character of modern communication give to one city of each state a predominance which grows almost automatically. If enough business executives work in New York or Milan, in Sydney or Melbourne, the smaller cities in many ways cannot compete. The basic decisions are made in the headquarters of great corporations, and more and more these headquarters tend to be, necessarily, in the great agglomerations. Only there are the real decisions made. This in turn makes it profitable, in the short run at any rate, for industries to be near their own headquarters. Proximity facilitates many problems of management. And (a point I think of great importance) many more of the social advantages of urban life tend to be concentrated in the great agglomerations than can be found in quite large cities of the second order. This affects the location of industry because the great city appeals, very often indeed, to the managerial class and to the wives of the managerial class. This choice is reflected in the great growth of opulent suburbs around London or New York or Chicago. It is also reflected in the attractions of the great market, the attractions which exercise a great pull on many industries which need a high income market. It is, I think, significant that one of the two most famous of English papers, the former *Manchester Guardian,* some years ago dropped "Manchester" from its title.[5] At a certain stage in the development of the economy it becomes essential, even for a very powerful provincial unit, to have increasingly important offices in the main economic center. And there is then a temptation, possibly an economic advantage, in having more than offices, in having branch plants in or near the main urban aggregate.

The concentration of managerial direction or representation in the main city imposes a serious handicap on the managerial class in the lesser cities. They can offset this only by very close contacts with the megalopolis. Inability to do this is an added handicap to the peripheral cities.[6]

It is not asserted that only capital cities can have these attractions. The obvious exceptions have already been noted. But capital cities normally do have these attractions, and these attractions are magnified by the fact that the city is a capital. It would be absurd to suggest naively that capital cities are parasites on the economy. But it is an inescapable fact that capitals do, in the nature of things, drain resources from the rest of the country. These resources are spent on various governmental activities, garrisons, bureaucrats, Court or Congress. As the interlocking between the political and

[5] At the time of this writing, *The Guardian's* plans for printing in London were not yet complete. The *Guardian* is now printed in London as well as in Manchester. It has a large London office and a larger circulation in London than in Manchester. It is a matter of speculation how long piety will keep the effective headquarters in Manchester. In the same way, the most important group of London department stores has recently passed into the control of the Glasgow firm, "The House of Fraser," but it remains to be seen how long the management is conducted by Sir Hugh Fraser from Glasgow instead of London.

[6] This is noted in the recent remarkable *Inquiry Into the Scottish Economy,* 1960–1961: Report of a Committee appointed by the Scottish Council, Development and Industry (Edinburgh, [1961]). "In this sense there is no first thing to be done, but it is sensible to begin with personal communications, the need for which has been a major factor in the concentration of growing industries in the south. With the postwar development of air passenger transport Scotland is now potentially one of the most accessible places in the country: good air services can reduce the disadvantages of distance from the main centers of communication and enable the many advantages which Scotland offers to industry to be exploited. The domestic air services have not, however, measured up to the need, much less to the possibilities. Damage has been done to the economy for reasons as simple as that industrialists cannot at short notice get air passages to make contact with their customers, to attend business meetings, or to get their customers to them. Existing business has been hampered, new business lost, and industrialists considering a Scottish location discouraged." *op. cit.,* p. 186.

economic spheres becomes more important, many economic decisions are necessarily made in the capital, and the same general forces
that lead to the growth of any megalopolis are especially potent in
the case of a megalopolis which is also a capital city. In the ancient
world Alexandria, and Rome and later, Constantinople, grew this
way, and London and Paris owe some, probably a great deal of
their economic preponderance to their ancient role as political
capitals, in each instance now nearly a thousand years old. This
can be noted and possibly offset by deliberate decentralization as
the central governments of the United States and Great Britain have
from time to time attempted, but these attempts do not come to
very much and have in general no more importance than the location of the Federal Mint in Philadelphia.

There are obvious exceptions to the identification of the political capital with the economic capital. One of the most obvious is
the city of Washington. George Washington's hopes for the commercial future of the city of which he is the eponymous hero have
been frustrated. Washington has not held the gorgeous West in
fee. The site was not as favorable as the first President thought, and
what advantages the region had were preempted by Baltimore. Yet
Washington does show the economic importance of being a capital. The whole urban area, the District of Columbia, and the very
rapidly growing suburbs in Maryland and Virginia, have made
Washington, if we disregard its remarkably rigid political boundaries, one of the largest cities in the United States. Washington was
an overgrown village for a long time because the United States was
a village power, with few civil servants, small revenue, no equivalent of the Prussian garrison of Berlin. As late as 1939, although
both Washington and the federal government had grown a great
deal, the character of the capital reflected the pacific character of
the United States. There were far fewer troops of all arms and
all ranks in and around Washington in 1939 than there are army
officers doing a regular tour of duty in the city today. The size of
the Pentagon is a symbolic revelation of this new fact and the
Pentagon itself is not nearly large enough to house all the service
departments. The close integration of government and the economy
helps the growth of Washington nearly as much as it does the
growth of London and Paris. A great many basic decisions are
made in Washington. Being President of one of the great New
York banks, or of the New York Stock Exchange, is not nearly as

commanding a role in the economy as it used to be, largely because the Secretary of the Treasury and the Chairman of the Federal Reserve Board are far more potent, as residents of Washington.

In many other ways Washington is becoming much more of a "real capital." It has gained a great deal in social variety from the large number of new diplomatic missions to the United States established since the last war. The post of American Ambassador to the United Nations is important, but it is not nearly so important as the post of Secretary of State. The Waldorf Astoria is not a real rival to Foggy Bottom. New York has, in fact, lost some of its old predominance.

And Washington has acquired some of the marks of a great capital. It now has in the National Gallery, in Dumbarton Oaks, and soon will have in the new Museum of Technology, cultural assets of the first order. With the increasing role of government in the advancement of science there has been an increase in the importance of Washington as a center of research, if only because a great deal of the research carried out elsewhere is commissioned, and inspected, and is largely paid for by such federal bodies as the Department of Naval Research. There has been not only a great improvement in the standards of the local universities, but also a great increase in the number of learned bodies which, like the business community and the unions, think it necessary to have powerful lobbies in Washington. And there are, of course, an increasing number of important independent research institutions located in Washington. The more institutions of this kind are located in Washington, the more other institutions of this type are willing to consider locating in Washington, if only because its now very important academic population is an attraction to other academics elsewhere.

True, Washington is not a complete capital. There is the nearly total absence of industry, not only in the District but in the surrounding urban developments. There is the fact, more depressing for some people than for others, that Washington is a second rate city musically, and not even that theatrically. Artists do not yearn to live there; art is not marketed there. It is not a first rate shopping center and even now has not enough very rich people or spenders of lavish expense accounts to encourage certain types of conspicuous consumption. Then, even as a political capital, it suffers from the fact that few of a political personnel, i.e., the members of

Congress of both Houses, Cabinet officers, and high federal officials, keep permanent establishments in Washington. But the number of important officials who have settled in Washington permanently, and remain in Washington after they have ceased to be high officials, is increasing. Also, it is often forgotten that one reason for the nomadic character of the life of the political personnel is the so called "locality rule" which limits representation in Congress to residents of States and districts. Senators and Representatives must maintain residence in their home states for legal if for no other reasons. They cannot, like English and French parliamentarians, live in London and Paris and make only occasional visits to their constituencies. But it should be remembered that sessions of Congress are now much longer than was customary, and the business of Congress is much less parochial than it once was. Only a few of the older and more tradition-encrusted politicians can now afford to admit that they have in mind only the residents of Bumcombe county.

And last, a very important novelty in the modern world, Washington is now by far the greatest news center in the United States and probably in the world. For the press, and for television, a spacious Washington base is a necessity. Out of Washington come many of the best stories and out of it come many of the decisions that make the best stories, stories about summit meetings or the latest news from Cape Canaveral. Washington will remain a mutilated capital, but it is and it will increasingly be a real capital and a real city of the first order.

In a sense Rome is an artificial political capital like Washington. Its main business is government. The city of Rome has not been an intrinsically important economic unit in Italy since about the third century. The concentration of Italian industry in the north has reinforced the predominance of Milan and Turin and with the steady drifting of population of South to North (the reverse of the situation in Britain), the economic predominance of the great northern industrial cities is reinforced. If the more enterprising and wiser unemployed peasantry of southern Italy go to Turin or Milan where there is a genuine demand for their labor, many thousands of less well advised peasants go to Rome because of its political prestige, although there is no effective demand for their services. The result has been the creation of some new slums as deplorable as the ancient slums of Naples or Palermo. Rome *is* the capital, and it is the capital, not because of any present advantages of its situation, but because of the great ghosts that inhabit it and made it impossible to locate the capital of united Italy anywhere else.

The same forces that made Rome the inevitable capital in the nineteenth century made the small Turkish city of Athens the inevitable capital of the new Greek state a generation before, and in this century the result has been to create in modern Athens a political pull of attraction even more difficult to explain on purely economic grounds than the position of Rome. The overwhelming preponderance of modern Athens in modern Greece (it has now almost a quarter of the total population) has provoked a vivacious reaction. It has even led to the suggestion that the capital of Greece be moved elsewhere. Pella, once the capital of Alexander's Macedon, has been suggested. Professor Kydoniatis, professor at the Athens Polytechnic, believes that "by moving the seat of the government elsewhere Athens would be decongested. Building sites would depreciate, and it would be possible, through expropriation, to uncover the entire ancient city. . . . History taught that concentration in cities and desertion of rural areas was the forerunner of catastrophe." (*The* [London] *Times,* February 2, 1962.) Another suggestion is the moving of Athens to the royal suburb of Tatoi. The immense growth of cities like Athens has led Professor Doxiades to coin the word "ecumenopolis"; his example is the threatened merger of London and Manchester. The example of Brasilia is being pondered in Greece. It is safe to say that the "eye of Greece" will not be demoted to being a tourist center in favor of Pella or Thebes. It is also safe to say that the possibly pathological growth of Athens is due to the fact that it became in the nineteenth century, for the first time in its history, the capital.[7]

Contemplating the position of the "city" (an ambiguous term, I freely admit) in the modern world, I am struck by two phenomena that are linked though possibly formally contradictory. The work of urbanization goes on but we are unwilling to face its implications and less and less does the traditional view that the city

[7] The case of new "invented" capital cities like Canberra and Brasilia needs mention. Canberra is set by law in an area not chosen for even fictitious economic prospects. The future of Brasilia depends on the future of the Brazilian hinterland. But there would be nothing but a village on the site of Canberra (which has, in 1961, a much bigger population, relatively, than Washington had in Lincoln's time), but for a political decision and there would not be on the site of Brasilia even a village were it not for political decisions.

appears or grows in response to favorable geographic conditions describe the realities of modern urban growth.

The unwillingness to face the urban problem is especially marked in the "Anglo-Saxon" countries. There is, for example, the astonishing refusal in Britain, not only to think about urban problems, but to admit that they really exist. Yet for many centuries, London and its suburbs have held between one-fourth and one-fifth of the total population. No political movement that London has opposed has ever succeeded; few that it has supported have failed. This simple truth can be illustrated from the text of Magna Carta and the history of the London Labour party. Yet, as I have suggested, there is still no adequate historical explanation of the growth of London, no tying together of the first great post-Roman water supply, the "New River" in the seventeenth century with the coming of the buses (here, Paris was the pioneer), of the underground railways (here, London and Glasgow were the pioneers) of artificial lighting (again, London was the pioneer). Yet the most startling sight to a citizen of a megalopolis like ancient Rome or Alexandria would be the glow on the horizon as you approach New York or London or Paris at night! I could multiply the examples. The City has never been taken as a phenomenon worthy of profound historical (not antiquarian or sociological) investigation, at any rate in the English-speaking world.

Why is this so and what are its consequences for us? In the case of Britain, especially of London, we have to allow for the fact that since the Middle Ages, English society has been "open." The successful city merchant—the successful city man of any kind—could return to the town he came from and settle down as a minor gentleman, as William Shakespeare did. He could and very often did move to a new place where his ambiguous social origins could be conveniently forgotten. How many English or Scottish noble families have recent commercial origins and have managed to implant themselves with their newly found or newly bought title far from the dark, Satanic mills where the money was made! If I were a cad, I could illustrate this theme at length, to the discomfiture of innocent Americans who are not as cynical about our nobility as the native Briton is.

This would not matter if it had not important social and economic consequences. The easy access to the gentry and to the nobility has prevented the formation in Britain of that interesting, important and valuable class, the continental "patriciate." In no British city, with two possible exceptions, do we find a class of wealthy men, with their economic and social roots planted in the same soil. As soon as they reach a certain level of economic success and social sophistication, they set up as gentry, buy a country house (which is not the same thing as a house in the country), buy, or in more recent years, earn a title by public benefactions and forget as soon as possible, the soil and "muck," as they say in the North of England, from which the money comes. There is a constant draining off of the richest, the most leisured elements of society. There are occasional individual exceptions: the Wills family in Bristol, the Boot family in Nottingham. But I can only give Manchester and Norwich as cities where something like a patriciate exists or did exist. And Manchester has been deeply and beneficially influenced by a large Jewish and German colony, used to civic loyalty. Norwich has, in its great Quaker families, something of the same type.

I am aware that the case is not the same in the United States (and it is not quite the same in France although the differences between Britain and France would require too much time to describe). The tradition of civic loyalty and service has not totally disappeared from cities like Boston or Philadelphia or San Francisco (not to speak of some smaller and slightly less famous cities). But even in the United States there are signs of decline, of the flight to suburbs and exurbs, of decay at the heart and dropsy, especially in the field of communications, at the center.

But to return to Britain, which I am using as a horrible example. Many of our troubles stem from a firm refusal to face the facts of our urban situation. We pretend that the English "love the country." They love gardens but they do not love the country as a countryman does. The vast majority of the English population cannot tell wheat from barley, an oak from a beech. The representative English farmer is not a character out of Thomas Hardy; he is a modern technician working to his great profit in the most highly mechanized agricultural system in the world. (I refer not to Iowa but to East Anglia whose true capital is the other Cambridge.) But because of this fiction we put up with atrocious transport conditions in London (not as bad as New York's but less excusable). With a smaller proportion of our population living on the land than any community in history has known, we still personify ourselves as John Bull or as Sandy McPherson, living off his home grown oats and home distilled whisky. Mr. McPherson is a slightly more plausible figure than Mr. Bull, but not much more. What we do not accept is the fact that, for over a century, we have been city dwellers. This has, as I have already suggested, led to a serious "déformation professionelle" in my own profession of historian. For example, Dr. G. M. Trevelyan, third in a great dynasty of historians, has quite rightly pointed out that Pope's lines: "God made the country but man made the town" are deceptive, for man made both. The carefully tilled and decorated English countryside is as much a work of man's hands as are the horrid cities. What Dr. Trevelyan does not note is that the British business classes to which he belongs on his mother's side felt no responsibility for the cities whence came the wealth, but a duty and a pleasure in decorating the countryside.

What I have already called the most remarkable phenomenon of urban history, London, distorts the picture. For into London (as into Rome in the past) pour the talents, the ambitions, the greeds of the whole country. Had I time I could give dozens of examples of the fatally magnetic attraction of the "Wen," as Cobbett called it, when it was about a tenth of its present size. I shall give one. The British Atomic Energy Committee bought a fairly recent office building in Lower Regent Street, tore it down and erected its new offices within a stone's throw of Piccadilly Circus. The eminent scientists who perpetrated this folly were not, I am almost sure, attracted by the night life of the area (the best strip clubs in the world I am told), but by the proximity of the Athenaeum Club to which most of them belong—as I do myself. The examples can be multiplied. What do they suggest? They suggest, I submit, that in an age of inevitable urbanization, we still do not accept its logic. We think, like Jefferson, of the city as a cesspool (here I am half tempted to agree), of the countryside as a stronghold of the virtues (here I am tempted to disagree). Blinded by our historical myopia, we neglect the basic virtues of the city life that led to its identification with "civilization." We may lament the decline of the old romantic and rural life in which it is likely our ancestors had some share and from which they fled, and are fleeing, to the cities.[8] It is

[8] This nonsense reaches its height in Australia, the most urbanized of the great European extensions. Not only are the lawns of Vaucluse, the smart suburb outside Sydney, as rich in wagon wheels as Fairfield County, Connecticut, but eminently bourgeois figures will sing songs of the back blocks of the convict days,

reasonable to ask, will the city grow or be replaced by vast "urban disseminations" to coin a phrase? Has the big city, the megalopolis, passed the point of good returns? If we link together the city and its suburbs, the city will grow, even if it decays at the center. The result may well be a series of areas like Los Angeles strangled in its freeways, a city without a center and, I hope but do not believe, without a future. Have the real advantages of city life which are overwhelming (they can be seen in the antithesis of Los Angeles: San Francisco) been lost in mere growth? I fear they often have. For example, some colleges of the "University of London" are fifty miles apart and one of the many disadvantages of Los Angeles, so an exile tells me, is that you never meet anybody accidentally. All the advantages of the city can be got in a community the size of Edinburgh or Dublin.

But I am not very optimistic that we shall escape the self-strangling of the city since we are not prepared, apparently, to think realistically about it. As for Professor Boulding's idea of a disseminated urban culture linked by T.V. channels, I can only say I don't believe it probable and hope it is impossible. I have done a great deal of radio and T.V. cross talk and it is never satisfactory. For one thing, you cannot do what Mr. Dean Acheson has recently reminded us is often desirable, namely take a poke at your inter-locutor. No, there are many things that must be done face to face, not as in T.V., "person to person." The reproduction of the human race is one of them and another is the using of the city for its high-est purposes, the civilization of mankind. But we can only do this if we abandon our agrarian myths and accept the fact that we are nearly all citizens of a city and that it is our historically given job to make it "no mean city"—as that highly urban character, St. Paul, put it.

---

of Ned Kelly and the bushrangers even in Adelaide, where one of the greatest and most successful experiments in deliberate city planning was made more than a century ago and where there were never any convicts, or bushrangers or many sheep shearers.

V

The City as an Artifact

Urban Forms

SIR JOHN SUMMERSON

I want to begin by trying to define the role of the historian in relation to the city as a physical and mostly visible entity. We may perhaps be under the impression that this role is a very ancient and large one which has been played for centuries and, at certain levels, grossly overplayed. If we think that, we are, I am afraid, confusing history with something else—with geography or with geography's little old sister, topography, or merely with certain kinds of illustrative and descriptive writing. The fact is that the history of the fabrics of cities is as yet almost unwritten.

What is the historian's task in dealing with, say, the fabric of one single city? How must he approach it? First, he must learn from the geographers the factors of site and situation and the general morphology of the city as it stands. Next he must take possession of whatever the political, economic, industrial and social historians can give him. After that he must master the whole corpus of topographical material—not only maps, but prints, drawings, photographs and descriptions of lost buildings. Last, he must know the city—know its modern face, its ancient monuments and equally, the scraps and fragments which are neither ancient nor monuments but still significant and instructive flotsam from the past. When he has done all this he can begin (though I need hardly say that any historian not totally inhuman will have begun long before).

The bulk of material before the historian of the physical city is, of course, enormous; but if he really is a historian he has got to deal with it all—or, if that sounds too like a catalogue, let us say *be aware* of it all. I stress this because I am disposed to condemn the kind of urban history which concentrates on architecture at the expense of total building output; such work may or may not be good architectural history but it is not the history of the city as an artefact. Our historian has to be on terms with the whole physical mass of marble, bricks and mortar, steel and concrete, tarmac and rubble, metal conduits and rails—the total artefact. He has to deal with all this and he has to deal with it within limits. What are these limits?

They are probably best defined in terms of exclusion. Thus, our historian must not be primarily concerned either with administration or with the social, economic and industrial life of the city. He will have to intrude himself constantly into those fields to discover causes, incentives and controlling factors but they are not for him the main issue. The main issue, all the time, is tangible substance, the stuff of the city, and that implies form. I am not going on from this to say that the historian of the city as an artefact must be an art historian, though it is very nearly true. He must be both less and more than an art historian. If he cannot maintain a lively interest in form or if his interest in form extends only to form which is produced as "art," he cannot possibly write the history of the city as an artefact. It is the study of urban form as the resultant of a complex of social, psychological, and economic forces which is the essence of the kind of history I am postulating. The role of the historian in relation to the city as an artefact lies here.

It is now proper to enquire how far historical writing about towns has tended toward the type of history I have defined. Before

1914 I doubt if we could nominate any works as fulfilling the necessary conditions because, before that date, city life was never seen in its organic character—that is to say as the life of a community with a class structure and furthermore as a community existing in time and continuously in a state of change. Some of the classic historians and topographers from the sixteenth to the eighteenth centuries did, indeed, describe cities with admirable comprehensiveness—Stow's *Survey of London* of 1598 is a noble instance. But they described cities as static entities plus historic antecedents. The conception of the urban community as a developing organism is the necessary condition of the ability to analyze the fabric correctly and thus to reduce the mass of raw material to historic terms. For the fabric of the city is the integument of an organic life; it is produced and increased by the growth and movement of the organism which it protects and of which it is, in certain aspects, the tool. If the city is not understood in this light, the history of its fabric can only be enumerative and therefore (short of outright cataloguing) incomplete.

The outstanding introduction to the study of the city as an organism was, I suppose, Patrick Geddes' *Cities in Evolution*, published in 1915. It did not pretend to be a historical work and was in fact intended to propagate the nascent town-planning movement of its time. But Geddes was the first writer to see the slum not simply as something to be wiped out in the name of hygiene but as a living part of the living city, with an intelligible past and a future which must be rendered intelligible in relation to the whole. In Geddes' eloquent pages the slum became as real, historically speaking, as the great boulevard or the palazzo. Twenty-three years after Geddes, in 1938, came Lewis Mumford's *The Culture of Cities* in which some of Geddes' ideas were taken over and elaborated. Mumford's book is a critical study of cities rather than a history, but for us it is particularly remarkable for the penetrating and imaginative handling of the fabric. These two books are certainly landmarks in the history of an attitude to the study of cities but they treat of cities in general. What I am more concerned with here is the bearing of that attitude upon the study of single cities or conurbations—and by "study" I mean systematic analysis leading to a historical portrayal.

The only book I know which could really be called the history of a city as an artefact is a book on London by the Danish architect-town-planner, Steen Eiler Rasmussen. It was published in Denmark in 1934 and in England as *London: the Unique City* in 1937. It has been republished since. Once again, this is not a strictly historical work in the professional sense. It is based largely on secondary sources but has the enormous merit of being the work of a critical and imaginative first-hand observer. Rasmussen arranges his material very logically to demonstrate and explain one fundamental characteristic of London's morphology; its diffuse and scattered pattern. He could have done this in two dimensions but he chose to do it in three. The result is an image of the London fabric which is quite unforgettable and which has, in fact, considerably modified the image of the city current before Rasmussen's book became well known. One would not consult Rasmussen on matters of historical process and detail, since many of the secondary sources on which he relied were inadequate, but his approach is, I think, one of the most fruitful which an urban historian can adopt at the present time.

Having reached the theme of London I hope I may be forgiven if I develop it independently; the literature of the London fabric being what has most concerned me in the past thirty years. The points I want to make can as well be illustrated by a study of London as of any other great city. After Rasmussen it is necessary to mention three books dealing with the fabric of London in restricted areas of time. N. G. Brett-James's *The Growth of Stuart London* (1935) brought together a mass of valuable evidence on the expansion of the capital during the seventeenth century but dealt with it almost entirely in two dimensions, so that the impression given is that of a growing map rather than a growing city. It is not a study of the artefact. Mr. T. F. Reddaway's *The Rebuilding of London after the Great Fire*, which appeared with sinister promptitude on the eve of the blitz, dealt superbly with the administration and economics of a critical phase but stopped short of physical description of the rebuilt city. My own *Georgian London* (1946), begun before the war and finished after it, errs in the contrary direction, being primarily a study of London architecture though seeking to place the architecture in a proper relation to the social pattern and the economics of metropolitan expansion. Written in two phases, first when documentary sources were just being put away, and second when they had not yet been exhumed from wartime repositories, it is sketchy and far from authoritative.

This brings me to the postwar period and work done on the London fabric in the past fifteen or sixteen years. By far the most important is the *Survey of London* and of this I would like to speak in some detail. The *Survey of London* was started in 1894 by a small group of architects and amateurs concerned with the recording and, so far as possible, the preservation of ancient buildings in London—especially east London where forgotten monuments were rotting in the swamp of poorer class nineteenth century housing. The leader of the group was C. R. Ashbee, a disciple of Morris and a designer of originality and influence. In 1896 the London County Council (governing body of the London area) took a share in the work of the *Survey* with the result that a series of volumes began to appear under the joint aegis of the Survey Committee and the L.C.C. These volumes consisted in part of monographs on single buildings and in part of parish surveys. They have been appearing at irregular intervals ever since. Over so long a period it is natural that they should vary greatly in character and quality. The early volumes are what one may call "artistic-antiquarian"—a little vague on documentation and rather artily printed at a private press. Some of the volumes of the 'thirties are decidedly more professional. During the 1939–1945 war the activities of the *Survey* were largely suspended, but in 1949 they were resumed. The survivors of the original committee surrendered their responsibilities to the L.C.C. and a trained editor and staff were appointed. Dr. Francis Sheppard and his team have now been responsible for four parish survey volumes. They represent the most remarkable work done on the fabric of London in recent years.

The principle running through most of the series of parish surveys has been, in the first instance, to trace the manorial history of the area and the process of its coverage with building and then to select those individual buildings or groups of buildings which appear to possess "architectural or historic interest" and to describe them in drawings, photographs and letterpress. This has proved a useful method within certain limits, but it does not, of course, measure up to the historical criterion which I proposed earlier. Dr. Sheppard has pushed the method far beyond its old limits by a sharp realization of the truth that *all* buildings are buildings of architectural and historic interest. In the two magnificent volumes on the St. James's area, published in 1961, nearly every site is dealt with both in the historic dimension and the architectural dimension. As the area has always been one of wealth and fashion, the result is extremely striking. But for my present purpose these volumes are less important than some of Dr. Sheppard's earlier volumes, dealing not with historically "important" central areas but remote and complex suburbs where growth and form are now for the first time subject to historical analysis.

The study of the suburb seems to me at this time particularly relevant. For a long time now the suburbs has been increasing at the expense of the city center, the outer suburbs increasing at the expense of the inner ring and the centrifugal movement, enormously intensified by the automobile, throwing the city far out over the country. If we are to see our modern urban problems in perspective, it is the suburb which needs to be studied, its phases sharpened into focus, its successive images realistically rendered. Where London suburbs are concerned, Dr. Sheppard and his team are doing remarkable work. Tracts of impoverished, blighted and blitzed housing in Lambeth and Southwark, dismissed by the town planner as so many hundred acres of sheer obsolescence, are decomposed into their original constituents, separate initiatives with distinctive social and architectural characters, often but not always ignoble. The buildings are examined and some of them drawn or photographed.

The *Survey of London*, which takes the whole county area for its sphere and is under an obligation to produce volumes of reasonably general interest at reasonably frequent intervals cannot, of course, work out the entire building history of every area it tackles. For a more intensive treatment of one suburban area I recommend a book by Mr. H. J. Dyos of the University of Leicester, published in 1961, and entitled *Victorian Suburb; a Study of the Growth of Camberwell*. Camberwell is one of the southern suburbs of London which was a village in the middle ages, a semi-rural resort of well-to-do professional men in the eighteenth century and which in the nineteenth century became completely builtup as a lower middle-class dormitory suburb. Sixty or eighty years ago the name of Camberwell stood for the uttermost depth of social mediocrity. More recently it has stood not even for that; it has stood for absolutely nothing, a forgotten shapeless tract of London—from the air, just a part of the interminable London carpet and a part with no decipherable pattern.

But there is always a pattern and Mr. Dyos has recovered the pattern of Camberwell in terms of building estates, the operations of speculators and land companies, transport, social structure and amenities. Nothing will ever make Camberwell a very edifying spectacle, but the truth about even the most squalid of human performances has a deep fascination. Furthermore, it is the stuff out of which current imagery is fashioned; and our imagery of the past has an incalculable bearing on our imaginings of the future.

From this review of the work which has been done on the fabric of London in the past thirty years you will understand two things. First that the efforts seriously to come to grips with the subject are fairly sparse—we have one continuing official history and just very occasional excursions by historians with architectural or social-economic interests. Second, you will observe that the *city-as-artefact-as-form* slips through the net almost every time. Even the *Survey of London* only gives us selective records and descriptions; Mr. Dyos gives us a few photographs and some neat elevations of Camberwell housing types, though he does not discuss them and he gives no house plans. Nobody except Rasmussen has ventured to disintegrate the boundary between social-economic history and art history and give us what really and truly could be called the "History of London as an Artefact." Rasmussen's work is, after all, a brilliant essay rather than a systematic study. Has the job ever been done or even attempted for any city? Not so far as I know. Is it worth doing? That, like so many projects in historiography, is impossible to answer until it has been done.

I should like in conclusion to put before you in brief outline two studies which have occupied me in recent years but are not yet in form for publication. Both are London studies and both involve, in different ways, that totality of historical considerations which seems to me essential to what we are about—the treatment of the city as an artefact. The first study is of Covent Garden, London, built between 1630 and 1638. The second is a study of the Chalcots estate in the Borough of Hampstead, London, an area of land belonging to Eton College and developed as a new suburb from 1843 onwards. The first has a formal conclusion of great architectural nobility; the second rather the reverse.

Covent Garden takes its name from the Convent of Westminster to which it belonged before the Reformation. In 1630 it was in the hands of Francis Russell, Fourth Earl of Bedford, a man of thirty-seven, a great landowner and man of business and a political figure of some consequence in those circles which were not too friendly to the Royal prerogative. Now this land of Russell's stood northwards of the Strand, about half way between the City of London and Westminster. It was therefore subject to the effects of a series of proclamations restricting the building of new houses in London and the suburbs. These proclamations, initiated by Elizabeth, culminated in 1625 with a proclamation of peculiar rigor, back-dating the control of expansion to 1616, ordaining materials and floor heights for all rebuildings on old sites, and totally prohibiting buildings on new sites. A commission of the same year (1625) appointed fifty-one persons to implement the proclamation. The text of this commission contains a loophole for new development not contained in the proclamation. If old houses were demolished they could be rebuilt on *new* sites, but such redistribution could only be effected with the sanction of four commissioners and of these the King's Surveyor of Works was to be one. Through this loophole came the principle of planning by Royal direction. The King's Surveyor at this time was Inigo Jones.

Now Francis, Earl of Bedford, was anxious to develop his potentially extremely valuable property; and we have the interesting confrontation of this powerful and able man of business with Inigo Jones, the agent of the Crown, a man of dictatorial temperament who was also incidentally a man of artistic genius. Bedford had already been in trouble over his building ambitions—he had laid out the street called Long Acre, where his buildings had been stopped, with the result that the street was a heap of rubbish. Now he was trying again and in a more calculating way. The mere redistribution of old sites would not satisfy him; he meant to build on an ample scale and this he could do only if he could obtain a Royal license setting aside the effects of the proclamations. He did obtain such a license in February 1631, and it cost him £2,000. Even so, the control of the Crown was not totally relaxed and we know from a document of the next generation that Covent Garden was built "by speciall direction of the . . . King and his Councell wth. much ornament and beauty and to a vast charge"—the charge being Bedford's, of course. We do not know how the personal relations between Bedford and Inigo developed, but Inigo certainly laid out the streets and designed the buildings.

Between the pressures exerted by the proclamations, the business ambitions of the Earl, the willingness of the Crown to make concessions for ready cash, and the architectural experience and initiative of Inigo Jones, two very remarkable things came to pass. The first was that the earliest formal and calculated piece of urban estate development in England was set in motion. The second was that Inigo Jones was supplied with the opportunity of executing a profoundly important study in the Tuscan order.

It was presumably the Earl with his sound business instinct who hit upon the formula for London expansion which was to be used all through the eighteenth and far into the nineteenth centuries; that is, the formation of a regular open space or square composed of sites attractive to the wealthier house hunters, the provision of a conspicuous church as a social symbol and, after that, the building up of side streets for the less wealthy whom wealth attracts. The Earl forgot just one thing—a market. (The market came, of course, and squatted under his garden wall—then it moved into the great square. Now, in ghastly revenge for being forgotten in the first instance, it has eaten up the square, the houses and the side streets, the church stinks of it and the Opera House barely keeps it at bay. There is, I believe, no urban chaos in the world today to compare with the chaos of Covent Garden.)

To this fragment of London history is added another feature: to look at the Bedford-Inigo achievement in the round and assess it as architecture. Strictly on the stylistic level it is a brilliantly erudite study of the Tuscan order. Why Tuscan? Does the question of style knit in with other factors? It does, and for two reasons. First, the Earl of Bedford's religious opinions tended toward puritanism. In building the first new London church since the middle ages he would want to strike a note at once simple and fundamental. The Tuscan is the most primitive of the orders. Second, in undertaking an extremely costly real estate speculation he had no great margin for conspicuous waste. The unembellished Tuscan fulfilled that need too. Now there is a famous story about the Earl instructing Jones to make the church of barnlike simplicity and of Jones's reply: "You shall have the handsomest barn in England." The real point of that story has long been mislaid. It is this. A barn is an agricultural building. The order appropriate for agricultural buildings, according to Palladio, is the Tuscan. It was from Palladio that Jones took his instructions in creating Covent Garden Church. They harmonized precisely with the instructions of the Earl of Bedford.

There is, of course, a great deal more to the Covent Garden

story; the drainage and water supply, the social impacts of the scheme, the special character of Jones's Tuscan, the extension of the theme to the arcaded square, the creation of a new type of London housefront and so on. I have said enough, I think, to exhibit an instance where a political and religious situation, the personalities of a great promoter and a great artist can all be shown to interact in a critical phase of town morphology which moreover expresses itself in three dimensions at a very high architectural level.

My second study is a far less promising affair. The farm land known as Chalcots was given to Eton College by Henry VIII in exchange for some land near St. James's which he required for his own purposes. Farm land it remained for some three hundred years, by which time the northern fringes of expanding London were almost literally within a stone's throw. In 1824, the Provost and Fellows of the College Royal of the Blessed Mary of Eton, a conservative and slow moving body, had their attention drawn to the possibility of increasing their revenue by developing the Chalcots estate. They moved, but very slowly and missed the real estate boom of the 'twenties by several years. Some rather wretched pairs of villas sprang up on one edge of the estate. Nothing more happened until 1842 when the Provost and Fellows again exerted themselves and instructed their surveyor to lay out some roads. This action attracted the attention of a builder, Samuel Cuming, who bargained with the College and took eight plots on building lease in 1843. He took more the next year. This was well timed for the building mania which reached its peak in 1847, by which time Cuming was well away with building along five new roads. He prospered and when he died in 1870 was worth £45,000.

Nothing, of course, could be more commonplace than this chain of events. The same sort of thing was happening all around London and, for the most part, the products of the process are still there, still being lived in (I live in one myself). It is a process which comes as near as possible to complete anonymity in its results, for it can truthfully be said that not one solitary soul was ever really interested in what the physical, visible results would be. The Provost and Fellows may never even have seen the field they owned. They relied on the reports of their surveyor. The surveyor's sole interest was to lay out convenient roads, mark off building plots and take his fee. The builder who took the plots borrowed money to build, mortgaged his houses as he built them, assigned the leases as soon as he could and so worked his way over the ground without leaving a trace of responsibility behind him. State or municipal control was lacking apart from the obligation to pay a poor rate, a highway rate and a lamp rate. People came and bought or rented the houses—a suburb was born. Thanks to the 1851 census returns we can see inside this suburb in its earliest days. A mixed lot—small manufacturers, solicitors, a Congregational minister, an architect, a painter or two, widows bringing up families on small incomes—lived there. It was not a social group with any cohesion. The houses are in pairs, semidetached; each pair was designed to look like one substantial villa. They were designed to sell. "Villa" was a catch-penny phrase in the 'forties, and the architecture helped out with stucco finish and wide Italian eaves, echoing John Nash's Regent's Park cottages of twenty years before. But around the main window of each house is an architectural frame which is not Italian but Greek—it comes from the fourth century B.C. Choragic monument of Thrasyllus. Catch-penny again? Yes, indeed. It was not necessary for the builder's architect (whoever he was) to go to the erudite folios of Stuart and Revett. This very design is given—not too inaccurately—in *The New Practical Builder and Workman's Companion*, whose author tells the reader that it is "highly esteemed for its correct proportions and decided effects when carried into execution." In these terms, the terms of a shopkeeper, was the genius of ancient Athens decanted among the solicitors, tin-bath manufacturers, and dissenting ministers of London, northwest.

The application of art history is, you see, as necessary to the proper description of a seedy Early Victorian suburb as it is to Covent Garden. It falls into place with the social and economic aspects. The whole scene becomes comprehensible. When we come to the church built on the Chalcots estate the incentives, economic and architectural, are a little more intricate. There was a local committee, spurred by a mixture of class consciousness and conventional piety. The College of the Blessed Mary of Eton, to whom ground-rents were beginning to accrue, could scarely refuse a modest triangle of ground. Cuming, the builder, knew that a church was the very thing to give "tone" to a new estate and offered generous terms. The Bishop of London gave a word of encouragement. And so a church was built—and, of course, it was not Italian or Greek but Gothic. Now the psychological reaction of the English middle classes to pointed arches is a subject altogether too large even for the most summary treatment and here I must break off.

I hope I have said enough to indicate the kind of historical studies which seem to me to be worth while if we attach importance to the city as an artefact. They are worth while because they tend to create real images of what our cities are. Which is not what the guide books make them—assemblages of statistical facts, and public monuments planted in an incomprehensible "sprawl" of housing. Today the sprawl is the city and its history is as important as the history of cathedrals. A city is a community of people who are continually creating and recreating their own environment. The tragedy of the modern city is that the processes of creation and recreation have been delegated not to the most responsible but often to the least responsible sections of the community. But "delegation" is not the right word. It is an oversimplification. The growth of cities, the forms into which they grow, the acceptability of those forms by the citizens and, I would add, the changes in acceptability which these forms undergo—all these matters are of the very essence of city life and we understand very little about them. Nor shall we understand more without strict historical enquiry.

Proprietary Philadelphia as Artifact

ANTHONY N. B. GARVAN

To speak of any city as an artifact is partially a perversion of terms. "Artifact," a word of relatively modern American origin (Brinton, 1890), is by archaeological definition "a product of human workmanship especially one of the simpler products of primitive art as distinguished from a natural object." In histology, it describes products found in the cell structures as a result of death or the use of reagents. Current usage has extended the term to include most of the simpler forms and fragments of hand tools used in any technical process, but no reputable authority has yet extended it to include not only simple tools but the processes, social structure, and infinitely complex relationships of even the smallest urban community.

In the accepted use of the term two qualities can be distinguished which are of considerable value. First, "artifact" as used by the archaeologist and anthropologist refers to material objects or tools near to their natural state which human use has altered and for which humans have found one or another cultural role. Gourds, arrow heads, tapa cloth obviously meet this definition while amphora, breech-loading cartridges and batik cloth might, owing to the complexity of their manufacture, lie beyond its limits.

Second, and of equal importance, it is clear that the definition is a relative one. An industrial culture might consider a trenching spade a mere artifact, the use of which it comprehended in only the vaguest terms. At the same time an agricultural society to which effective drainage meant the difference between survival and starvation would view the same instrument as a highly complex tool to be used in a skillful and thoroughly sophisticated fashion.

If, therefore, the term can be applied to an urban complex at all, it should be applied in such a way as to seek all those aspects of the city and its life for which the material structure, buildings, streets, monuments were properly the tool or artifact.

The simplicity of the analogy at first seems very attractive. But the simplicity is deceptive. The structures, the selection of sites, the building materials used, the styles of architecture, the subdivisions of the city, its nomenclature, these and many other sorts of data must be analyzed to arrive at any assessment of the city's technology, its economy, its religion, its value system, its strata of society and its daily life. Moreover, all of these taken together give evidence of the way in which the daily habit patterns of the inhabitants were related to each other and structured as a culture. These and many more relationships must be reassembled and made as meaningful to the interpreter as the trenching tool was to the seventeenth-century English yeoman. The artifact and its technology must be understood as inseparable aspects of the same process. If the city as a whole can be structured as an artifact, it is an artifact of the whole culture and not of its economy, social standing, politics or any other aspects of urban life taken singly or alone.

At this point it may be redundant to point out that in order to achieve a reasonable view of the culture of which the city is an artifact, a high degree of detachment is required. The usefulness of the term, "artifact" in describing the tools of a more primitive society arises from the general characteristics which the more complex society finds shared by all the implements of the primitive people. These are often not apparent to the natives who use these artifacts and appear only as a result of an epistemologically detached and deliberately broadened view, a view, which in some instances, sacrifices detail to an over-all interpretation but aims at a valid appraisal of the artifact tool within the culture that produces and uses it.

In many respects colonial Philadelphia meets these requirements for a modern researcher. Enough buildings and monuments survive to demonstrate the visual and concrete outline of that city. Letters and pamphlets document the intent of its founders; maps and views indicate its realization. In short, viewed from the complexities of modern Philadelphia the colonial city is an artifact of the religious, social, and economic intentions of the Proprietor and his colonists, an artifact for which documents provide the equivalent of craft manuals.

Moreover, such an inquiry has validity and importance for the modern town planner. Since Philadelphia was from 1682 a planned city, later changes in its original outline may suggest the limits and direction of successful urban modification of a planned community and, equally important, the character of those which failed.

When on Sunday morning of March 5, 1682, William Penn reviewed his charter granted the previous day at Westminster, he found listed therein precisely the sort of powers and privileges he felt most competent to exercise.[1] His grant of "a province of Seigniorie"[2] held of the crown "as of our Castle of Windsor, in our County of Berks, in free and comon (sic) socage by fealty only for all services, and not in Capite or by Knight's service"[3] must have seemed to him a nearly perfect instrument for the creation of new settlement in America. Not only were its boundaries vast, but the powers it granted "the true and absolute Proprietaries" were pre-

[1] *Pennsylvania (Colony) Laws, Statutes, etc. The Charter to William Penn, and the Laws of the Province of Pennsylvania, 1682–1700, preceded by the Duke of York's Laws in force from 1676 to the year 1682* (Staughton George, Benjamin Need, Thos. McCamant, eds., Harrisburg, 1879).

[2] "Seigniorie." "The fee, dominions, or manor of a seignior" in a seigniory, i.e., a "lordship." "In English law a lordship; a manor. The rights of a lord, as such in lands." *Black's Law Dictionary* (West, St. Paul, Minnesota, 1951), 1523.

[3] *Minutes of the Provincial Council of Pennsylvania* (Jo. Severns, Philadelphia, 1852) I, 18, 19, hereafter cited as *Minutes, I.*

cisely the ones which Penn felt most necessary but which were at the same time circumscribed and reinforced by royal concern with the excesses and independence of Puritan colonies and governments, a concern which Penn shared both as a favorite of the Duke of York and as an intimate of Quaker sufferings in New England.[4]

The nice balance of palatine privilege and royal concern for colonial conformity appears nowhere more clearly than in the passage relating to justice and legislation. These offer a long recital of the rights of William Penn and his heirs to appoint justices, publish laws, pardon all crimes and offenses (save wilful murder and treason). The charter provided that the said laws be agreeable to the laws of England and, more important, reserved the right of receiving, hearing and determining appeals "touching any Judgement to bee (sic) there made or given."[5] Thus no transfer of the Proprietor's person to America nor any other fiction could long deny the operation of English law in the colony.[6] Moreover, in order to guard against the development of a local custom repugnant to the laws of England the charter specified that all laws of any sort whatever "Within five yeares after the makeing thereof, be transmitted and delivered to the Privy Councell (sic)."[7] The review of legislation and appeals to that body thus insured the consistency and conformity of the new colony.

Penn seems to have perceived at once that the terms of the charter, designed to insure the absolute operation of English statue and common law relative to estates, would at the same time guard his property and that of his heirs in a way wholly foreign to the corporate colony.[8] Although he seems to have enjoyed an anachronistic pleasure in the feudal aspects of the charter Penn recognized it for what it was—a legal device to encourage settlement of foreign parts and the growth of Penn's personal estate.

[4] William Sewall, *The History of the Christian People Called Quakers* (London, n.d.), 650, 651.

[5] *Minutes,* I, 20.

[6] The Charter of the Massachusetts Bay Company permitted the making of laws and ordinances "soe as such lawes and ordinances be not contrarie or repugnant to the lawes and statutes . . . of England." *Records of the Governor and Company of Massachusetts Bay* (N. B. Shurtleff, ed.: Boston 1853–1854), I, 12.

[7] *Minutes,* I, 20–21.

[8] *Minutes,* I, 20. "Soe as the said ordinances bee consonant to reason and bee not repugnant nor contrary, but so farre as conveniently may be agreeable with the Lawes of or Kingdome of England." ". . . and our further will and pleasure is, that the lawes for regulateing and governing of propertie . . . as well as for the descent and enjoyment of lands, as likewise for the enjoyment and succession of goods and chattels, and likewise as to felonies, shall be and continue the same as . . . the general course of the law in our Kingdome of England."

Taking full advantage of the terms of the charter which gave him the power to "Divide the said Countrey and Islands, into Townes, Hundreds, and Counties," and to erect and incorporate Townes into Borroughs and Borroughs into Citties." [9] Penn's first offer of terms of settlement implied most of the basic outlines of the province and at the same time showed a matured and well developed philosophy which sprang not only from the Utopias of his library shelves but from a life spent in the saddle as an itinerant Quaker and landed estate manager.

Of his bias Penn was perfectly aware and, far from hiding his intentions, made them quite specific. Writing in 1681 to interest English and Continental settlers, he saw English rural distress relieved, not aggravated, by the peopling of the colonies with country persons "who were low here if not poor and now Masters of Families . . . and some after their Industry and Sucess there made them wealthy, they return and empty their riches into England." [10]

The kind of countryside which Penn visualized for America had almost equal Utopian vision and nostalgic longing for the past. A stern critic of the absentee landlord and courtier-gentlemen, he compares the excesses of wealth and wasteful labor of the former to the ". . . old time . . . Nobility and Gentry" who "spent their Estates in the Country, and that kept the people in it; and their Servants married and sate at easie Rents under their Masters favour, which people the place." [11]

Penn deliberately framed his terms of sale to attract such rural wealth. Knowing from long experience in Ireland and England that wild exaggeration would draw only speculators and men of no experience he deliberately wrote the description of his new grant in sober and restrained prose, proofread by mariners and settlers of the Delaware Valley.

The fact that Penn's terms seemed to his fellow Quakers to be very attractive, if not inevitable, should not obscure the selective nature of their appeal. Although couched in the simplest terms of land sale, in fact this initial offer laid the basis for the colony's road

[9] *Minutes*, I, 21–22. "to doe all and every other thing and things touching the premises which to him or them shall seeme requisite, and meet, albeit they be such as of their own nature might otherwise require a more especiall commandment and warrant, then in these presents is expressed."
[10] *Original Narratives of Early American History* (J. F. Jameson, ed.), XIII, 206. Hereafter, *Original Narratives*.
[11] *Original Narratives*, XIII, 206.

and land system and by implication its entire rural and urban administration until 1712.[12]

To "all my dear Country-Folks who may be inclin'd to go into those Parts" Penn offered a relatively restricted choice.[13] First of all he guaranteed all titles and rents free from "any Indian incumbrance," on the surface an obvious and necessary provision operating solely to the benefit of the purchaser.[14] However, since only his personal funds might extinguish Indian titles and since he himself must be a party to all purchases or conquests the proprietor thereby gained a considerable measure of control over the location of the frontier. In fact neither Penn nor his immediate successors ever thought of the entire province as open to simultaneous settlement. Rather for the improvement of their own estates and the safety and prosperity of the settlers they conceived the edge of settlement as a treaty line held fixed for a period of years and only to be overrun when a new and equally rigid but more distant boundary had been erected. In no sense did the Penn Proprietary visualize a constantly advancing frontier of squatters and frontiersmen; rather they saw a province which might from time to time be enlarged by purchase much as the English conquest had enlarged the Plantation of Ireland between 1550 and 1660.[15]

Moreover, Penn read his charter quite literally since the Crown had regarded the Irish lands as Crown property to be disposed

[12] William W. Comfort, *William Penn 1644-1718* (Philadelphia, 1945), 65, 66. "On account of the number of properties and the number of heirs involved, Penn's will, though brief, was somewhat complicated. He left to two Earls as trustees the government of Pennsylvania and territories, to be disposed of to the Queen or any other person to advantage. That provision, when the will was drawn, involved presumably the twelve thousand pounds which was a little later agreed upon with the Lord Treasurer. But . . . the government never passed from the family . . . To seven trustees in England and five in Pennsylvania Penn gave and devised his Pennsylvania property with instructions to sell enough to pay all of his just debts; next to convey ten thousand acres to each of the three children of William, Jr. and to Penn's daughter, Letitia Penn Aubrey; next to divide all his other lands in Pennsylvania among his children by his second wife, as she might think fit. All of his personal estate and arrears of rent due he left to Hannah Callowhill Penn, whom he also named executrix. Thus, in general, Penn's interests in England and Ireland passed to his second wife and her children."
[13] *Original Narratives*, XIII, 215.
[14] Samuel Hazard, *Annals of Pennsylvania 1609-1682* (Philadelphia, 1850), 510.
[15] By 1726 it was estimated that 100,000 persons had settled without a shadow of a right. William R. Shepherd, *History of Proprietary Government in Pennsylvania* (New York, 1896), 38-41, 49, 50, 53. The English Act of 1623 gave a large importance to the Common Law doctrine of adverse possession which was not diminished until 1833. See William Holdsworth, *A History of English Law* (London, 1924), IV, 485, 486.

according to the kings' wishes[16] and since Charles II had, for whatever cause, specifically granted Pennsylvania to Penn then Penn reasoned all lands in the province were his personal and private property and in fact the bounds of the province marked nothing more than the limits of his personal estate.[17]

What frontier Penn fixed arose in large measure from the quantity of land he sold in England. Since the offer of unlimited or excessive amounts would at once depress the American value of purchased land and depress the English sale, he chose to offer land for a limited period in England, then to close his books, proceed to America, there complete the purchase of sufficient land from the Indians to cover his sales, and finally, by lot and survey to locate the properties he had sold and leased.

Although Penn's procedure can be explained in forms of economic self-interest, at every step he so carefully defined his terms as to produce an offer nearly as satisfactory to the settlers as to promoter. On July 11, 1681 he published certain conditions or concessions which clarified the procedure of survey and allotment. The earlier pamphlet *Some Account of Pensilvania* had indicated his terms. Purchasers of a share in the province received 5000 acres for £100 and 50s quit rent, payable after 1684. Leasees paid ld per acre annual rent on 200 acres or less. For each servant carried, more

[16] See generally Sir Thomas Phillips, *Londonderry and the London Companies, 1609–1629* (Belfast, 1928). Also George Hill, *An Historical Account of the Plantation in Ulster* (Belfast, 1887). Sir Arthur Chichester, Lord Deputy of Ireland, 1604–1616, gave the conditions that land was to be held in "free and common socage as of the castle of Dublin."

[17] *Laws of the Commonwealth of Pennsylvania* (Philadelphia, 1810), I, 479; The Act of November 27, 1779. ". . . whereas the claims heretofore made by the late Proprietaries to the whole of the soil contained within the bounds of the said charter . . . cannot longer consist with the safety, liberty and happiness of the good people of this commonwealth . . . Be it therefore enacted . . . that all and every the estate, right title, interest, property, claim and demand of the heirs . . . and other claiming as Proprietaries of Pennsylvania . . . together with the royalties, franchises, lordships, and all other hereditaments . . . are hereby vested in the commonwealth of Pennsylvania." The eighth section confirms to their owners the private estates and proprietary tenths or manors. The ninth section declares all other quit rents and arrears void. The fourteenth section enacted that £130,000 was to be given the claimants and legatees of Thomas and Richard Penn, "in remembrance of the enterprising spirit of the founder, and of the expectations and dependence of his descendants." See also *Laws I*, 133, 134, 135, 136, 137; The Act of May 21, 1722. By this act, the power to establish courts and nominate judges, which had resided in William Penn and his heirs, was vested in the governor. Before this time, "the Justices of the County-Courts, were empowered to lay out cart-ways to the public road to appoint viewers of partition fences, to superintend the erection of bridges, and the laying out of highways." These powers were not withdrawn by this act, but remained vested in the existing courts.

than fifty acres were alloted to the master and fifty acres to the servant at the end of his time.

No property of any kind was to be free of some service, however nominal.[18] All purchasers as well as renters were in Penn's view tenants subject to quit rents forfeiture and escheat. To support his contention he quoted the charter which granted him the right to make grants "as of the seignory of Windsor by such services, customs and rents as shall seem fitt to said William Penn his heirs and assignees, and not immediately of us our heirs and successors." [19] In any instance, while Penn held the rents low, it was his hope that their great number would assure him a reasonable return, and neither he nor his heirs ever abandoned their privilege.

Inasmuch as Pennsylvania tenure was basically feudal its economic attraction for English, Irish, and Welsh Friends lay elsewhere. Prospective purchasers knew little of the country. They were offered an archaic title and yet, before a year was out, nearly 600,000 acres had been sold to some 470 first purchasers,[20] and by 1701 Penn could without serious exaggeration estimate his colony's population at 20,000 persons.[21] Pennsylvania's lure for both purchasers and settlers lay in Penn's thorough understanding of the rural landholder of his day. Unable to purchase or lease British land in sufficient amounts to justify the new economies of enclosure, he found his own modest holding could not compete in a market controlled by great estates. To such a person the offer of, say 1000 acres, for £20 and a low annual quit rent seemed ideal. Not only would all his land be contiguous so as to permit easy management

[18] William R. Shepherd, *History of Proprietary Government in Pennsylvania* (New York, 896), 14–16 "Penn was empowered to grant the land in such proportions as should seem fit. The grantees were to hold it in their own right, not directly of the King, but of the proprietor, in fee simple, fee tail, or for a life or lives, or a term for years, and by such services, customs, and rents as might appear to him expedient, the statue of quia emptores notwithstanding . . . in order that no subinfeudation should be permitted in Pennsylvania, it was expressly provided in the charter that upon ensuing alienations the lands should be held of the same lord and his heirs of whom the grantor had held, and by the same rents and services . . . Purchasers of the soil held immediately of Penn, not of the King, and that by socage tenure . . . the estate held by the grantee would thus be a tenement, not an allod. It was subject to quitrent, to forfeiture, and to escheat. Pennsylvania may be viewed as a seignory, but divested of the heaviest burdens imposed by feudal law, and endowed with such powers of territorial control as distance from the realm of the lord paramount required."
[19] *Colonial Records of Pennsylvania* (Philadelphia, 1852), V, 24.
[20] Hazard, 637–642.
[21] *Original Narratives* XIII, 260. See also E. B. Greene and V. D. Harrington, *American Population before the Federal Census of 1790* (New York, 1937), 114.

and consequent economies, but the quantity would be sufficient for both the original purchaser and his heirs for at least two generations (Penn owned 12,141 statute acres in Ireland in seventy-two pieces, largest 386, smallest fifteen).

Gregory King has estimated that, in 1688, out of some 1,350,-000 households in England, 445,000 had incomes between £40–£100 per annum; only about 50,000 had incomes in excess of this sum, but 849,000 had incomes of £20 or less. Clearly Penn's offer consciously or unconsciously tapped the numerous middle class.[22] For such persons their chief expense lay in the cost of the voyage. The sale of English goods or lands would amply compensate them for their American purchase.

Beyond the mere acquisition of land there lay the promise of easy improvement and betterment. No apparent bar to the purchase of land existed in Pennsylvania like the New England township or the southern plantation. Land was plentiful and its division in the interest of the rural landowner. To encourage the larger wealthy holder who could purchase 500 acres, Penn added the inducement of a city plot within a large town or city, later Philadelphia, thus providing for the class of men like himself who, though they enjoyed country life, were no stranger to the city's trade.[23]

Moreover, this provision had far-reaching effects upon urban life of the city. In the first place unlike virtually every other British city in America, its owners were widely distributed throughout the 600,000 acres of the province which meant a close connection with surrounding rural counties. Second, since only original purchasers were given town lots with their rural land, it meant that these persons, together with the Proprietor, were given a handsome share in the rise of urban real estate and in the port's commerce. Placed in a position to dominate its future growth much of the continued

<hr />

[22] Charles D'Avenant, *Political and Commercial Works* (London, 1771), II, 184.

[23] Samuel Hazard, *Annals of Pennsylvania 1609–1682* (Philadelphia, 1850), 516–517. "That so soon as it pleaseth God that the above persons arrive there, a certain quantity of land or ground plot shall be laid out for a large town or city, in the most convenient place upon the river for health and navigation; and every purchaser and adventurer shall, by lot, have so much land therein as will answer to the proportion which he hath bought or taken up upon rent. But it is to be noted, that the surveyors shall consider what roads or highways will be necessary to the cities, towns, or through the lands. Great roads from city to city not to contain less than forty feet in breadth, shall first be laid out and declared to be for highways, before the dividend of acres be laid out for the purchaser, and the like observation to be had for the streets in the towns and cities. That there may be convenient roads and streets preserved, not to be encroached upon by any planter or builder, that none may build irregularly, to the damage of another.

eminence of Morris, Shippen, and like families rests in part on this early advantage.

Since Penn closed his English estate books in 1682 he had to provide some kind of buffer against the immediate expansion of his colony. This he did in two ways: first by retaining some 60,000 of acres as a Proprietary reserve to be sold by his agents in America, and second by the erection of a number of manors. These manors, though they lacked the vitality of independent manorial courts, served a real purpose in the management of the proprietor's interest. Holme's map of the province dated 1687 shows the manors granted to members of the Penn family or to especially favored persons. Such grants served two purposes. Penn could thereby bypass the terms of his printed conditions and he could make large grants to persons whose influence he wished to court or whose settlement he wished to attract.[24] Altogether he granted eight manors; one to himself, and three to his family.

By this device he removed certain lands from the province's land office and granted this land to himself or his family not in his office as Proprietor but as a private individual. A royal contest over these grants would have opened the entire land history of the colony to review and for this reason the Assembly forbore even under the strong inducements of revolutionary fervor to touch the Penn manors. The manor thus preserved a part of the Penn properties from any threat to disallow the charter, since such properties were held apart from the Proprietary undivided lands. Finally, the distribution of manor lands among the members of Penn's family guarded them against the danger of forfeiture, a serious threat after 1688 when Penn's friendship for James II placed him under suspicion of Papal and Stuart learnings. Though in most instances the lands were sold before their value appreciated, their sale did provide modest sums for both Letitia and William Penn, Jr. and contributed to the costs of their American visits.

Penn provided for three additional types of land allotment,

[24] Shepherd, 45–47. The body of patentees known as the Free Society of Traders in Pennsylvania were established in the Manor of Frank, and a manor house erected on the land of its president. Also a 5000 acre manor was granted to Eneas MacPherson of Scotland, creating the power to erect the barony of Inversie. Manors were also granted to Nicholas More and William Lowther. See also John E. Pomfret, "The First Purchasers of Pennsylvania," *The Pennsylvania Magazine of History and Biography*, LXXX; 2 (April 1956), 158 and Thomas Holme, *Map of the Improved Part of the Province of Pennsylvania . . . begun in 1681* (engraved by E. Lamb, London, 1687. Facsimile, Philadelphia, 1846).

each important to his provincial plan and the direction he wished urban growth to take. First for persons of common background and interests he offered townships of 5000 acres which he would sell to constituted companies or associations of planters. Within the boundaries of such towns the company was free to allot lands as it saw fit, keeping only in mind the proportions of its members and averaging about 500 acres to a family.

Penn did not endow the Pennsylvania township with any of the powers made familiar in New England. Indeed, 5000 acres seems modest enough when compared to the six mile square of the average Connecticut town.[25] Further, in order to benefit by a lot in Philadelphia, the allotment of township land had to be recorded at the Proprietary land office. This hastened the disposition of land within the township and weakened the position of its first purchasers, since they soon disposed of the townships' unallotted land. In most instances before 1687 the inhabitants of a township were assembled chiefly by lot from among purchasers who wished their land surveyed. As a consequence, most of the province was settled by individuals who came to know their neighbors only after they took up land. Such persons naturally tended to rely upon the Proprietor and the county courts to give leadership and settle disputes.

In a few instances, however, Penn used the township for clearly defined social ends. The most famous and successful of such experiments, Germantown, was described by Daniel Pastorius seventeen years after its foundation. He recalled with gratitude Penn's "good advice and convincing reasons toward the first beginners" which caused the township to be "laid out not in plantations as the most part of the Province but in lots and more compacted settlements." In consequence Pastorious estimates that upon

[25] *Minutes*, I, 27. "That where any number of purchasers, more or less, whose number of acres amounts to five or ten-thousand acres, desire to sit together in a lot or township, they shall have their lot or township cast together, in such places as have convenient Harbors or navigable rivers attending it, if such can be found, and in case anyone or more Purchasers plant not according to agreement, in this concession to the prejudice of others of the same township upon complaint thereof made to the Governor or his deputy, with assistance they may award (if they see cause) that the complaining purchaser may, paying the survey money, and purchase money, and interest thereof, be entitled, inrolled, and lawfully invested in the land so not seated."

"That every man shall be bound to plant or man so much of his share of land as shall be set out and surveyed, or else it shall be lawful for new comers to be settled thereupon, paying to them their survey money, and they go up higher for their shares."

his 5700 acres of land three score families and some other single persons then dwelt and had begun to exhaust the timber. At the same time both Penn and Pastorius took satisfaction in the fact that the isolation of the Germans and Hollanders had enabled them to keep their religious meeting, their language and their customs for nearly a generation from their first settlement. The township had thus proved a means of preventing the too quick dispersion of peoples and intermingling of nationalities.

Honorable Gov.

May it please thee to remember these seventeen years ago this Township by thy good advice and convincing reasons towards the first beginners thereof was commenced to be laid out not in Plantations as the most part of this Province but in lots and more compacted settlements which method being after followed by our Countrymen who from time to time arrived here it fell so out that there are now upon the 5700 acres of land this our township consist in three score families besides several single persons and some dwelling so close and near one to the other that they have not half as much timber as will fence there small spots of ground.

Germantown 17, XII mo. 1701 Daniel Pastorius

By 1682, 600,000 acres had been sold at £100 each, £5000, or £12,000 total.

Penn entertained similar hopes for the Radnor and Haverford townships which he visualized as pockets of Welsh settlements. Three of these, Haverford, Merion, and Radnor he allocated to companies of settlers, who, under the leadership of well to do Welsh Quakers, had subscribed to approximately 5000 acres of land for each company.[26] Penn treated each of the purchasers of the Welsh company tracts as trustees and gave Philadelphia lots and Liberty lands only to those Welsh individuals whose personal properties exceeded 500 acres. Moreover, he did not intend that the Welsh grant should carry manorial rights and though he encouraged the compact settlement of Welsh colonists he sternly denied them the right to hold their own courts independent of the Quarter Sessions of Chester County.[27] He unwisely used the Irish term

[26] *Original Narratives* XIII, 228, 318, 451, 452. Radnor, Merion, and Haverford were the three townships of the Welsh Tract, although Holme's map shows only Haverford and Radnor. The Welsh purchase was later expanded to 40,000 acres, known as the Welsh Barony.

[27] *Minutes*, I, 265–267, see also Shepherd, 46. The Welsh claimed a distinct barony and refused to consider themselves within the counties of Philadelphia or Chester. However, they were not numerous enough to occupy the whole of a

"barony" to describe the Welsh holding and this subdivision of a county was assumed by the Welsh to carry English prerogatives. In fact Penn quite clearly intended his concessions to the Welsh settlers to be limited to contiguous survey of their lands. He did not intend that Welsh law should govern the descent of property or that the Welsh have special treatment in the allotment of urban land.[28] Unfortunately by so doing Penn alienated in large measure Welsh support and at the same time gave to the Proprietary opposition a vigorous Welsh leadership in Thomas Lloyd and David Lloyd, the latter's executor and kinsman.[29]

At the heart of his county land, manors, and townships Penn proposed to lay out a "great town." Writing his commissioners on September 30, 1681 Penn described the town he wished them and his surveyor to lay out. They should choose a spot "navigable, high, dry, and healthy"[30] and there lay out 10,000 acres as the bounds and liberties of the said town. Each share of 5000 acres was to have 100 acres of these lands and each fraction of a share its due proportion.

No other land was to be surveyed until the city plot was laid out and this was to have uniform streets from the river to the "country bounds." The houses should be built in a line and he, as Proprietor, should have a plot "not the tenth part" but "less than a thirtieth part, to wit, three hundred acres, whereas several will have two by purchasing two shares, that is, ten thousand acres." His personal hesitancy may be measured by his final line: ". . . and it may be fitting for me to exceed a little."

That Penn visualized a very unorthodox city becomes even more clear by his fifteenth instruction.

"Let every house be placed if the person pleases in the middle of its plat, as to the breadth of it, that so there may be ground on each side for gardens or orchards or fields, that it may be a green country town which will never be burnt and always be whole-

---

country. Therefore, the governor and council declared that several baronies might lie within the same county. The Welsh plea to be regarded as a manor was also denied and the unsettled part of the tract granted to other purchasers.

A "barony" is in England, a quantity of land amounting to fifteen acres. In Ireland, it is a subdivision of a county. *Black's Law Dictionary*, 190.

[28] Hazard, 518.

[29] *Minutes*, I, 266. See also Comfort, 153. "David Lloyd headed the Quaker Party that claimed the province was losing its privileges and immunities through Penn's administration of government."

[30] Hazard, 528.

some." When one realized that the "plats" would run from ten to one hundred acres, it is clear that Penn neglected the urban center for his gentlemen's seats. He visualized, not a city, but a residential district of regularly arranged parks with uniform streets down to the water from the country bounds. His sole concern for commerce was that a "place for the storehouses be on the middle of the key which will yet serve for market and statehouses too." [31]

In order that this complex scheme of land allotment might be carried through Penn sent Thomas Holme, his surveyor, a list of purchasers early in 1682. Between that date and August, 1682, Holme and the commissioners surveyed and allotted the city's lands, apparently substantially as described in his printed letter to the *Free Society of Traders* published in 1683. Little remained of Penn's original plan and instructions. Instead an extremely interesting and complex plan evolved which owed little to the Proprietor except the partial achievement of his intent.[32]

Thomas Holme, an Irish settler under Cromwell and resident at Waterford in 1682, had already some twenty-two years of colonial experience as soldier, surveyor, Quaker writer and land owner in Ireland.[33] Penn's instructions to Holme, however vague, reflect the Proprietor's confidence in his surveyor-general. The paucity of the changes he effected after October, 1682 show the plan met his approval as an inevitable compromise, but its background Penn probably understood only very imperfectly.

He must have known as did Holme that similar plans were common in Ireland. There the conquest of stubborn and resourceful natives had forced the development of English cities, sometimes upon a cleared site, more often adjacent to an Irish citadel. Oxmantown in northeast Dublin, the English town of Limerick, the southern quarter of Cork built out over marshy islands were familiar enterprises to the Irish Quakers to whom Penn entrusted his American enterprise.[34] Quite appropriately both he and they adopted the

[31] *Ibid.,* 530.
[32] *Original Narratives,* XIII, 224 and map (Holme) opposite 243. It is possible that Penn approved the changes in Plan of his commissioners but hardly likely in view of travel time. He does appear to have renamed streets. Trees for individuals, High and Broad following common practice notably at Oxford. See also Hazard, 594, 595.
[33] See generally Penn, Holme MSS in the Historical Society of Pennsylvania. See also *Tercentenary Commemoration of Captain Thomas Holme, 1624–1695* (Philadelphia, 1924), 5–40.
[34] Maurice Craig, *Dublin, 1660–1860, A Social and Architectural History* (New York, n.d.), 84–85.

most advanced town design of which they had knowledge to the Pennsylvania problem.

English experience in Irish town design arose out of the necessities of conquest and as a consequence was often entrusted to an artillery officer who had all the requisite skills. Thomas Stafford, writing in 1683 of the conquest of Munster some thirty years earlier, shows the familiar military camp of seventeenth century English forces. Within a large rectangular enclosure, simply fortified, the tents of the troops are arranged in blocks along long avenues broken by regular cross streets. At the center of the enclosure is an open parade ground upon which the commander's tent stood. A peculiar hallmark of these military designs appears in the design of the central open square. This is often cut into by enclosures devoted to markets and officer quarters.[35] When adopted to civil purposes as at Londonderry by Raven the square cuts into the four surrounding blocks so as to provide additional frontage and a large free area for the town's main cross-axis.

That Holme knew Raven's plan for Londonderry cannot at present be demonstrated although it is likely that as an itinerant Quaker he visited Friend's meeting there.[36] Moreover Thomas Phillips' survey of Ulster had furnished the hub for the crown's investigation of the City's administration of Irish lands and gained a kind of infamous renown thereby.[37] In any instance Londonderry's plan by the end of the seventeenth century had become sufficiently well known to be used as a cartographical symbol for the city by Rocque, the celebrated map maker.

Faced with the immediate problem of Philadelphia's design, Holme made decisions based more upon Irish experience than proprietary instruction. First he chose to give first purchasers a narrow but central plot in place of the ten acres promised in the 1681 conditions of sale.[38] In order to compensate for this deficiency he then laid out near the city proper some 10,000 acres of liberty lands.[39] Such lands, following London and Irish precedent, lay beyond the physical boundaries of the city but within the limits of its jurisdiction. Those of Cork, Waterford, and Youghal even in

[35] Thomas Stafford, *Pacata Hibernia* (London, 1633), plate 1.

[36] See generally Isabel Grubb, *Quakers in Ireland* (London, 1927).

[37] Sir Thomas Phillips, *Londonderry and the London Companies, 1609–1629* (Belfast, 1928).

[38] Hazard, 517. See also *Original Narratives*, XIII, 243.

[39] Shepherd, 19.

1810 remained much as they were in 1680, rural districts physically indistinguishable from the county baronies which bordered them, but carrying with their properties the privileges and immunities of the town or city which they bordered. Higher annual rent, a denser population and the presence of a few villas seemed to the average traveller more a difference of degree than of kind.

On the other hand the liberty lands of Dublin and Philadelphia, like those of London, had in the same period become the site of urban expansion favored by their administrative identity with the city itself. In each instance a series of speculative ventures had extended the city's street pattern out over neighboring fields, and small estates along which uniform housing of various classes quickly sprang up. To English colonists in Ireland and Pennsylvania liberty lands continued to be a kind of speculative suburb which urban political control made more valuable and which meanwhile might be enjoyed as gentlemen's seats or modest estates too small to be profitably farmed or leased but large enough to preserve rural delights for wealthy merchant or fashionable wife.

The city itself gained a wide, greenbelt of rural parks upon which speculators might slowly encroach for two centuries, and these same liberties linked the distant enclosures of the county with its Philadelphia center. First purchasers in 1682, for the most part like-minded Quakers from a scant half dozen English counties, had substantial holdings in city, liberties and surrounding county. Such purchasers reflected a concrete image of Penn's hope for the union of commercial and landed interests and gave a sure safeguard for the continuance of a Quaker oligarchy by their descendants.

Having widely dispersed purchased promised urban holdings in the Philadelphia liberties, Holme saw fit to contract purchasers' city lots at the ratio of about one acre to every 5000 acres purchased and about half an acre for smaller purchases. In all these allocations the largest purchasers received the most valuable sites.[40] He laid out some 470 such lots to almost as many purchasers. The balance of Philadelphia's two square miles he retained for the Proprietor and the land office. By so doing he assured the city of a concentration of wealthy merchants near the two river fronts and to both Proprietor and lot holder the prospect of a steady rise in the value of their Philadelphia real estate.

[40] *Original Narratives*, XIII, 243. The original conditions gave ten acres for every 500.

In one aspect his plan was not realistic. In order to prevent undue crowding Holme had surveyed the full acre and half acre lots for the holders of full and partial shares and carefully placed the former on waterfront and high street sites. Unfortunately the requirement of locating several hundred lots with some degree of equality made the lots unduly deep and narrow, a fault that led to serious consequences in ensuing years.

Holme's other measures gave more lasting benefit. Most renowned were the five squares. Holme laid out a ten acre municipal square at the crossing of the city's principal streets and four lesser squares of eight acres each two blocks north or south and five blocks east or west of the principal square. These lesser squares "to be of like uses as the Moore-fields in London" had a very curious design which clearly indicated their intended purpose. The two southern squares, now Washington and Rittenhouse, had streets along only two of their sides, the two northern along three. In each of the squares this device prevented roundabout traffic and assured residential quiet. Town plots were allotted about the squares so as to assure varied façades, some being lengthwise. More important the Proprietary retained at least one side of each square possibly with the hope of erecting a Proprietary mansion after the fashion of the Russells at Covent Garden.

Holme seems to have derived Philadelphia's central square directly from the Londonderry plan. Its location on the principal axis of the city, an axis asymmetrically placed, the notched design of its surrounding blocks, all follow Londonderry and military practice.[41] In fact the market and city hall which appears on the 1687 map of the province strongly recalls the armed town center of Thomas Phillips.[42]

On the other hand the parentage of the lesser squares is less apparent. The legal use of Moor Fields, to which Penn refers, was as an unrestricted playing field for young men similar to that of Lincoln's Inn fields with which Penn had become familiar as a student. Their small extent, the use of the term square as opposed to fields and the allocation of surrounding property all suggest the intimacy of the residential squares of Bloomsbury, the pleasures of which were reserved for tenants of the square's owner.

St. Stephen's Green in Dublin, a common of fifty-seven acres,

[41] *Original Narratives*, XIII, map opposite 243.
[42] Phillips, plate, 12.

furnishes the closest comparison though again with some differences. In 1663 shortly after the arrival of James Butler, Duke of Ormonde, the corporation of Dublin leased some thirty acres of lots around the perimeter of St. Stephen's common and designated its center, a square of twenty-seven acres, as a municipal green, tenants of which had to provide some shrubbery but which after 1709 was administered as a private park. Since Penn vested title to Philadelphia's squares in the city and retained only the unallocated perimeter lots, and since (like both Moor Fields and St. Stephen's Green) the anticipated use of the green area was general and not tenants' only, it is not unlikely he followed an Irish precedent with which his friendship for James Butler had made him thoroughly familiar some sixteen years earlier when the Duke of Ormonde had acted in his father's behalf, and again in 1669 when the Duke protected Irish Quakers from civil punishment.[43]

One further subtlety of Holme's plan should be noted. In every instance he selected street widths appropriate to the intended function of that thoroughfare and at the same time he introduced great variety into the dimensions of the building blocks. In this the plan marked a great advance over New Haven, Connecticut, the acme of British seventeenth-century use of the rectangular grid in Colonial America. Dock Street was divided into two streets of thirty feet each separated by a canal. Front Street required sixty feet, the equivalent of London's broadest streets. High and Broad streets each measured one hundred feet, an almost fantastic affection for the provincial city and an indication of both Penn's and Holme's hopes for the youthful metropolis. It would take nearly three centuries before these powerful arteries began to constrict their city.

Elsewhere the plan was ample and generous but not romantic. Spruce, Vine, Sassafras, Chestnut, and the numbered cross streets measured fifty feet. Mulberry oddly was laid out sixty-six feet in breadth.[44]

The size of Philadelphia blocks seems to rest more upon the

[43] Craig, 19 sqq. and map, post. William Penn, *Irish Journal* (London, 1952), 12–13, 25, 26, 59. A full legal and historical review of the Moor Fields is given in *Dyer vs. Philadelphia*, 276 Penna. 348 ff., 1923; also see *Wheeler vs. Rice*, 83 Penna. 232, 1877 *Commonwealth vs. Albarger*, Wharton 469, 1836.
[44] Nicholas B. Wainwright, "Plan of Philadelphia," *The Pennsylvania Magazine of History and Biography*, LXXX: 2, 209. Parson's map shows Mulberry (now Arch) as one of the original 9 east-west streets.

necessity of providing frontage for each landholder than upon clear social or visual objectives. Blocks varied widely but generally were constructed on modules of fifty-one feet or forty-nine and one half feet which represented the shortest street frontage. The depth of blocks generally varied between 195 and 300 feet but in many instances a block depth of 198, or its double 396, were used. The rationale behind this aspect of the design deserves further study.

Clearly Holme understood what Penn had misconstrued; the practical requirements of transportation, land values and commerces and their relation to actual survey. On the other hand, he firmly agreed with Penn's objectives to create a regional plan suitable for Quaker worship in which the Proprietor's interests would be secure, the wealthy holder of metropolis and country inseparably linked and the best economic theories of Petty and Penn himself put into practice. Between Penn's idealism and Holme's practical survey there was no conflict of objective but only a difference in execution.

With a nice combination of English land policy and continental vision Holme's plot showed the metropolis stretching from river to river a distance of twenty-two blocks or two miles.[45] Although the colonial city only built compactly some eight blocks westward, the Penn Proprietary guarded jealously against unregulated building upon the remaining land, all of which they retained. Before the conclusion of their century of administration they had the satisfaction of seeing their Philadelphia properties command a high price near the Delaware, and beyond eighth street, a fair one. Rents had in general risen throughout the city; a commerce of eight million dollars in 1261 ships per annum testified to the adequacy of the plan.[46]

As a consequence behind these commercial values a very real aesthetic grew up for the city, one which bound the dockside to the great central square and its four satellites and one which from the outset seems to have impressed visitors.

Although it is apparent that Penn's plan was a success as a social and economic device, its religious significance becomes more clear when we contrast the plan with that of New England settle-

[45] Thomas Holme, *Map of the Improved Part of the Province of Pennsylvania . . . begun in 1681* (engraved by E. Lamb. London, 1687).
[46] James Mease, *The Picture of Philadelphia . . . in Arts, Sciences, Manufactures, Commerce, and Revenue* (Philadelphia, 1811), 52–53.

ment. Two major differences are at once apparent. In the first place the settlement is widely scattered and settlers isolated from one another. In the second place settlement did not advance in steps but instead spanned the whole of three counties in less than five years and soon covered two more. Only a population predominantly free of dependence, either upon a fixed ministry or a place of worship, could make so rapid an advance. Friends free to worship with one another in their own houses found the scheme totally agreeable, while their contemporaries disputed in New England legislatures the precise location of Puritan meeting houses and adjacent home lots.

Second, the rapid and complete initial allocation of land over a wide area assured for many years the local control of Quakers or like minded Continental worshipers. As a consequence the demand for new and multiple towns so strong in New England was, until mid-eighteenth century, muted in Pennsylvania, and Philadelphia as the seat of the Yearly Meeting remained the uncontested municipal religious center of the colony.

Based upon the long rising vista to Fairmount, Philadelphia waited for the topographical artist of the nineteenth century to capture its quality in paint. As seen at the end of the eighteenth century great rows of uneven and varied brick buildings marked the uneven plot lines of the original purchasers. At the first crest of the rise the recent Lombard poplars marked the cite of Penn's too distant meeting house. Beyond, the horizon was broken not harshly by the subdued picturesque rock of Fairmount. The gentle landscape seemed confirmed by the regularity of brick and white sash varied with the novelties of Palladio but everywhere decorous. The wild indecencies of European courts seemed not only distant but beyond belief. The lusty joys of lesser Franklins never tempered the architectural façade; their manners excited no more curiosity than the masochistic rites of Indian natives.

All this and more William Penn foresaw. Here was the modest architecture of Wycombe and Rickmansworth set upon straight and rational streets and enjoying the prosperity of five counties. No London palaces or even great houses crowded the merchant or the landed Proprietor. No clear line separated city from country. Beyond the straight streets lay gentleman's estates and charming liberties. A little farther off the rich pastures and farms of Chester, Philadelphia, and Bucks. In short all that Penn loved in the England

and Ireland of his youth had been transplanted and had prospered in Pennsylvania.

The dominant force in the shaping of Philadelphia was the philosophy of William Penn. Because he was able initially to exert a strong selective policy, despite English concepts of toleration expressed in the Acts of 1689 and 1692, he attracted to the colony colonists who were genuinely allured by his plan of settlement and who found its material and perhaps aesthetic reward very great indeed. Since it drew a wide cross section of English faiths, Penn's agricultural, mercantile, and social system must have been basically sound for his time. But behind all of his planning and design lay the fact of Proprietary control exerted both directly in the purchase of new lands from the Indians and the sale of land to white purchasers; indirectly through the daily decisions of the court of Quarter Sessions which reviewed all new road petitions, requests for mill sites, and enforced highway maintenance. Herein of course lay the danger. The scheme, though a strong one, rested principally upon the Proprietary and not upon the legislature.

It is not surprising, therefore, that the American Revolution had a very great effect upon the efficacy, indeed survival of the Penn-Holme plan. Obviously the holdings of the land office became the property of the Commonwealth, and what had been an economic and social administration for the benefit of the Penn heirs became a political administration for the benefit of democratic voters and settlers. This alone would not have been fatal, but it became compounded with the political appointment of justices to the court of Quarter Sessions, the rapid sale of Philadelphia land for the benefit of short term office holders and the assumption by the city of private rights of way as municipal alleys.

The result was not difficult to predict. Road maintenance in rural areas declined as soon as the justices of the courts of Quarter Sessions became subservient to the voters, and until the introduction of turnpike roads the main trunk system declined in quality if not in mileage. The rapid and almost unplanned increase in lesser roads strengthened local communities, towns and townships at the expense of the metropolis.

The rapid auction by the legislature of land in the City's Northern Liberties, designed to bring immediate revenue to the Commonwealth, led to a substantial reduction in relative land values and with it the open invitation to the speculator to build long rows of not similar but identical housing in which shoddy construction often offered the most economical use of cheap land. Moreover ownership now became extended to many new large landlords without rural holdings or mercantile interests whose speculation demanded quick profits and wide profit margins.[47]

Extended slums, if not already created by these chaotic pressures, were given a final push by the assumption (again under pressure) of the municipal voter of many small alleyways, made necessary by deep lots, which hitherto had been sternly regarded as private right of ways. The assumption of these narrow passages into the city's plan delayed and made difficult their closing, encouraged multiple subdivisions for rent and sale and, in the absence of strict legislation as to use, permitted commercial and heavy traffic totally foreign to their dimensions.

It would be at this point quite easy to condemn the *laissez faire* city and point out that as an artifact of the mature philosophy of William Penn Philadelphia's end was near. But this view may oversimplify the problem, for in fact the city remained as an artifact of an altogether different society whose growth in population and wealth became, if not independent, largely separate from the countryside which surrounded it. Moreover, population growth was given impetus and direction by the introduction of public water and sewer works, the cost of which would have determined the Penn Proprietary's opposition to their installation. Significantly the chief works of the new Philadelphia of the early nineteenth century became the waterworks, and the Pennsylvania Hospital; each enterprise quite beyond the largess of any single man. To establish any absolute measure of the value of the postrevolutionary city compared to its colonial predecessor seems impossible if not ridiculous. Both cities served useful and different ends.

There remains, however, one great distinction between them. Colonial Philadelphia owed little to Swedish or Indian settlement. Their traces were easily accommodated or subdued. Post-Revolutionary Philadelphia could not so lightly dismiss the colonial city. Like the street pattern of London in 1666 it remained an integral part of the form and the outline of the nineteenth century city. The

---

[47] This sale of Liberty lands was administered by the city between August 1781 and June 1782. Over 1400 separate lots were offered. This monumental sale changed the pattern of Philadelphia real estate and is the subject of a separate study by the author. City of Philadelphia Patent City Lots. Mss. Book. 12.

city as artifact was altered to new uses by the American Revolution but as artifact it also retained continuing life of its own independent of the merits of its design, an aspect of its existence which Henri Focillon would call a "Vie des Formes."

Moreover the post-Revolutionary city surveyors and planners can be scored on one serious failure. They apparently regarded the city's plan which they inherited solely as functional tool of Penn's land office. They rejected any larger social implications of the Proprietary policy in their zeal to democratize and disperse the Penn holdings; they destroyed the ultimate planning power of the courts, created no substitute, and finally to please the local voter extended municipal custody to a vast network of hitherto private alleys, thereby introducing metropolitan traffic into some of the narrowest urban pockets of the nineteenth century. Despite the light, the water and the hospitals, the post-Revolutionary plan of Philadelphia exacted too high a social price for its improvements. In short it altered the cultural artifact it inherited without understanding the history and social uses of the city's plan—its cultural meaning.

In modern times this element of historical heritage cannot be ignored unless the planner be willing to destroy totally, as did Pennsylvania's first planners, the whole living pattern they wish to improve. Nor will it be sufficient for him to give an anecdotal account of the city's past, of the history of its various subdivisions, of its visual prospects and handsome monuments. Instead if he is to acknowledge the value of the city as artifact he must explore each aspect of its remaining structure, understand as an anthropologist its cultural role and the whole culture of which it is a part, and only then with a full and mature philosophy endeavor to alter and improve it.

Any effort to shorten this process, however humane and understandable in a bureaucratic sense, will only lead to the kind of solution which Pennsylvania's Revolutionary legislators advanced: a solution which met popular, selfish and uninformed approval and had the advantages of happy coincidences but left deep and terrible, chaotic conditions as its principal heritage.

Planning for a town, city, or region is a cultural process of the greatest consequence. Its background must be based upon cultural history which is neither art history nor sociology. Instead it combines something of each of these with an anthropological concept of culture. It seeks to establish a system which relates in an orderly pattern the observed pattern of all customs or repeated human actions not just those related to commerce, architecture, or street design.

If in fact this wide structure has been long acknowledged by the best planners they have been less willing to recognize that the social conditions which they can and have observed in their own lifetime have definite chronological boundaries as real as the geographical limits which they conscientiously apply. Past historical cultures are not illustrations of present cultural theories. They must be examined in their own light as full and valid working systems. The decision to emphasize or destroy one or another existing structure service, street or community must rest upon a full understanding of its history and purpose. The immediate past should not be given undue emphasis and importance.

Certainly increasing publication of urban planning analyses, both historical and of modern cities in Asia, Africa, and South America, cannot fail to increase the perspective given by comparative techniques. Only when historians of the city have become personally aware of the vast range of possible forms planning can take will they be able to evaluate the range of solutions from which any particular plan emerges. If Philadelphia, for example, be compared to New Haven, Connecticut, one sees at once that religious considerations, although a part of the planning process, never dominated it nor created any aspect of the plan which was as socially and economically inflexible as the relation of the nine large squares of New Haven to the distant harbor.

In comparison with a Catholic plan like that of Philip II for Spanish cities, only the use of the grid plan suggests similarity. Government and the established church played no dominant role in this early English city. Even the land office had no important site. Rule was by custom, not power and prestige, and had but small effect on the site plan.

If the advantages to the interpretation of Philadelphia given by its record of surviving buildings and documents is to be exploited elsewhere, some cautions should be observed. Among them none is more important than the recognition of the selective process of survival. Some elements of the distant past survive because they are of use in the more recent past; to understand another epoch each survival, whether it be a street, a park, building, or a local custom, must be weighed in terms of its over-all role and then the value of its evidence assessed. This is of particular importance in the use and preservation of historic buildings since a modern *post hoc* view of their importance may give them a role for which their design is quite unsuited. In any instance the great and probable impact of the taste of intervening periods must be assessed in order to understand the importance of what remains.

Moreover each part of the historic plan must be analyzed for the light it sheds on the whole of the culture. The same building may give important evidence on class structure, technological development, foreign contacts, ritual, weights and measures, family values, and many other categories of human experience. In order to be evaluated it should be studied from all these viewpoints and its evidence interpreted. The techniques of anthropological cross-cultural studies are available and wholly or partly useful to this end.

Underlying the whole foregoing discussion has been an important tacit assumption, namely the premise that any urban community which exists for a period of years develops an over-all culture which in part at least dominates the subcultures and individual differences of its residents. This assumption may not be universally acceptable and may lack validity for contemporary town planning. Certainly much planning has been based upon national or regional principles, upon economic improvement or social betterment or even upon speeded transportation alone. Whether a measure so taken will appear as sound a cultural artifact after three centuries as Thomas Holme's and William Penn's Philadelphia must await the judgment of time.

Meanwhile the historian can feel some sympathy for his contemporary who must like the physician operate upon the broad body urban with an awareness that "life is short, the art is long, the occasion instant, decision difficult and experiment perilous."

The Form of the Modern Metropolis

WALTER L. CREESE

Observe one slight difference between the manner in which Sir John Summerson spells "artefact" and the way Americans spell it, "artifact," and the warning is out. The barriers in a "common language" imply that we should also be on guard not to misinterpret his basic meanings. Let us beware particularly of mistaking his ease of delivery and clarity of thought for innocence.

What he has to tell us of the city as an artifact is masterfully concentrated in the passage about the mid-nineteenth century Chalcots estate near London. He first assays the routine meanness of the suburb. He describes the surveyor laying out the roads and marking the plots, then pocketing his fees and departing. Next comes the builder who puts up the houses, mortgages them, assigns the leases and moves on in his turn and as soon as possible. Our hearts are further hardened against aristocratic Eton College which sold its land for this "catch-penny" purpose just as the most callous speculator might. (Here, of course, the historian in the audience is intellectually hobbled since he already knows that Eton College was later to sell under similar conditions the land for Hampstead garden suburb and that turned out the greatest of them all.) The qualifying condition is that no one cared about the Chalcots suburb.

Then Sir John quietly calls attention to the carefully copied Greek frame about the main window of each house "from the fourth century B.C. Choragic monument of Thrasyllus," and we are touched. They didn't *have* to do it, he says. The decoration becomes pathetic and a little funny, in the English way, as the "genius of Ancient Athens" is "decanted among the solicitors, tin-bath manufacturers and dissenting ministers of London, north-west."

He mentions how the Neo-Gothic church there came to be built and concludes: "Now the psychological reaction of the English middle-classes to pointed arches is a subject altogether too large for the most summary treatment and here I must break off." The whole clumsy apparatus of a newly dominant class striving to promote the good and the beautiful through Victoria's long reign is conjectured by this single concluding sentence.

The writing of urban history as a specific art has hardly begun anywhere, Sir John suggests. But Britain does have one distinct advantage in the field, which his own fine scholarship appears indirectly to reflect. It is, of course, a tradition of urban criticism, much of it with a historic reference. It began with the Neo-Gothic Pugin and passed on to Ruskin, Morris, Lethaby, Parker and Unwin, Geddes, and up to the present with men like Sharp, Osborn, and Holford. The *Architectural Review* marches on ahead with its banner line of "Outrage." My personal explanation for the root source of this continuum would be that further back than Pugin's "Contrasts," the thoughtful Englishman had been brought up on the romanticism of the late eighteenth and early nineteenth centuries. He already saw reality as a series of pictures to which he had been trained to respond emotionally. The general approach can still make a visual success of a Roehampton.

When the burgeoning of the industrial revolution appeared suddenly before the eyes of this country-bred novelist, poet and essayist, he naturally began to conceive of the urban environment as if it were a potential landscape. Read Dickens or Disraeli, Wordsworth or Blake and the mood is plain. It is intriguing to notice how often this attitude turns up in the writing of the American, Lewis Mumford, and it seems not too much to say that the brilliant talent of the Dane S. E. Rasmussen, in observing cities (especially London) also derives in part from this effect. Back of this was the tacit wish to reintegrate communal life, the village symbol, which had been so violently disrupted by population growth, agricultural change, and technological advance. The symbol in this instance owed its vitality to the fact that it nourished an essentially classless dream of a return to medieval harmony. Thus appears the British spectacle of the educated and often upper class reformer accomplishing the most difficult political, social and economic maneuvers while discoursing on how they ought to be achieved with such a popular esthetic as was readily available in the Middle Ages (the supposedly superfluous "pointed arch" again). How can he occupy himself with esthetics when the grimmest realities are at stake? The long and short of it is that the British intellectual has never been constitutionally able to consider urban reform *except* in broad visual terms.

The catch phrase in Sir John's paper is "the organic city." The theory of an organic unity, modelled along Darwinian lines, must have been first applied to the slum by the former botanist and Huxley pupil turned regional planner, Patrick Geddes, as Sir John says. It also appears true that as modern cities have expanded and the ability to control them has diminished, we have had to search much harder for abstract formulations of their most elementary workings, such as "organicism." These factors had to be, and will continue to be, totted up.

Yet a major contribution from the British experience could still arise from the momentary exploration of the intimate rather than the more grand and abstract pattern. At this stage there is a certain opportunity to be had from the study of the actual broken bits of the modern city, no matter how grubby. Even Geddes had to rotate his *camera obscura* atop the Outlook Tower rather slowly in order to instruct his pupils. To outline too quickly and thoroughly the entire content of the city is to risk a further numbing of the perceptual faculties. Genuine conviction is only earned by repeated experience. As Glenway Westcott remarked about photographs of America during the Depression, because the act of looking itself was so important, ". . . I go on looking until the pity and the shame are impressed upon me, unforgettably." Or as Sir John put it more impersonally, "The main issue, all the time, is tangible substance, the stuff of the city, and that implies form." He insists on a reexamination of actuality in order to reach historic authenticity.

His latent condemnation of "the kind of urban history which concentrates on architecture at the expense of total building output," marks a special distinction in his plea for comprehending urbanism as a process. He seems not so anxious to prove that the humbler artifacts belong by right of continuance, a type of squatter's right, within the present urban complex, as to demonstrate that they are the result of an accretion begun in the nineteenth century by people who could not hope to know what they were about. His contrast between the Earl of Bedford's speculative Covent Garden, a magnificent conception of that seventeenth century artistic bureaucrat, Inigo Jones, and the equally speculative but more anonymous and improvised Camberwell and Chalcots estates amounts to just that. The moral is that although urban responsibility may be culturally postponed, as it often was in the nineteenth century, it cannot be permanently avoided by the society as a whole.

Sir John's admonitions may sound slightly remote to our ears. Bear in mind a little longer that the educated Englishman is a romantic by inheritance. Sometimes his otherwise useful sensitivity to local color can be painfully misdirected as after the Boer War when it was seriously argued that if the London slums had been earlier removed, the humor, courage and, most important for national security, the fighting ability of the Cockney soldier would have vanished with them. In World War II while these same slums were being flattened by buzz bombs his thumbs-up attitude was again commended as a national asset. Yet all we have learned so far merely reinforces what Sir John has contended is the evidence for a universal as well as a local need. Fundamentally required is a quicker sympathy for the city acquired under the guidance of expert discipline. After the better instincts of tradition have dissolved there is no other resort than to reason and historicism, but it is, or should be, reason made potent by feeling. This is the essence of the original historic position of romanticism, I believe, and its creative possibilities are as limitless as its nostalgia.

When the British urban historian picks up a fragment of the broken city and rotates it in his palm, we are not repelled by its crudity and desolation as much as fascinated by its subtle shadings: ". . . even the most squalid of human performances has a dignity of its own and furthermore is the stuff out of which current imagery is fashioned." Our foreign eyes become as busy as the Impressionist Monet's when he kept scores of canvases going in his London hotel trying to capture the elusive British light.

Our ability to relate scale, proportion, color, texture, direction, and tension among the component parts of a given urban situation, which must stretch far beyond the physical limitations of the dynamic Baroque, the most recent age to fulfill its urban purposes, could thus be more effectively cultivated. No major expressway, for example, would then be permitted to gut the ancient and honorable heart of a metropolis, simply because it would appear so incongruous in the setting. By the same token, the Roosevelt Memorial would be built without further acrimonious debate because it would seem so supremely logical as a modern urban symbol in a city long dedicated to public symbols.

The very process of modern specialization and abstraction, another manifestation of which has been the suburban sprawl of which he speaks, has been allowed to contradict itself in terms of efficiency, to deny that the city is any longer a physical entity, just as it is not a social, financial or an administrative one either. This is where our basic anxiety about the existence of the city arises, it seems to me.

The classical city, according to Aristotle, was a place where men dwelt closer together in order to pursue a noble purpose. The medieval city was, insofar as it was beautiful, a City of God. The baroque city in its visual perfection was a positive emblem of an absolute ruler and his hierarchical state. These cities were visually functional in that they represented some central aspiration of their own cultures, not realized in all aspects perhaps, but nevertheless recognizable. The visual functionalism of our own age is more one of transfer and dispersal of meaning into a thousand channels of power and motion, enhancement of worth, or frequency of creation and replacement. The speed and precision required for this act of distribution robs the visual arts of their older fecundity and power of resolution except when the final object is reached. In design the suburb is esteemed above the city, the house above the suburb, and the automobile above the house. And we know from history that the distributive function of the street was given a high priority long before the appearance of the automobile. The fatal scintillation in the environment has undermined confidence in the permanent and stable urban form, choking off the possibility of its visual reintegration, the true organicism for which it ought to be renowned. Sterility and ugliness have crept into the vacuum.

If we were to encourage him one step further, Sir John might urge us to rivet our attention upon some tiny portion of the city for practice in accord with present habit so that we could come again to believe in the possibility of a human community, much as the mystic seeks a deeper identification with the universe by contemplating a single blade of grass. It is difficult not to turn in some degree mystical about urban planning affairs if one has ever had to handle their day to day workings. Those who control the physical character of the contemporary American metropolis by the investment of initiative and capital resemble those who oppose or resist them in the name of public interest by their overwhelming commitment to limited areas of reference and early termination of debate. It is always a matter of getting on to the next crisis. The professional planner can help hardly at all because he is responsible for everything and nothing at once. While the architect has been able to take advantage of a new esthetic consciousness of spatial freedom to refine his interiors, for the planners the liberty of modern dimension has resulted in little more than volumetric license and anarchy. He has become a busy shaper of the shapeless. All three of these types of urban agent, because they do not clearly see the city, cannot quite believe in it either.

This would be less alarming if it were not for the fact that the art and architectural historian, like so many other contemporary scholars, is forever at it storing up knowledge and polishing techniques. As the image of the contemporary metropolis grows less discernible, that of the past becomes more appealing—manifests itself in "full living color!" A visit to Old Williamsburg, for instance, is now a more refreshing experience for most, than a visit to Old Boston, in spite of the richer store of actual historic events in the New England city. One can absorb the splendid details and the whole satisfying picture of communal life together in the Virginia capital and feel better for it. It may be artificial in some of its aspects, but it is at least comprehensible.

This is merely to call attention to the possibility which historic restoration offers in fulfilling a need, which modern city planning has not, of making the environment visually convincing. What labels both the restoration town and the modern community as contemporary, of course, is their preoccupation with the immediate relevance and impact of circumstance. The real power of tradition which has been so sadly neglected, however, lies in its toughness rather than its brittle, instant perfection, its ability to bridge, bend, modify, and alter without breaking. No nation has the resources to build its cities anew in each generation. That only happens in a world's fair exhibition, the poor man's utopia. Generation must be joined to generation in our everyday cities or a consistent urbanism can never result. The perspective of urban history is now required to activate rather than inhibit the progress of urban creativity. Unless we come to understand the history of the more recent as well as the distant past, we shall never hope to abandon our prejudices against the future. Our concern with problems of growth has persuaded us that the modern era casts its mold mainly in quantitative assumptions, whereas Sir John has reminded us, and accumulating evidence in all the Western European and North American cities since the turn of the industrial revolution would corroborate him, I think, that some of the most radical, exciting and persistent questions in regard to having taken that turn remain highly qualitative.

The Visible Character of the City

HENRY MILLON

Tthese remarks will be to some degree complementary to the views of Walter Creese, at least those about the function of an historian. But I am astonished that we have been at this conference for three and one-half days now and have been talking about a city that is a three-dimensional object which we all think we know something about, and we have yet to see any visual material of any sort. It seems to be an obvious thing to have done, to have shown pictures of something. Yet here, too, I am, from the visual field, not showing any slides.

My remarks will be advanced particularly as those of one who is interested in comprehending the sensible form assumed by the city in its development, or, for that matter in its subsidence. In other words, my attention will focus on the visible character of the city as it is determined by the shapes and sizes of the urban spaces, its circulation pattern, its structural system or even its intestinal tract. It is in this light that I would like to examine Sir John's exposition of the way the social, political, and economic factors interacted with matters of purely artistic interest to produce a precisely defined environment in Covent Garden, and in contrast to this, as Mr. Garvan has shown, the way religious, social, and economic factors were acting in the development of the plans for Philadelphia.

But before we begin with such a discussion, allow me to preface these remarks with a few words that will second those of Sir John and Mr. Garvan. A study such as that outlined by Sir John, and to a degree achieved by Mr. Garvan, is precisely what is needed. The studies emphasize the patterns of growth, rather than static achieved situations. From this point we must move eventually to the fully developed study of a much larger picture—the development of an entire city, the pattern of civic growth and contraction. Perhaps here we ought to emphasize that while we always study growth of cities, we never study contractions. Yet there are cities that are dead or very nearly dead. It would be interesting to know why they died and what it was that happened. Why is Richelieu today smaller than when it was laid out in 1635? What has happened when a section of a city that was established as a fine upstanding residential district, with all of the well-heeled swells living in it, turns out to be a slum one hundred years later? The dynamics of this would be an exciting thing to look at.

The question of the ultimate value of such a study is, I believe, of minor importance. It is nice that the historian is allowed by the world to illuminate things for it, but I think this is not really necessary. I think we need not conceive of history as being of topical interest, or of having topical value—as a utilitarian science that sees as its aim the betterment of the present condition of man in general. I see no reason why competent, sensitively conceived, and executed history should not be immensely rewarding as an exposition of some of the multifacets of man, rewarding to the writer and the reader as it deepens his consciousness of himself and his environment. In short, I see no need for the historian to apologize for his pursuit of knowledge or to prove the value of his work for the contemporary world of practice.

Rasmussen, in *London—The Unique City* which was cited by Sir John, says that: "To us, the city of London is not the end, but the means. And only the part of it that can help us understand the city of the present day more clearly is of any interest to us." Now it is to just such an attitude that I think we must, as historians, be opposed. All of the city is of value, and all of it worthy of documentation. But a study such as both of the writers have emphasized has to be built on the accumulation of data. The stuff of history is really made from these data. And this is most gravely needed. A great portion of the material is available in public archives. Most of the matter of the construction of cities was of public concern, and these archives need to be plumbed. They simply have not been examined in a way we now know they ought to be.

For example, even of Rome, the city that probably has had more written about it than any other city in the world, there is no more than a fragmentary account of the periods which have the fullest documentation.

Here I should like to cite the example of one period which has received some attention—the Rome of Sixtus the Fifth, from 1585 to 1590. Professors Giedion, Krautheimer, and Ackerman have each recently spent some time studying the development of the city during the sixteenth century, culminating in the vast changes wrought by Sixtus, and his architect, Domenico Fontana. But even then the admirable work is only fragmentary. Years must still be spent in the archives to fill out the skeleton we now have. Moreover, and I think this is even more important, we have yet to have a clear picture as to just what Fontana and Sixtus the Fifth intended with their streets and obelisks. Professor Argan has made some perceptive comments about the significance of Sistine planning, of streets internal to a city, lined with buildings, and the visual importance of perpendicular foci formed by the obelisks at the main pilgrimage centers. But we still do not have more than just a vague idea of what it was Sixtus and Fontana wanted to do by placing these obelisks. Why obelisks? Why not columns? And above all, where does the idea originate, the idea that an urban complex can be described and bounded by a series of crucially placed stone needles?

I offer this only as an illustration. There are many other factors such as the condition of the forum at the time that certainly come into consideration in the problem. But Rome is a major city, to some people *the* major city; next to St. Peter's the obelisks are the most conspicuous features of the city, and we simply don't know why they are there. We badly need a collection plan, an outline of what it is that needs to be known. We need to found some kind of a central group that could, in consultation with scholars, outline what the fields are that really need study next, what direction is indicated to bring together the information that is so badly needed.

In Sir John's paper are clearly outlined two entirely different degrees of architectural intervention in the formation of the city, or of the suburb, as it happens. I suggest that there are perhaps three gradations here which we must distinguish. The first one is the completely coherent designed environment in which one man or, at the most, two men define a very precise architectural environment for a particularly desired effect; in other words, a completely created situation in which very little is left undecided. Covent Garden is an example and so are the Piazza San Carlo in Turin, the Place des Vosges in Paris, and the Place Royale in Nancy; you know them all, they are the standard city planning examples.

A second type, which is quite different, is the development that gives rather little thought to coherent, over-all design. Development is achieved simply by selecting designs from a handbook. An obvious example is Sir John's second of Chalcots, in which the buildings were not new architectural designs, but were actually selected from books and built according to a system, producing a kind of environment which is familiar, and has at least a certain kind of architectural quality.

The third type is one which we should not ignore, although we seem to be ignoring it. Here absolutely nothing is done in the way of design. The buildings occur. I suppose the examples that most easily come to my mind are the medieval, small Italian towns. There, when a house was added you built a shelter, and you built it with the methods which had been around for hundreds of years, and you simply added the rooms that were needed, and that was it, and this agglomeration went together as it might. Thus a city is produced which has accidental characteristics sometimes attractive to the eye, sometimes not. An example might be Camberwell. Perhaps this was what Sir John was suggesting. Bagnaia in Lazio, or

Bra in Piemonte have the same characteristics, being just natural accretions, and not at all the result of design.

These types are on three entirely different levels. They create three different kinds of environment. Needless to say, each type may provide an environment which is vulgar or sophisticated, satisfying or unpleasant, stimulating or stultifying. The visual quality of the result depends in a good measure on a kind of imponderable sensibility that has to be there in order to create an environment of high visual quality. It may exist, it may not.

Certainly the first two groups of three-dimensional solutions that we talked about are to a degree independent of the plan of the city. The first group is clearly much more allied to the plan, but it is perfectly possible to imagine a plan having been set up for the development of an area, and then the quality of the environment or the architectural character having been changed to a marked degree with a different choice of architectural designers. It would be possible to imagine one architect or surveyor laying out a residential addition to a town with streets sixty feet wide at 200-foot intervals and yet using strikingly different formal solutions, such as row, semidetached, or single-family houses. It was in fact to forestall these unforeseen possibilities that façades alone were built in many places, such as the Place Carrière in Nancy, which suggest that the façade was built to define the exterior space in which the designer was interested.

This is to say that while a plan *may* determine the shapes, size, and character of an urban solution, it does not necessarily do so unless stringent regulations are laid down to enforce the desired end. In fact such regulations designed to fix at least the dimensions of external city spaces have been laid down throughout history. In Turin, for example, when a new addition to the town was laid out in the 1660's, the Madame Regent stated that all the buildings in the new development had to be at least three stories above the ground floor, but on the property line adjacent to the street. These regulations should not be confused at all with the most common building edicts such as those that regulated the layout of buildings to minimize fire hazards, for example, as they did in ancient Rome. Instead they were regulations designed specifically to force the landlords to build the buildings to a particular size—no lower, no higher—in order, as the Madame Regent states herself, that the result would be more pleasing to look at. The consideration was clearly aesthetic.

I have led you away from the main path, just for a moment, to illustrate a relationship between a plan and a resulting physical environment. Mr. Garvan did that even more clearly. This detour that I have made is to suggest that the history of city plans can also benefit by being analyzed according to the degree to which they are conceived with attendant limitations. Mr. Garvan has presented a clear summary of the religious, social, and economic factors behind the organization of Pennsylvania, particularly Philadelphia. The present disposition would perhaps be incomprehensible without this kind of analysis. Most interestingly he pointed out that a rigidly controlled system guaranteed land values and prohibited speculation by anyone else other than Penn and his heirs.

The most astonishing thing to me was the fact that Penn was apparently indifferent to the aesthetic character of the city or its "urbanity." He gave instructions for free-standing, single-family houses each on its plot of ground, providing, as Mr. Garvan stated, not a city, but a residential district. Holme made out a different plan, a city plan, as you have seen—a city plan, for instance, that is virtually identical with the city plan of Savannah—and Penn approved this new plan, even if there was little remaining from Penn's original plan. It seems that the basic form of the city did not interest him at all but rather the land distribution, the city houses, liberty lands, and farm lands. Most of what we would like to think of as the amenities of that 1682 plan seem to me due to Mr. Holme's ideas, and not to the religious, social, or any other ideas of Mr. Penn, even though, as Mr. Garvan says, Penn selected Holme because their ideas coincided on these points.

I find this interesting, because it suggests that in this particular case and in this particular city at least there is no necessary direct continuity at all between the so called background ideas that for two and one-half days we have said are essential to the study of the form of the city. In fact, it makes me wonder about the ultimate value of all of the bolstering we must do to study the final form in an instance such as this. I certainly agree with Sir John that it is primarily the visual material that we must analyze; in other words, the visual aspect of the city. Well, let us suppose, though, that we are as completely and throughly acquainted as we are able to be with social, political, economic, religious, and intellectual factors that have contributed to the making of the community—as for example, let us say the Place des Vosges in Paris, Beacon Hill in Boston, Trastevere in Rome. We can draw on rich background material to explain the physical phenomena, perhaps even some of the visual phenomena.

But as historians of, if you will allow me, "urbitecture" we are still left with our most difficult assignment, which is the assessment of the visual character of the environment and in what this particular visual character resides—in other words, what it is that forms the environment itself, and how the walls, the surfaces themselves, are modulated, articulated to give a specific character to the city, to define the space or the group of spaces of the city. Then beyond that lies the most difficult thing of all, the value judgment on the quality of this environment. This judgment will certainly include the factors previously mentioned, but also will include a final assessment of the relative quality on a scale of good to bad of the physical, visual environment that has been created. This is yet to be done for any city anywhere, and it may well be a task that should be left to an historian of "urbitecture," if ever one should come up. But even though we do not have one at this moment, if one did come along, he would certainly have to develop a new analytical technique. We simply have not developed any technique for this kind of problem, and I believe this new historian would have to develop a whole new critical vocabulary.

VI

Planners and Interpreters of the City

The Customary and the Characteristic: A Note on the Pursuit of City Planning History

CHRISTOPHER TUNNARD

In his recent inaugural lecture at the University of Leeds, the economic historian M. W. Beresford began by pointing out that although this subject had been taught in English universities for over fifty years, it was only since the end of World War II that economic history had entered its "frock coat" period and become eminently respectable. "We historians," he added, "are getting nearer that specialization and division of labor that Adam Smith noted in the pin factory. . . . We even have our subspecialists: agrarian historians, business historians and transport historians, to name only the subspecies who publish their journals." [1]

Professor Beresford then proceeded to deliver an illustrated

[1] M. W. Beresford, *Time and Place* (Leeds, 1961).

lecture on the history of a street in Leeds, the excellence of which qualified him to assume the mantle of "urban historian: subspecies topographical."

It is with a variety of urban history (since species rank cannot be claimed for it as yet) that the present remarks are concerned. I refer to the history of city planning, which is now beginning to receive attention as a specialization in a few universities in different parts of the world.

First, the parent species. (I am leaving aside for the moment the question as to whether city planning history more properly belongs with the history of art and architecture.) What is urban history? Its range is on the one hand wide and vague, and on the other specific and parochial. It cannot be said to have achieved the status of economic history, and the lack of systematized knowledge of the history of the city is probably one of the reasons for holding the present conference. Political and religious philosophers—Plato, Aristotle, St. Augustine, More—have variously used it for their own ends. Art historians have toyed with the city, but cannot accept it as an art form.[2] In spite of this, the historian Burckhardt remarks that the worship of the relics of art and the indefatigable combination of the relics of history form part of the religion of our time.[3] If so, the history of cities, in which man's esthetic and economic endeavors mesh so closely in corporeal form, is not yet a part of this religion, to judge by the status accorded to it by modern historians. The city has been a focus of civilization, although not in all countries simultaneously, since the middle of the fourth millennium B.C. Who but Burckhardt himself, Pirenne, Spengler, Rostovtzeff, Childe and a few others have ever given it the attention it deserves?[4] For example, Toynbee's *A Study of History* pays considered attention to the general environment, but fails, as Mumford points out, to recognize the critical importance of the

[2] Pierre Lavedan, the most distinguished of contemporary city planning historians, in advancing his concept of the *ensemble urbain*, gives first place to its esthetic content. See his *Histoire de l'Urbanisme: Renaissance et Temps Modernes* (Paris, 1941), 5, 6.

[3] J. Burckhardt, "On Fortune and Misfortune in History" in J. H. Nichols, ed. *Force and Freedom* (New York, 1943).

[4] Certain cities could scarcely escape deification: the history of France is the history of Paris after the sixteenth century; there is Venice and the Venetian Empire, and the cities of the Hanseatic League. As an example of overconcentration on the city, modern historiographers cite Gibbon's preoccupation with Cosmopolis itself as blinding him to the real reasons for the Fall. (See D. R. Dudley, *The Civilization of Rome,* New York, 1960.)

city in the development both of institutions and of personal life. Historians of science and of ideas (two rapidly evolving subspecies of the genus Historian) have been on the other hand closely preoccupied with urban institutions, particularly in their examinations of the ancient world.

This leaves us with historical studies of individual cities. These are legion, and I need only mention Molmenti on Venice, Poëte on Paris, A. J. H. Jones on the Greek city, and Carcopino on Rome to underline the excellence which has been achieved. Perennially useful, although seldom sufficient for the purpose under discussion, are the thousands of local histories, often compiled by amateurs or antiquarians in the form of memorials for centenaries and other occasions. The bibliographies of the Urban History Group, so ably begun at Rochester under Blake McKelvey's direction, are evidence of the growing numbers of works devoted to the urban scene in this country alone. Many of these, of course, are devoted to the various functions of the city, in which it forms the locus rather than the generator; thus we have studies of the garment industry in Manhattan, histories of port activities, or of political parties and power groups.[5] Among the better-known historians, Bridenbaugh, Schlesinger, and Wertenbaker have paid special attention to the American city.

Among these thousands of works, a proportion may be classified as topographical history, which sometimes comes close to being the history of city planning. As Nikolaus Pevsner has pointed out, topographical history is not often well done.[6] At one extreme are the inventories of the Royal Commission on Historical Monuments and at the other Henry James' *Portraits of Places.* Really good topography demands a rare mixture of talents and interests, according to Pevsner; good writing is one essential, and an eye for the characteristic is another. It is rare to find a work as useful and at the same time as well presented as H. J. Dyos' *Victorian Suburb,* which John Summerson has commended elsewhere. An American counterpart, although somewhat less comprehensive, is Walter Muir Whitehill's *Boston: A Topographical History;* which, if read with Walter Firey's *Land Use in Central Boston,* gives the city planning historian much that he needs to know.

[5] The contributions of sociologists should not be overlooked. A recent addition here is G. Sjöberg, *The Pre-Industrial City* (Glencoe, Ill., 1960).

[6] N. Pevsner, "The Topography of England," in *The Listener* (January 11, 1962), 81.

Yet it is to topographical history, to the accounts of travelers in the less well recorded places and periods, and above all, to archaeological evidence that the historian of city planning must turn. For theory and interpretation he will be indebted to archaeologists and classical scholars; to writers like Wycherley, Castagnoli, and McKendrick, who have tried to unravel some of the mysteries of the orthogonal plan, its origins, persistence, and transfer. Until, that is, he is retained to make his own investigations, and delve into old Florentine tax records, British registers, or the *topographie* collection of the Bibliothèque Nationale in Paris; or to take part in archaeological expeditions, as city planners are now beginning to do in Latin America.

The historian of city planning is concerned above all with the physical, yet behind each physical form lies an act of will . . . of a society, a group, or an individual. City planning embraces more than the artifact of the city (if indeed the whole urban fabric can thus be described). It is to be distinguished from an art form by practical considerations, by custom, by overriding political and social content, and by its ties with economic geography. It is less capricious than art, and at the same time subject to external forces which shape the city in often quite arbitrary ways. "Napoleon's armies were great makers of conquests," wrote Wilkie Collins in 1861, "but the modern guerilla regiments of the hod, the trowel and the brick kiln are the greatest conquerors of all; for they hold longest the soil that they have once possessed . . . with the conqueror's device inscribed on it—'This ground to be let on building leases!' " [7] Perhaps the city plan can be described as a mosaic, but far too often without the grand design that the builders of the Persian mosques were able to create out of a multitude of tiny pieces.

To avoid the merely descriptive, to ascribe motivation, cause and effect, are the tasks that lie before this specialized branch of history. Otherwise topography would suffice. But if we are passionately curious—as I assume we are—as to why certain societies used the plans they did, what is the explanation of their persistence or transfer to other societies, what is the relationship between the plans of colonizers and those of the parent country (important to those new nations which are now making their own plans) or what relations can be discovered between the growth of urban

[7] Wilkie Collins, *Hide and Seek* (London, 1861).

centers and regional or national settlement patterns, then a path will have to be chosen which leads to the historian's objective more directly than the meandering routes that have been followed in the past.

An illustration here may suffice to point up the basic knowledge that we need. When the city of Thurii was founded by Pericles, the Delphic oracle was consulted and responded with the riddle: "You must found your city where you shall drink water by measure and eat barley cakes without measure." On rich alluvial land on the Gulf of Tarentum the colonists found a spring from which water issued through a bronze pipe, which the natives called *medimnos*. *Medimnos* was a dry measure in Athens, and thus the colonists thought they had found an answer to the riddle. This mystical site selection was followed by a laying out of the city along the rational lines of a Hippodamian grid (the famous planner from Miletus was supposed to have been a member of the expedition). But in addition to this information we know that Thurii was as carefully preplanned as modern Periclean science could make it. The site was a strategic one along the trade route to Sicily and the Athenians had probably decided well in advance where the general location should be. Thurii was founded in a spot where the passage of overcrowded boats in bad weather through the Straits of Messina could be avoided by debarking the men, sending them across land and the ships around to meet them. This strategic importance, coupled with the fact that the inhabitants could grow more than they were able to eat, enabled Thurii to flourish until it was finally reduced in status by the Roman subjugation of southern Italy.[8]

Myth or ideology—environment—technology—power. All contributed to the plan and the settlement pattern. All are first on the list of controlling factors that must be examined in the city planning of any society, including the contemporary.

The second category in this hypothetical "construct" concerns the morphology of the plan, or the study of organic form. "Growth" is the key factor here, of course, from the earliest nucleus to the extent at the period under review. Were earlier street patterns extended? Did new concepts determine radical differences in the plan of enlargement? Questions of this nature must be asked, and also "use" factors should be looked into, for they may have

[8] K. Freeman, *Greek City-States* (New York, 1950), 26–43.

some bearing on the disposition of the planning elements. In our example of Thurii, for instance, there is some evidence that the city was divided into blocks for different ethnic groups, including one for the Sybarites, who were there when the colonists came. This may be the first example of a city with ethnic zoning, as distinct from former natural ethnic groupings in cities. The possession of such a characteristic gives Thurii far greater importance in city planning history than many other Pan-Hellenic foundations of the period.

We next come to the third dimension, or the "build" of cities, as the geographer R. E. Dickinson has aptly termed this aspect of the plan. First, there will usually be a hierarchy of streets, with differentiation between important and less important arteries of interior communication. This is evident long before the *cardo* and the *decumanus* begin to dominate all Roman planning (with the curious exception of Rome itself) and is the key to the identification of many planning types in all periods thereafter. Societies have clearly expressed their intentions in the hierarchy of street patterns imposed on the land; but no less important is the block, or building pattern, which they enclose. Excluding the agglutinative pattern of most earlier city development, this block pattern is strikingly revealed to us in the excavations at Olynthus. For some periods, notably the later islamic and the medieval, an understanding of the building pattern is a prerequisite to unravelling the plan form, but it occupies an important place in every age. One of the chief characteristics of the 1811 plan for Manhattan Island is the close relationship between the block size and the town house and lot dimension established previously by speculative builders.

In our examination of the build of cities, it is legitimate to speculate on certain esthetic aspects. Were the profusion of fountains and commemorative tablets in Greco-Roman cities mere incidents in their "build" or did they dominate the visual impression? Were the one-thousand foot blocks of Alexandria as monotonous as E. M. Forster thinks they must have been? [9] Or did the placing of the many public buildings and the glistening whiteness of the ensemble produce an opposite effect on visitors to the greatest city of the then known world? But here we are trespassing on the history of urban design, for which I shall reserve a few concluding remarks.

[9] E. M. Forster, *Alexandria: A History and a Guide* (New York, 1961).

An important element in the history of city planning, and certainly the most neglected, is the influence of urban institutions. We must thank the historian of ideas for underlining their attractive power. Beginning with religious institutions in ancient civilizations (the mountain temples of Sumer) the physical embodiment and placing of ritual, governmental, cultural, commercial, and in modern times industrial, institutions have had as yet incalculable effects on the planning of cities. "As yet incalculable" because so little work has been directed toward the problem. Brinckmann was aware of institutional influence, Poëte dwells on it in his analysis of the Paris plans, and Mumford rightly stresses it throughout *The City in History*. Granted that the form of any city can be considered as the product of all of its institutions, and, especially since Athens, of its political institutions, their physical disposition has received scant attention, except in the case of certain dominating fabrics like the medieval cathedral in the urban bishopric. Certain plans, such as those of the islamic cities of North Africa and Spain, cannot be understood except in the connotations of institutional placement, and changes in the city plan are frequently the result of new institutions arising either within or without the older pattern. Investigations of this aspect of urban planning should be extended to establish a corpus of information of the role of institutions in regional settlement patterns as well; attention could be given especially to Mayan ceremonial centers, medieval rural monasteries and modern national road systems.

To sum up, the study directives start with the settlement pattern and general site considerations, viewed from the standpoint of value systems of the society (philosophy, ideology, myth, legend), environmental factors, the state of technology, and political power. These are followed by morphology (the study of organic form of the city or city group), with special reference to the ground plan and "use" zoning. Next comes the "build" of cities . . . the hierarchy of streets, the block and building pattern, and their esthetic considerations. Finally, the role of institutions must be given due thought. The whole is to be brought into focus by emphasis on origins, persistence and transfer, and seen with an eye for the customary and the characteristic. It is, I hope, clear that other considerations should not be excluded, and that nothing can take the place of insight in any type of historical investigation. But a certain amount of systematization would appear to be of help in a not very systematic field.

Moral judgments should at all costs be avoided. In the recent past, moral prejudice has resulted in extraordinary distortions of historical fact.[10]

Earlier the question was raised on the milieu in which city planning history might be pursued. It is probably evident that I consider this type of history as somewhat separated from the history of civic or urban design. Twentieth-century city planning history has been written mostly from the esthetic or architectural point of view. Sitte, Hegemann, Gromort, Bunin, Kimball, Rasmussen, Feiss, and Zucker are among those who have made contributions to the history of urban design. It is to be hoped that this type of study will flourish in the new climate provided by expanding history of art and architecture departments of world universities and institutes since the last war. My point is that the elements of city planning history described above should receive more attention, and that is why I would prefer to consider it as a special discipline for the purpose of academic study.

Although the concepts of city planning and urban design are interrelated and in my opinion should never be separated in practice, in the historical context it is essential to set up a differing "construct" for urban design. For one thing, urban design more frequently deals with the parts rather than the whole, and matters of quality and criticism enter the picture more strongly. We are concerned here less with the direct effects "of man on his environment and his environment on man," to use the phrase of the historian E. H. Carr, than with relative questions of symbolism, real and apparent size, texture, light, color, and other esthetic phenomena, which are appreciated through the senses and do not always have a direct appeal to the mind. Qualitative measures of proportion, perspective, and order of pattern, form, and space must be considered, as well as kinetics (movement in space of people, things, the observer) and the physical sequence of the objects under review.[11] We are also preoccupied with a range of specialized artists and

[10] See Ch. 2, "The Hydra," in C. Tunnard, *The City of Man* (London and New York, 1953).
[11] For a simplified analytical method, see C. Tunnard, "The City and Its Interpreters" in *Journal of the American Institute of Planners*, XXVII: 4 (November, 1961).

designers, whereas in the broad scale history of city planning we must include whole societies of nondesigners, who nevertheless have left important imprints on the land.

Not that we should consider the history of urban design as a lesser variety of the genus *Historiographia*. Improvement in the art of urban design is of paramount importance in today's environment, with its low visual standards and constant violations of esthetic principle. The surest method we can find for public education in this art is through comparative analysis of important examples of the past. If we are to ensure that in our generation man's imprints will change from the careless to the premeditated, then the history of urban design is one of the most important tools at our disposal. Recognition of the fact that it has a related study in the history of city planning can only increase the influence of both.

Urbanization and Social Change;
on Broadening the Scope
and Relevance of Urban History

ERIC E. LAMPARD

There is a prevalent dissatisfaction with the writing of urban history: some confusion as to its scope, some doubt about its relevance. The present conference, therefore, is addressed to a crucial point. At a time when urbanization is proceeding rapidly throughout the world, "knowledge of man's past experience with urban life . . . is severely limited." This is notably true for the industrial period since the eighteenth century. To be sure, there is a large literature of histories of individual cities and of case studies of particular aspects of urban life "but owing to the fragmentary nature of this work such studies have provided little cumulative knowledge of urbanization." [1] Dissatisfaction with the existing

[1] Harvard Summer School Conference on "The City and History," Statement of Purpose, July 24–28, 1961.

literature is not so much with things done as with things left un-done. Appropriate boundaries for urban history today are perhaps more difficult to define than those of the city itself. The present paper discusses the need to broaden the scope of writings in urban history and then outlines an approach to the study of recent urbani-zation in the context of social change.

(For the most part urban history remains a branch of local history.[2] It is actively pursued for its own sake and assumes a wider relevance only when a city is itself important by virtue of its size or of the outstanding events and personalities associated with it.) National capitals are obvious examples. Alternatively, local case histories sometimes serve as a corrective to sweeping interpretations of "mainstream" history or to generalizations from sources that have no particular local identification. A large number of deviant cases, however, does not of itself provide any intellectually sound framework against which to construct new interpretations. The distinguished social historian Asa Briggs suggests that historians are in fact "more confused in purpose than most other specialists who have turned to urban studies." Reserving judgment about whether the historian is more confused than, say, the urban so-ciologist or the city planner, it is true nevertheless that the bi-ographer of a city often does not know "whether he is fitting local history into a stock national framework or whether he is helping to construct a new scaffolding." [3]

Even when the more adventurous scholar attempts a com-parative history of two or three places having some experience in common, his frame of reference is usually commercial competi-tion, reaction to outside events, or political reform and only rarely comprises the social movements that create cities or give a generic character to the urban life of a period. The principal con-cern with city and society in modern times has come from outside the self-imposed confines of urban history. It originates in a deriv-ative kind of social history that is largely an offshoot of writing in

[2] Recent surveys of literature in urban history are: e.g. W. H. Chaloner, "Writings on British Urban History, 1934–1957, Covering the Period 1700 to the Present," *Vierteljahrschrift für Sozial- und Wirtschaftsgeschichte*, XLV (März, 1958), 76–87; Erich Keyser, "Neue Veröffentlichungen über deutsche Städtege-schichte, V," *Blätter für deutsche Landesgeschichte*, 95. Jahrgang 1959, 290–329, and previous numbers; Blake McKelvey, "American Urban History Today," *American Historical Review*, LV (July 1952), 919–929.

[3] Asa Briggs, "The Study of Cities," *Confluence*, VII (Summer 1958), 107–114.

economic or intellectual history; its attention has been focused on the *problems* rather than the *processes* of social change.

The emphasis of this social historian was very much upon the history of social policy from the standpoint of reform: on organized efforts to revive and rehabilitate the physical and human debris battered by industrial urbanization and economic change. The change created problems which required solutions. Recognition of this need gave rise to reformist ideas and movements through which the new urban-industrial society accommodated the transition from a rural-agrarian society. Amelioration, when and if it came, was usually attributed to the more active intervention of public authorities stimulated by purposeful interest groups. For the social-economic historian the key to the study of change was the conflict of interests; for the social-intellectual historian, it was the conflict of ideas. But neither focused directly on social organization or the structure of social institutions and, as a consequence, they gave only scant attention to relationships of individuals to their families, communities, and larger groupings except the state. The relation between the burgeoning city populations and a larger society was conceived in terms of the impact of the urban-industrial upon a relatively stable rural-agrarian order, leading to a dissolution of the latter after a prolonged and inequitable conflict between opposing ways of life.[4]

Studies of urban impact first gave the modern city a place in historical writings commensurate with its importance in society. Their authors succeeded, where more parochial-minded city historians had failed, in making the growth of nineteenth- and twentieth-century cities a central focus in the history of social thought and policy. Cities were thereafter treated both as distinctive molds of thought and behavior and as the loci of special urban problems. Urban impact historians investigated a narrow range of effects on the assumption that their causes were well understood.

The first social historians, therefore, dealt almost exclusively with the city problem. In Germany, Great Britain, and the United States, materials collected in public inquiries and community surveys by early social scientists (mostly philanthropic and practical investigators) became the primary source. Evidence gathered ini-

[4] Eric E. Lampard, "American Historians and the Study of Urbanization," *American Historical Review*, LXVII (October 1961), 49–61.

tially for political campaigning or legislative prescription was thus adapted, together with local newspapers, pamphlets, social manifestos, and descriptive statistics, to furnish the substantive history of urban-industrial life: city problems were virtually the stuff of social history as they were of social science. With such materials, historians were able to throw fresh light on political movements and changes in social thought. Insofar as they dealt with real people in actual places, their work had both charm and credibility. They avoided the unattractive and, in their opinion, unnecessary resort to sociological categories which served only to complicate the obvious. Eschewing the jargon, historians nevertheless adopted many of the same lines of inquiry, asked broadly similar questions of the same types of data, and came up with much the same results as their counterparts in sociology.[5] The sociologists meanwhile came to regard the study of social history as a useful antiquarian pursuit which might occasionally provide background to the purposeful investigations of more methodical scientists. Not surprisingly, many of the early sociologists and social historians were themselves reformers and sometimes avowed partisans of a political cause: *Kathedersozialisten*, Fabians, and Progressives. People who had lived through such transformations and studied their outcome were understandably involved. Of itself this was no disbarment but it riveted attention on problems to the neglect of larger processes. Since most of the critics of this writing were *"Kathederliberalen,"* the first social history was very much present politics.

Bias in the data was compounded by the weighting of reformist thought. The fixation with problems—public health, housing, nutrition, poverty, vice, and their corrupt consort, public apathy—led social thinkers to identify the pathological with the generic character of urban life. Judgment on the new society was often the expression of reformist animus in terms of rustic imagery or a lost corporate world. Disgust with urban conditions joined with an ingrained romanticism or a hope for reconstruction to

[5] Elizabeth Pfeil, *Grossstadtforschung* (Bremen, 1950) is a useful summary of the early German literature on the sociology and social history of cities. On international aspects of social theorizing and reform thinking, see Don Martindale, "Prefatory Remarks: The Theory of the City," in Max Weber, *The City* (tr., Glencoe, Ill., 1958), 9–62, also Arthur Mann, "British Social Thought and American Reformers of the Progressive Era," *Mississippi Valley Historical Review*, XLII (March, 1956), 672–692. See also, M. D. Hirsch, "Reflections on Urban History and Urban Reform, 1865–1915," *Essays in American Historiography*, Donald Sheehan and H. C. Syrett, eds. (New York, 1960), 109–137.

nourish the conviction that cities were costly deviants from some natural, more verdant, order of community life. By implication rather than inquiry, the country remained a place for natural, personal, and hence "normal" relationships. As if its municipal deficiencies were not enough, the city milieu was said to isolate the individual and decompose all the corporative affiliations of work and family that had hitherto sustained him. Hence, if urban environment were the culprit, housing standards should be imposed and neighborhoods countrified. Insofar as density was the real villain, population should be progressively dispersed to garden cities where optimal conditions would obtain.[6] More radical reformers found industrial capitalism at the root of the "social question." Passage to the city had involved not only a loss of innocence but of humanity itself. Cities were but giant factories and their streets assembly lines for mass-producing labor. That cities generated more varied opportunities for a growing population which might compensate for its congestion and strain or that their meanest streets were also avenues to social and cultural improvement was for a long time overlooked; the redeeming features were discounted, virtues disallowed. It was as if to consider the apologists' claims would disarm the critic. But that critics had also appeared in the countryside and proclaimed against similar rural woes seems to have been ignored in most writings on the city.[7]

So often the familiarity which the contemporary historian feels for his subject breeds not contempt but oblivion. In the inter-World War years the urban-industrial society became so much a part of the established order that scholars took it for granted. The urban impact had been absorbed. If isolated pockets of rural intransigence might be found fighting an ideological rearguard action against the twentieth century, conflict of that sort was no longer a very convincing framework for the analysis of social change. Society went on changing but the city ceased to provide a central focus outside of urban sociology. Social history degenerated into the study of everyday things, a popular genre of lighter nonfiction.

[6] William Ashworth, *The Genesis of Modern British Town Planning* (London, 1954), 118–146, 167–190; more generally Lewis Mumford, *The City in History* (New York, 1961), 482–524, and Pierre Lavedan, *Histoire de l'Urbanisme* (3 vols., Paris, 1926, 1941, 1952), especially vol. 3.

[7] E. E. Lampard, *loc.cit.*, 57–59; E. deS. Brunner, *Growth of a Science: A Half-Century of Rural Sociological Research in the United States* (New York, 1957).

Even as professional urban history (local history) was finally coming into its own, the city was dropped from accounts of contemporary events and reappeared only in the aftermath of World War II as a vantage point for viewing the rise of suburbia and its impact on the central city's core.

By the 1950's the memories of older citizens as well as the extended chronicle of reform achievement bore witness to an amelioration of the grosser features of city life. Amenities and services had become diffused among the more accessible rural communities and the urban way of life was no longer encompassed by city or even metropolitan bounds. To be sure, new problems had emerged with the automobile, affluence, and the unplanned flight to suburbia, but these were mostly of an administrative or technical nature —highways, public transportation, pollution, schools, recreation, and urban renewal. But without relaxing the community's dependence on the central city's core, the withdrawal of comfortable residents and profitable business had accelerated neighborhood decay and drastically reduced the local tax base relative to the mounting urgency of *metropolitan problems*.[8] While the city's work force often increased, the number of its inhabitants fell off; their composition reflected a rising share of the aged, the minorities, the impoverished. Otherwise, urban affairs had become questions of service and efficiency: the unit cost of public facilities, priorities in social overhead and, the only unavoidable political issue, who was to pay? Of old-style problems only the endless task of housing the city's poor (complicated as much in some areas by racial tensions as by low incomes) still called for the creative passion of the reformer to supplement the competencies of the planner.

Although measurable socioeconomic differences between town and country have been reduced, the older compartmentalization of society has been reinforced and sharpened by psychological interest. Improved facilities and manifold opportunities notwithstanding, the urban way of life is still characterized by social disorganization and personal breakdown. Many of the alleged symptoms—from mental illness to delinquency—are shared with residents of suburbia, however, and are no longer considered peculiar to the newcomer or the *nouveau arrivé*. Originally, deviant

[8] A review of developing metropolitan problems in the United States is given in Lloyd Rodwin, ed., *The Future Metropolis* (New York, 1961). Up-to-date studies of the planner's art are: Kevin Lynch, *The Image of the City* (Cambridge, Mass., 1960) and Gordon Cullen, *Townscape* (London, 1962).

behavior was ascribed to the competitive striving for place and preferment in the capitalist vortex, then simply attributed to the generic impersonality of the city which precluded genuine personal relations. Most recently, it has been linked *via* Freudian metaphors to the intrinsic instability of secularized urban and suburban family life.[9] For many, the receding countryside still remains, inferentially at least, a distinctive folkish place, the natural mold of closer, more satisfying contacts.

No known form of organized community available to today's citizens appears in itself to secrete the long sought elixir that combines material well being with psychic balm. There is evidently much room for improvement in the city-region, if only a limited interest on the part of its citizens. There is even greater need for renovating the concepts and tools of those practicing community therapy. So many of the early prescriptions of political scientists—from "home rule" and city managers to the American Progressive's trinity: initiative, referendum, and recall—have proven weak or vain things. Most of the established sociological maxims concerning reformed environments and redeemed people have become otiose, if not discredited. Once received, notions of town planners have not only been refuted (on paper) by later planners but have been rejected or, worse, ignored by the very people they were intended to save.

Yet without the reformer's long struggle to civilize human life in the industrial society, we would know even less about modern urban development than we do now. Reform has always been a major stock in trade of local and social historians. The business of urban history is not now to belittle what it once commemorated and confirmed. Merely to reverse the bias and shift the weights the other way would not broaden the historical study of the city in society.

The task confronting urban historians, therefore, goes beyond revisionism. Reform ideas and achievements constitute only a part, possibly a minor part, of the amelioration. They scarcely touch the nature of underlying movements in society that have trans-

[9] For example, Georg Simmel, "Die Grossstadt und das Geistesleben," *Die Grossstadt*, Th. Petermann, ed. (*Jahrbuch der Gehe-Stiftung*, IX, Dresden, 1903), 187–208; Louis Wirth, "Urbanism as a Way of Life," *American Journal of Sociology*, XLIV (July 1938), 1–24; M. A. McCloskey, "Urbanization," *Dilemmas of Youth in America Today*, R. M. MacIver, ed. (New York, 1961).

formed both town and country. The analytical framework of urban-rural conflict is but one political timber in a potentially much large scaffolding. While acknowledging the contribution of impact studies, it is well to remember their shortcomings as social history: compartmentalization of society on the basis of question-begging criteria, the recourse to political metaphors in default of sociological categories, the neglect of the process of urbanization.[10]

If professional urban historians, local historians for the most part, are to be exempted from many of these strictures it is testimony to their industry rather than their imagination. A myopic view of the general is not corrected by holding a mirror glass to the particular. Much of what is reflected lacks precision or pertinence. Though city histories and local cases supply a more rounded picture of urban life in particular contexts, they do not furnish the needed framework for understanding social change. Not enough is known of urbanization and urbanism in general to enable the microscopic case worker to determine what is unique or otherwise in his cherished specimen: he cannot tell us why one Athens, one Florence, one Vienna, or New York. Variance in the data cannot be defined, let alone appraised, until it is examined in relation to a framework of analysis. Microscopic work in local history, though monumental in detail, rarely furnishes its facts in forms that are amenable to macroscopic treatment. Urban history, therefore, lacks not only general frameworks but consistent and comparable data relevant to them.

Such are the general grounds for dissatisfaction with the scope and relevance of much writing in urban history. If many practical and professional studies of cities remain, as Asa Briggs contends, "imperfectly grounded in more general urban studies" and if, as this paper maintains, most administrators, architects, welfare workers, and planners have not fully grasped the nature of changes they attempt to order, reasons are not hard to find.[11] Social historians

[10] E. E. Lampard, *loc.cit.*, 54–57; A. J. Reiss, Jr., "An Analysis of Urban Phenomena," *The Metropolis in Modern Life*, R. M. Fisher, ed. (Garden City, New York, 1955), 41–49. See also the later views of Louis Wirth, *Community Life and Social Policy* (Chicago, 1956), 173–174.

[11] Asa Briggs, *loc.cit.*, 108–111. Briggs emphasizes the importance of visual and subjective elements in urban studies to supplement the social science approach. He recommends the anthologies of Bayrd Still on New York and Bessie L. Pierce on Chicago. See also, Anselm Strauss, *Images of the American City* (Glencoe, Ill., 1961).

and others concerned with the long run have not begun to examine the social processes that create cities. There are no studies of modern urbanization and urbanism nor, until recently, very pertinent studies of particular aspects and cases.[12] Bureaucrats and "problem solving" social scientists have been working, for the most part, with concepts and tools inherited from the last great period of creative thinking about cities—the years before World War I.

Historians have failed to order the recent urban past in either a comprehensive or relevant way and have, in fact, often confused matters by a ritual insistence that they only study "particulars." Although there are limits to which any one discipline could or should treat urban developments in their entirety, it is time surely to frame a broader approach to urban history, one that elucidates concrete local situations in the *same* terms that are used to treat more generalized transformations in society. Individual cities, for example, can be treated as particular *accommodations* to a many-sided societal process: urbanization. Interest lies in so reformulating the generalities of urbanization that they can serve as principles for organizing and evaluating the range of materials found in the diverse, but rarely unique, experiences of particular towns. The scope of historical urban studies should thus be broadened and more systematic efforts made to relate the configurations of individual communities to on-going changes that have been reshaping society.

At stake in a broader view of urban history is the possibility of making the societal process of urbanization central to the study of social change. Efforts should be made to conceptualize urbanization in ways that actually *represent* social change. For this purpose urbanization may be regarded as a process of population concentration that results in an increase in the number and size of cities (points of concentration) and social change as an incremental or arhythmic alteration in the routines and sequences of everyday life in human communities. The method will be to explore possible interrelationships between the phenomenon of population concen-

[12] The only general work on urbanization in English is the comparative study by Adna F. Weber, *The Growth of Cities in the Nineteenth Century* (New York, 1899). Paul Meuriot, *Des agglomérations urbaines dans l'Europe contemporaine* (Paris, 1897). An essay in the classic tradition of French demography "Urban Agglomerations and the Social Evolution of Countries" was contributed by Louis Chevalier to R. M. Fisher, ed., *Metropolis in Modern Life*.

tration and certain apparent trends in social organization, structure, and behavior.[13]

(Historians are accustomed to speak of continuity and change in human affairs and, in ordinary discourse, the implication is often given that change and alteration are wholly circumstantial, if not chance, events.) But continuity may be viewed as the periodic or regular recurrence of routines and sequences in the affairs of households and communities, and change as their cumulative or net outcome. Throughout history much of everyday life has been patterned according to repeated or periodic sequences: familiar daily, weekly, monthly, annual, and other recurrent cycles, such as the passing of the seasons and, in case of life histories, the passage of the years. Recurring cycles are, nevertheless, subject to alteration and eventually to trend—otherwise, barring chance, there would be only continuity and never change.

Consider some of the implications of this view for a description of social change. Work and rest in European culture, for example, having usually been instituted in a diurnal routine with some regular interruption on the Sabbath and the further likelihood of seasonal variation.(Labor and leisure have alternated in some conventional division of hours of day and night until something occurs to increase or decrease the span of one in relation to the other.) Many such occasions come to mind: the introduction of artificial illumination, restrictive legislation, a shift in residence or job. But the alternating routines may also be affected by the unfolding of a given person's life cycle as when he becomes too old to maintain the schedule or type of work of his prime. The regular experience of major life sequences follows the same broad recapitulation through the patterns of childhood and maturity to those of old age and beyond *via* sequential rites of passage. Alterations in this basic progression are effected through the rephasing of sequences either by social or natural modification.)Categories such as the length of apprenticeship or age of retirement may be redefined. The achievement of new legal or social "class" status by marriage

[13] In what follows the author wishes to acknowledge his indebtedness to the work of Otis Dudley Duncan, Leo F. Schnore, and Norman G. Ryder: especially O. D. Duncan, "From Social System to Ecosystem," *Sociological Inquiry*, XXXI (1961), 140–149; Leo F. Schnore, "Social Mobility in Demographic Perspective," *American Sociological Review*, XXVI (June, 1961), 407–423, and other unpublished papers by Duncan, and Ryder, especially the latter's analysis of "age cohorts."

or acquisition of property, for instance, may have the same effect. Improved diet or hygiene represents joint modification by society and nature and has its effect, for example, in an increased average life expectancy.

Such routines and sequences in the lives of individuals and groups are repeated or recapitulated as the case may be within a customary interval but both are subject to alteration and to trend. Sooner or later routines and sequences are recognizably changed in a determinate direction that appears irreversible. The daily round changes with age or by social qualification. Men growing up learn trades, later they may change them, and eventually work part-time and retire. Women work too but expect to marry and spend much of their time in raising children. With greater or lesser involvement of the community, the family fits the children in turn for their life's career. The unfolding of *life sequences* changes the everyday patterning of *life routines* for each individual and there is a striking modality observable in people of the same broad chronological age. Gradually, the enmeshing sequences of parents' and childrens' lives alter each other's routines and thereby the routines and structure of the family group. Over the years, the organization of the family is affected by the changing structure of its internal relations. Finally, the changing patterns of domestic routine and family structure will measurably affect the patterning and structure of routine activities in the community that are more or less age-specific—from school attendance and job entry to the establishment of new households and propagation of the next generation.

Differences in routines and sequences between generations are particularly revealing of social change brought about by divergence from the routined ways of parents. Migration, shift of occupation, change of status and social mobility create the interstices through which change takes form in the patterning of people's lives. Organization and structure of both family and community activities are affected in the same way. Departure from the ways of parents may be viewed not only as the alteration of routines by age and social modification in the life-span of a single younger generation but also as variation in a trend of alteration over a longer sequence of intergenerational change. If such nonrecurrent movements in a population can be identified and separated from the recurrent ones, then trends of social change may be identifiable. These in turn may be analyzed into their various strands or components whose interaction and *net* alteration is registered in the trend. Thus a partially quantified expression may be given to an essentially qualitative social change.

All this, to be sure, may seem to be a matter of statistical manipulation and outside the sphere of the historian's interest. But it is a principal contention of this paper that social historians must begin to explore the underlying movements in community structure and organization that go much deeper than the epiphenomenal patterns of politics or the ferment of ideas. An autonomous social history ought to begin with a study of population: its changing composition and distribution in time and space.[14]

Economic history has already faced this necessity in its own development and, as a consequence, the discipline has been made over during the last twenty or thirty years. Little or nothing has been lost in the course of this evolution and a great deal has been gained. If the decomposition of trends into component movements can be accomplished in the analysis of such complex phenomena as the business cycle and capital formation or such demographic changes as social mobility, then some historians must begin to think in these sorts of terms even though requisite data may not yet be at hand. One obvious area in which this new kind of social history would be pertinent is the comparative study of economic growth. Were the requisite data at hand, there is no reason why they might not be expressed in terms of the distributional change from rural to urban residence; that is be given a spatial referent. Here then is the unmistakable relevance of urbanization to the study of social change. If sufficient data were recovered or reconstructed, the urbanization of population could be correlated with structural characteristics of an economic or social kind, their associations analyzed, and clothed in all the rich detail of historicity. Historians are as likely to discover these kinds of data for single places over short periods of time (registration records are a good example) as other social scientists are to find adequate coverage for their purposes in national and state enumerations.[15] The point is that, if the

[14] Useful introductions to population study are Maurice Halbwachs, *Population and Society: Introduction to Social Morphology* (tr., Glencoe, Ill., 1960) and Philip M. Hauser, *Population Perspectives* (New Brunswick, N. J., 1961).

[15] For example, Domenico Sella, "La popolazione di Milano nei secoli XVI e XVII," *Storia di Milano*, XII (Milano: Fondazione Treccani, 1959); J. D. Chambers, "Population Change in a Provincial Town: Nottingham 1700–1800," *Studies*

same sets of terms are used, similar techniques of analysis may be applied to both micro- and macroscopic situations and there is every reason to believe that the little world will illumine the large.

No doubt the resulting structures of urbanization and associated activity will present an array of diverse developments having significant features in common. Each urban situation will be measurably distinctive but its distinction is a matter of degree, not of kind. It will represent not so much the exception to a rule as a deviation within a trend (or general movement in the population) that needs understanding in historical-contextual terms.[16] Urbanization is the societal process that creates cities but each city is an accommodation of the general movement to a particular set of demographic, institutional, technological, and environmental circumstances—including the contingencies of events and personalities. Insofar as this approach is designed to measure variation it puts people and places back into history. The population is no longer an anonymous crowd dragged on to a stage to celebrate the doings of great men or news of great events. Everyday mundane life led in anonymity in nameless places contributes in its time to the great alterations of history.

What is at stake in this broadened view of urban history is the possibility of examining one of the most comprehensive, profound, and unprecedented manifestations of social change: *the urbanization of society.* Urbanization of society is a particular phenomenon of the last century and a half but, to grasp the nature and magnitude of the changes involved, it is necessary to draw a much longer perspective in order to bring the connection between urbanization and social change into bolder relief. Over the four or more centuries since 1500 it may be possible to discern which of a given set of factors at any time has prevailed in shaping an alteration in the character of the modern city. Was it, for example, the centralizing polity of the nation state, the pricing calculus of

in the Industrial Revolution, L. S. Pressnell, ed. (London, 1960), 97–124. Also perceptive commentary by Bayrd Still in "Local History Contributions and Techniques in the Study of Two Colonial Cities," *Bulletin of the American Association for State and Local History,* II (February 1959), 245–250. For community "problems" aggravated by demographic crises before the industrial revolution, see Pierre Goubert, *Beauvais et le Beauvaisis de 1600 à 1730* (2 vols., Paris, 1960).

[16] An analogous view of deviations in the study of economic "backwardness" is given by Alexander Gerschenkron, "Reflections on the Concept of 'Prerequisites' of Modern Industrialization," *L'industria: rivista di economia politica,* No. 2 (1957), 357–372.

the rational capital-using business system, the enormous increase in calorific energy unleashed by the application of fuel-burning machines to production and communication, or the population explosion of the countryside that was decisive, in Oscar Handlin's terms, in shaping the reorganization of the city's space, the reconstruction of its social order, and the adjustment of its citizens? [17]

No single approach is likely to provide a satisfactory explanation of this many-faceted phenomenon. But in the course of this longer inquiry it will be possible to develop three salients from which to advance on the modern city: the demographic, the structural, and the behavioral. The first deals with the growth and distribution of population in space; the second pertains to the organization of communities and society; the third has reference to the conduct of individuals. Although structural and behavioral characteristics provide essential clues to the nature and direction of social change, the demographic approach appears to offer at once the least ambiguity and the most promise from the standpoint of observation and measurement. As Schumpeter remarked: "We need statistics not only for explaining things, but in order to know precisely what there is to be explained." [18]

Human populations have been forming into cities of one kind or another for almost seven millennia but at no point before the eighteenth century did urban centers themselves contain more than a small fraction of the total. For much of that time, moreover, recognizable urban settlements were confined to a few widely separated parts along the rim of southern Asia. Cities, leagues of cities, urban civilizations may later have flourished elsewhere but never an urbanized society. [19] Great cities, to be sure, with populations that at times reached several hundred thousands had appeared in remote antiquity; one fairly late example, Seleucia on the Tigris, probably exceeded 500,000 inhabitants during the third century B.C. Around 1300 A.D., at the peak of the medieval flower-

[17] Oscar Handlin, "The Modern City as a Field of Historical Study," *supra.*

[18] J. A. Schumpeter, *History of Economic Analysis* (New York, 1954), 14. A much fuller treatment of these issues of conceptualization and method is given in E. E. Lampard and L. F. Schnore, "Urbanization Problems," *Research Needs for Development Assistance Programs* (Washington, D. C.: Brookings Institution, processed, 1961), LS 6–14.

[19] For a review of urbanization in the ancient Near East, see Carl H. Kraeling and R. M. Adams, *City Invincible: A Symposium on Urbanization and Cultural Development in the Ancient Near East* (Chicago, 1960).

ing, there were probably only five cities in all Christendom with more than 100,000 residents. London may have exceeded half a million in the third quarter of the seventeenth century and Paris may have during the next century but, in Europe and probably the world, they remained comparative freaks.

As recently as 1800 only about three percent of the world's estimated population of 906 millions resided in some 750 local centers of more than 5,000 inhabitants; more than half of this urban population was to be found in forty-five great cities (of 100,000 or more inhabitants) more than half of which again were located outside Europe. Asia had almost sixty percent of this great city population and Edo (Tokyo) may well have been the largest single agglomeration in all human history up to that time.[20] At the close of the eighteenth century only in Britain and the Netherlands did the proportions of total populations resident in towns and cities much exceed ten percent. There was no urbanized society—having from a third to half its people in cities—anywhere in the world.

Between 1800 and 1950 world population increased nearly 165 percent but world urban population resident in cities of 5,000 and over had risen by 2,535 percent. This striking disparity of rates provides a rough quantitative expression of the phenomenon of urbanization. By 1950 the number of cities with more than 5,000 inhabitants had risen to 27,600 and they now contained almost thirty percent of the estimated 2.4 billion world population. At this date the number of great cities, 100,000 and over, was 875 and forty-nine giant agglomerations surpassed the million mark. A larger proportion of the greatly increased world population resided in *Millionenstädte* in 1950 than in 1800 had dwelt in all cities of 5000 and over. In 1950 Australasia, the Americas, and Europe contained the largest relative concentrations of great city dwellers in that order but the growth of such cities was already proceeding at a much faster rate in Asia and Africa than in any other of the major continental regions.

Since about 1800 the world has witnessed a growth in the

[20] Kingsley Davis and Hilda H. Golden, "Urbanization and the Development of Pre-Industrial Areas," *Economic Development and Cultural Change*, III (October 1954), 6–26; P. M. Hauser, ed., *Urbanization in Asia and the Far East* (Calcutta: UNESCO, Tensions and Technology Series, 1958), 55–63. W. W. Lockwood, *The Economic Development of Japan* (Princeton, N. J., 1954), 4, and Irene B. Taeuber, "Urbanization and Population Change in the Development of Modern Japan," *Economic Development and Cultural Change*, IX (October 1960), suppl., 4.

number and size of cities with repercussions and ramifications which mark that turning point as one of the crucial disjunctions of human history. Whatever conditions of natural and social environment had hitherto checked the growth and redistribution of population had suddenly been relaxed. The appearance of urbanized societies, with well over half their populations resident in cities, represents the most far-reaching social change since the "urban revolution" of Neolithic times.

The most obvious structural movement associated with this unprecedented demographic change was the industrial revolution. Prior to the acceleration of city growth in the later eighteenth century, it is doubtful if urbanization had ever affected more than three percent of world population or more than ten to fifteen percent on a restricted regional or local basis. We know, nevertheless, that profound social transformations had occurred in Europe and elsewhere without benefit of sustained urbanization. A shift of four or five percentage points in levels of urbanization in the later Roman world or the high middle ages of Europe probably sufficed to mark important turning points in the unfolding of Western civilization. Such a transformation took place in the market city of northern Italy when "the market and public square became one thing." Merchants superseded landowners as the acknowledged fathers of self-governing mercantile communities.[21] Men of commerce acquired, not only wealth and influence, but status and dignity. Clearly, deep-seated changes take place wholly disproportionately to the numbers of people actually moving in and out of cities even on a local basis.

A general decline in population after the fourteenth century marked a disintegration of society that did not much abate before the sixteenth century. Activities in the market place were significantly depressed and cities surrendered a large part of their civic autonomy and their populations. The prolonged declension was relieved only by a gradual process of personal emancipation and the cultural flowering of the Renaissance which consolidated certain intellectual foundations of the ensuing era of geographical and scientific discovery epitomized in the new technologies: gunpowder, mining, printing, and navigation. But not before political allegiance, economic interest, and moral authority had been redefined in a viable unit of social organization and expressed in

[21] Robert S. Lopez, "The Crossroads within the Wall," *supra*.

terms of novel legal rights of property and contract were energies and resources effectively channeled to a common end, to the structuring of a new social order. Centralization of political, economic, and religious initiative in the princely nation state had, for the moment at least, the special virtue of linking technological novelty to commercial operations in more systematic efforts to improve production. Mercantilist polity contributed initially to national wealth and power but, outside the colonial areas (notably the Americas), the crowded ports and ostentatious capitals, it did not foster a growth of cities. The most that can be said quantitatively before the eighteenth century is that variations in rates of urbanization locally rather than levels generally provide suggestive clues to underlying currents of change.[22]

If the historian looks only for conspicuous changes in rates and levels of urbanization before 1700 he will overlook important structural movements in society that were scarcely reflected in the city. He must study developments in the country as well as the town and divorce between the two, even for analytical purposes, may lead to serious misunderstanding of urbanization itself. Raising of market crops, for instance, led to a more rational pattern of land use in accessible country districts: a conscious effort not only to maintain the fertility of the soil but to increase its productivity. Rising capital-output ratios rendered old routines inherited from communal land management irrational in the sense that social (as well as technical) limits on output represented a lowering of potential returns on fixed investment. Since mining and many branches of pre-industrial manufacture were also country or village pursuits, their reorganization along capital-intensive lines away from restrictive craft traditions likewise did not affect the internal order of the city nor disrupt the daily circulation of its people. Credit, information, and initiative might be channeled through the centers but reorganization of production in farm, mine, and mill went on mostly in the outlying places. City dwellers provided more of the

[22] Heinz Stoob, "Kartographische Möglichkeiten zur Darstellung der Stadtenstehung in Mitteleuropa, besonders zwischen 1450 und 1800," *Historische Raumforschung, I, Forschungs-und Sitzungsberichte der Akademie für Raumforschung und Landesplanung,* VI (Bremen, 1956), 21–76, for alternative ways of representing urbanization. Roger Mols, *Introduction à la démographie historique des villes d'Europe du XIVe au XVIIIe siècle* (3 vols., Louvain, 1955) is an excellent guide to demographic problems and materials before the nineteenth century. On town settlement in the New World: Richard M. Morse, "Some Characteristics of Latin American Urban History," *American Historical Review,* LXVII (1962), 317–338.

specialized commercial and administrative services needed to integrate a slowly evolving territorial division of labor.[23] By the seventeenth century there was nothing generically "urban" in the adaptation of a profit-seeking capital-intensive regimen nor in the rational evaluation of people and places in terms of their relative income-earning capacities. Few of these functional relations between town and country or among the cities were altogether without medieval precedent; the range and intensity of later developments marked them off from their predecessors. These were portentous indicators of transformations outside the city's limits that would shortly become concentrated and intensified within its own constricted space.

Thus preindustrial division of labor, centralization, and hierarchical organization were institutional means to implement a larger comity. They were not so much results of social change as its immanent forms: the modes by which it unfolded. Around 1700 small cities performed broadly similar central place functions (trade, civil and ecclesiastical governance, defence, some manufacture) with regional variations across wide areas of territory. Country districts were largely self-sustaining for the bulk of production and service needs. Work, work places, and the working day were scarcely articulated from the domestic routines of everyday life and living. Provincial manners combined with local building materials to give an outwardly variegated texture to a broadly similar social fabric. Large cities, including political capitals, provided only the more specialized services of interregional or international significance; they were the emporia for provincial staples and exotic specialties. Transport and communications factors sufficed, among other things, to mitigate the sense of interdependence for the vast majority. Low rates of urbanization but higher levels locally were a consequence of centripetal organization and the intensive utilization of special sites. The industrial revolution was nourished in countrysides such as these and not before the large-scale application of fuel-burning machines to production and com-

---

[23] For this term "integration" in relation to "effective space": John Friedman, "L'influence de l'intégration du système social sur le développement économique," *Diogène*, XXXIII (Jan-Mars 1961), 80–104; *id.*, "Cities in Social Transformation," *Comparative Studies in Society and History*, IV (November, 1961), 86–103. For the profound insight of a contemporary: Giovanni Botero, *A Treatise Concerning the Causes of the Magnificence and Greatness of Cities* written in the late sixteenth century and translated into English, London, 1606.

munication in the nineteenth century did industrial-urban disciplines impose any wholesale rationalization on population or space.[24] The rationalizing centripetal movements of industrialism, however, were immanent in the social order that had emerged before the perfection of the steam engine (Industrial urbanization did not destroy an old order; it fulfilled the new one.)

There is no need to rehearse the marvel of technological unfolding from water wheels and steam engines through turbines to electric generators and internal combustion engines. Each would in turn have its peculiar influence on the morphology of city growth.[25] Both the accelerated pace and the altered form of urbanization after 1800 were determined by the newer technological component of industrialism that imposed an exacting regime of technical efficiency based on the relative work performance and operational requirements of machines. But, insofar as the trend of change was the *net* outcome of variations in existing routines and sequences, the technological component was made effective through the institutional component of the price system.[26] Relative technical possibilities expressed through the more comprehensive and value-laden calculus of bookkeeping reinforced the movement of population and economic activity (other than agriculture) out of the countryside and into the town.

The same exalted conventions, however, did not enter the full cost of a firm's business decisions to the community. "External" as well as "internal" economies, for example, accrued to the firm but not the diseconomies created by the firm's own operations.[27]

[24] E. E. Lampard, "History of Cities in the Economically Advanced Areas," *Economic Development and Cultural Change*, III (January 1955), 86–102, proposes that, since functional specialization leads to areal differentiation, the degree of interaction among activities distributed in space may be taken as a significant index of the relative maturity of regional urban structures. Thus, during the industrial revolution in England, cotton, wool, and iron districts became more sharply differentiated, each proceeding within its own cycle of technical and organizational development. For comparisons with regional urban structures in France: *ibid.*, 110–115. Also, S. G. Checkland, "English Provincial Cities," *Economic History Review*, n.s. VI (1953), 200, and F. J. Fisher, "The Sixteenth and Seventeenth Centuries," *Economica*, n.s. XXIV (1960), 2–18.

[25] W. F. Cottrell, "The City in the Age of Atoms and Automation," *The City in Mid-Century*, H. W. Dunham, ed. (Detroit, 1957) for a perceptive analysis of relations between modes of energy conversion and the forms of cities.

[26] E. E. Lampard, "The Price System and Economic Change," *Journal of Economic History*, XX (December 1960), 617–637, for the social and ecological embeddedness of market pricing institutions.

[27] Shigeto Tsuru, "The Role of the City in Technological Innovation and Economic Development," *supra*.

Some of the latter no doubt fell on other firms and were duly accounted as items of "internal" cost; others were transferred to the household which was now separated institutionally and spatially from place of work. But the balance, and probably the largest part, of "external" diseconomies was carried by the community in the form of "city problems." Political adjustments in the form of regulation and taxation later moderated some of the more dysfunctional aspects of industrialism. Thanks to an increasingly flexible and productive technology, the price system operated *via* rising average levels of personal income to relax the older centripetal pressures somewhat. Built-up areas are now flung out across the countryside without visible unity or identity; city problems are dissolved into metropolitan problems: nobody's or everybody's concern.

Thus the social system of pricing, giving expression to whatever cultural and psychological principles are operative in human scientific creativity,[28] accounts in part for the particular demographic phenomenon of the urbanized society and its characteristic structural order of activities differentiated in space and time. The most evident mutation of this principle of social selection was an artifact which creates wealth, the industrial city. Linked externally to a functionally specialized countryside and to other differentiated urban centers, the industrial city was reorganized and reshaped along institutional lines into spatially-segregated areas of residence (households) and work (firms), with sharply differentiated time for labor and domesticity and with necessary interchanges of population from productive to consumptive roles at conventional, albeit temporally specific, points in daily and weekly schedules.

Evolution of this kind of city out of earlier prototypes was variously affected at times by national polity, capitalist business, fuel-burning technology, and not least by the sheer increase in population itself. When death rates declined without a sufficiently rapid change in family structure and size, population boomed. The nation state centralized the polity, renovated property and contractual relations, reduced the autonomy of local institutions, and the strength of traditional ties: it emancipated the individual. The community was even more closely affected by the flowering of rational capital-using business guided along profit-making lines

[28] William N. Parker, "Economic Development in Historical Perspective," *Economic Development and Cultural Change*, X (October 1961), 1–7. Also, A. P. Usher, *A History of Mechanical Inventions* (paperback ed., Boston, 1959), 1–10, and Chapters 2 and 3.

by market competition and conventional accounting technique: it represented people, places, and things as factors of production substitutable in almost infinitely variable proportions to the point of diminishing returns. The technological variable governed the rate, level, and direction of the urbanization trend subject only to modulation in the event of politically-serious dysfunction: technology reinforced and magnified the tendencies of political economy. The remaining variable is population itself. In some respects it is independent of the others but in many ways responsive to them, to the level of urbanization and the spatial-structural organization of family and community life.

This last point touches the least tractable of all: the effect of urbanization on human behavior. Urbanization has concentrated unprecedented numbers of human beings into cities of different size and density and, as a consequence, their daily routines and sequences have become radically changed through progressive differentiation. During any day, a person is obliged to play out many specialized roles in his family, at work, on the journey between, and in the community at large. In great cities these roles are often functionally, institutionally, spatially, and temporally specific. Over any life sequence the specificity of roles is modulated with age or change of socioeconomic status. Over generations both periodic routines and sequences become radically changed. Clearly urbanization must have affected human behavior in myriad ways. The fall in the birth rate, for example, and the trend toward smaller family in most urbanizing countries was not only a profound demographic and structural phenomenon, it mirrored a radical alteration in family behavior. Similarly, insofar as rural-to-urban migration brought rising socio-economic status to many families or their offspring, social mobility may have further modified behavior. Such changes, however, can be apprehended in the same way as demographic and structural alterations; they are often obverse and reverse sides of the same thing.

Nevertheless, it is said that urbanization "is more than a shifting of people from country to city and from landbound work to urban types of work. . . . Urbanization involves basic changes in thinking and behavior of people and changes in their social values." The reference, of course, is to the individual person. If he should display certain patterns of behavior—urban ways of thinking and urban values—he may be said to be urbanized. Indeed, if he exhibits such traits, he need not necessarily "leave his rural work or habitat." [29] Some city dwellers, on the other hand, do not yet manifest these traits. Such an approach has the great advantage of not restricting urbanism to the city milieu and seems to be in accord with many obvious facts of contemporary life. Yet it raises again the same difficult questions of definition and measurement that have plagued urban sociology and social history from the beginning. This kind of behavioralism is especially vulnerable when hypothetical urban traits have obvious counterparts in nonurban communities or are even more obviously related to a particular historic situation that may once have existed, for instance, in Berlin or Chicago. Finally, most of the behavioral studies have so far focused on urban pathology without ever establishing a very clear notion of what constitutes normal behavior in a normal community; hopefully, they never will. But if urbanization does produce notably higher rates of personal breakdown they may well be the consequence of adjustments people have been required to make in the routines and sequences of everyday life. This is especially true of newcomers in which case might not the symptoms be better treated as aspects of migration than of urbanization *per se?* Thus, some of the slum and near-slum neighborhoods in which immigrants to the United States experienced the trauma of their Americanization have apparently developed a richness of ethnic tradition and local cohesion that is personally and socially more therapeutic than the sanitary Superblock. Critics of urban renewal programs deny the need for bulldozer surgery on precisely these grounds.[30] One wonders whether this kind of phenomenon is not more responsive to forms and styles of literature and the arts than to any of the categories and techniques of social science.

From another standpoint, human beings and their communities are highly adaptable. The community is the social institution for human adaptation. Perhaps the predicament of both town and country dwellers in urbanizing societies is that adjustments are required at too great a pace in too many directions, most of which seem irresistible and irreversible. There are simply too many choices to be made and few generally accepted rules, other than those of the price system, to apply. Surely these are among the profoundest dilemmas of modern "Western" man—not simply the distinctive traits of urban thought or values.

[29] Nels Anderson, *The Urban Community* (New York, 1959), 5.
[30] Jane Jacobs, *The Death and Life of Great American Cities* (New York, 1961).

In the light of serious shortcomings in the concept, urban, and of the broad connotation we have given to the term social change (it is difficult to resist a conclusion that many of the problems and attributes commonly identified with the city or urbanization represent no more than a concentration of the effects of changes which are otherwise dispersed and less visible.) Not only are such problems as housing and public health intensified in a city milieu, they are more conspicuous there and the contrast with urban wealth and well-being made more reprehensible. (Urbanization concentrated age-old problems of poverty and ignorance and, in great cities, aggravated conditions that were as endemic to civilization as the city itself: congestion and artificiality.) In the city they are displayed for all who care to look. It is not surprising that the city becomes a locus for discontent that is by no means generic to urbanism itself.

The high visibility of social changes in the city is a consequence, not of population concentration and spatial segregation alone, but of narrow and near-sighted vision as well. What an observer sees in the city can be established only by relating the focus of his interest to a larger framework of understanding; the proportions of what are seen are determined by the observer's stance and perspective. The casual observer may see nothing of note; a reformer what his predilections allow him to see; an expert sees what he is trained to see. This is the fundamental reason why the practical student of urban affairs needs a filter for penetrating beneath the surface problems to the deep seated processes that create cities and transform them before his eyes.

The broadened perspectives on urbanization and social change sketched in this paper form no more than a partial framework of explanation. They need careful application to both micro- and macrohistorical contexts before they can yield a fuller sense of satisfied understanding. Doubtless, there are many other processes at work in recent history on which very different perspectives would be more revealing. But, in view of the importance of the modern city in society and its rapid spread throughout the world, more effort should be made to interpret social change in terms of urbanization as a process of society. The particular view of social change and the suggestions regarding demographic, structural, and behavioral approaches advanced in this paper are put forward not for acceptance, but hopefully for use.

The Building Blocks of Urban History

FREDERICK GUTHEIM and ATLEE E. SHIDLER

It is useful to think of the house of urban history as constructed from two sets of building materials: one for the exterior and the other for the interior. Cities, like ideas, have both an internal and an external history. The building blocks of internal urban history are monographs on individual cities. Those for external urban history are studies of historical periods and the process of urbanization in particular regions, societies, or civilizations. There is a much larger current supply of materials for the interior than for the exterior, and they have been neither plentiful nor strong enough to give the structure stability or shape.[1] Building blocks for the

[1] See Eric E. Lampard, "American Historians and the Study of Urbanization," *American Historical Review*, LXV (October 1961), 49–61.

interior need to be redesigned; those for the exterior need to be hewn out. Each effort will greatly strengthen the other.

On the internal side, we must ask in what respects the existing city histories fall short, and how criteria can be developed that will lead to better and more useful monographs on individual cities. A related question must also be asked. What comparative studies can be undertaken by urban historians in which existing monographs on individual cities would be most useful?

Before exploring these questions briefly, we would disavow any suggestion that this is the whole of urban history. There will always be other themes, such as impact studies and histories of ideas about, and attitudes toward, the city. We do argue, however, that the concept offered here defines the basic structure of urban history; and we suggest that it is from this structure that the main paths will emerge linking urban history to social, economic, political, and technical studies of urbanism.

Local history is the scene of extensive labors. State, county, and municipal historical societies and archives contain rich documentary deposits, well arranged for research. They have substantial support for such research, and they are in fact publishing substantial amounts of material related to urban history. But almost none of this vast effort is of immediate value to the urban historian. How can it be redeemed? Moreover, admirable as the leading city histories today are—Pierce's *Chicago*, McKelvey's *Rochester*, Green's *Washington*—they are not models for all the different types of monographs on individual cities we need. Works that are more sharply focused, more organizational in model, more methodological in theme are also needed.

A typology of cities, usable in other fields of urban studies, appears a prime requisite for comparative urbanism. Industrial towns are valuable in the context of economic history. They are also useful in the history of cities.

The question of comparability is inseparable from the data, and data in turn establish what can be done by interpretation. Here we need considerably more work on such powerful common denominators as the Census, federal legislation affecting cities, and great national developments—whether in politics, technology, or ideas—that have enveloped cities. It would be particularly instructive to see how cities have individually responded to certain common problems that all have been obliged to face. How different cities have received the city manager plan, the payroll tax, public housing subsidies, or the highway program profoundly reveals their institutional bias and system of values.

On the external side urban history may be expected to contribute strongly toward meeting the fundamental need of all urban studies—a general theory of urban growth. How has the historical process of urbanization varied relative to technology, natural resources, topography, military needs, governmental structure, and culture? Here again we need comparative studies as well as monographs on individual regions, nations, and civilizations.

In this connection, historians of North American urbanization should give serious attention to Rowland Berthoff's article, "The American Social Order: A Conservative Hypothesis," in the April 1960 issue of the *American Historical Review*. Berthoff invites the study of urbanization in relation to other major forms of mobility in American history: immigration, the westward movement, and movement up and down the economic and social ladder. Also, his article, along with such other recent works as Jean Gottmann's *Megalopolis*, underscores the urgency of studying the history of American urbanization in relation to the ever accelerating technological change in production, transportation, and communication.

VII
Conclusion

Some Afterthoughts

JOHN BURCHARD

The conference of which these papers are a partial record was a pleasant one—and I believe profitable. It had to meet the problem so many conferences now have to meet as all the world tries to be interdisciplinary. This was a confrontation of historians and other scholars (economists, political scientists, and a philosopher) with doers and partial doers, men who help to make cities or write polemics for or against what has and has not been done. The floor for the formal papers was given to the thinkers rather than the doers and that was a good idea, as, I am sure, a full tape of the conversation would demonstrate.

No one can really say whether any planner or critic will be a better planner or critic because of what he learned in those few days; whether any politician will mend his ways, or, if his ways are good, work at them harder; whether any historian had his view changed as to what he ought to be doing. Every one, I suspect, may think a little more about what he is up to. That others may share in this advantage is probably the principal reason for publishing a group of papers which, however excellent individually, cannot be claimed to provide a coherent and organized discussion of the topic.

The planners of the conference expected no more than that some ideas might emerge as to the state of the art of urban history, and what sort of work would be well to do. No one tried at the time to make a report and a checklist out of what was said then, and I am not going to try now.

Not long ago I was talking to a Russian historian about the desirability of having some discussions between Russian and American historians at the level of the many science conferences which have bloomed at Pugwash, in Geneva, and Moscow, and Stowe, and goodness knows where else. He agreed at once because "then we would find out who is right." We did not find out who was right in the days at Harvard Square. The conferees, like most other conferees, showed that each of us, in his own way, has some of the remarkable talent revealed by the fascinating, friendly streetwalker of the Piraeus who adored the Greek tragedies, who laughed and cried always at the wrong time and for whom in the end Medea, Jason, Oedipus, Orestes, Cassandra, Ismene, Antigone, Haemon, and all the gallant rest got together for a gala on the seashore. Each of us in his own way spent some time on the beach, which is another way of saying that scholars are human and therefore capable of playing the same set of notes to form tunes consonant with their several prejudices.

I, for example, was always talking about the fountains of a city, but others emphasized race riots. If one wanted Voltaire as his mouthpiece, another preferred Montesquieu. I have never heard so many different and fascinating, if not always convincing, references to and interpretations of William Blake. More than one tried, idly, to bring the papers closer to what was presumed to have been their subjects. In one instance Carl Friedrich suggested that if we had been talking about the University in the History of Ideas we would certainly not have talked instead about Ideas concerning the University; and he was trenchant when he remarked that history is what we remember and that what we choose to remember is affected by our present concerns. So it happened that some of the topics, too, went to the seashore. Even the planners were criticized, probably fairly, for thinking that a city could even be called an artifact.

I felt nearest to the wetness of the surf when Richard Meier began talking about the Role of the City in Technological Innovation and Economic Development. Almost before we knew it, he had introduced an analysis with graphs of what technicians might want in the way of the good life and how a city might be planned to lure them to it. He did this to build up a case for the thought that though, when you pandered to these needs, you might not speed up innovation, you might nevertheless be able to make a city out of Ann Arbor after all. Anthony Garvan objected to this by saying that Meier was defining a problem-solving city, but not solving the problem of a city, i.e., Ann Arbor. This exchange caused me to wonder whether a close study of the history of Ann Arbor, in the manner of Sir John Summerson, would have shed any light on Meier's propositions. And so my mind wandered to the lovely and whilom functional city of Montauban and what the denouement had been for the Counts of Toulouse who brought it into being.

The epitome of the beach picnic was provided by Martin Meyerson when he discussed an engraving from a nineteenth century book about the Mississippi and the West, republished in Henry Nash Smith's work on the American agrarian myth, *Virgin Land*. Called "The Garden of Ceres," the dominating central figure is that of Ceres, agrarianism personified, displayed against a background of progress containing a steamboat in the middle ground while, almost invisible in the remote distance, a few men are chopping trees. To Smith, the engraver had three main symbols in mind, Ceres, her plow, and the axe, all agrarian. He does not even mention the boat. But Meyerson saw the steamboat and having seen it, the axe might lose importance in relation to the logs which the men *might* have been levying from the forest as fuel for the boat. As one remembers the steamboat, it is hard to remember the axe and vice versa. Yet history should somehow contrive to remember both. All this goes to show merely that there is more than one solution to a riddle, or anyway to some riddles—and that ours was one of this type.

The conferees had the conventional contemporary semantic difficulties. There was no real effort to define what we were talking about, either history or the city. The definition of the latter was of course the more slippery. It may be supposed that we would have talked of nothing else had we sought consensus about it— and still not have achieved it. We all knew, I hope, that everything one might say, for example, about Athens before Themistocles could not be truthfully or usefully said about fortress Carcassonne, commercial Venice, residential Karlsruhe, or megalopolitan Los Angeles (read any other contemporary city you don't like, since to find another whipping boy than Los Angeles is long overdue).

I usually tended to support those who define the city as the congeries which multiplies the opportunity to exercise choice but not all cities have this diversity, only most of the great ones. It is moreover a definition of purpose rather than of a place. Perhaps the people of a few great cities eschewed diversity; certainly Sir Thomas More did not covet it for Amaurot; and it is, alas, possible that many people may not want even the freedom to be eccentric any more, if they ever did.

Moreover, Robert Lopez, for example, spoke against diversity as definition by speaking of the diversity of a Carolingian manor and asking, therefore, how much diversity you had to have before you had a city. For the sociological description he substituted an economic one. Following Pirenne, he insisted that without a market you cannot speak of a city. No one asked him how big the market had to be or whether it must serve more than the intramural necessity. This is cited simply to reveal that one or another of us tried to define the city by qualitative measures of economics, of politics, of ideology, of art, of density, or of law, and that none of these definitions met any general acclaim. The one positive, measurable definition, provided by the statistics from the Bureau of the Census, seemed almost the least useful for our purposes, even if urban population, like real wages, could be calibrated on a relative scale. We said nothing of other scales, for example, the number of minutes it might take a city dweller to move from the forum to the open country. Perhaps even this would need to be corrected to a time scale since, thanks to modern medicine, an hour was a bigger hunk of the life of an Augustan Roman than it is of yours or mine.

It must be said that we did not discuss definitions very much and no one felt like challenging Lopez when he said that each city was unique and that there had been only one Athens, one Florence, one Paris, one Rome; no one asked if there were a determinable difference between the uniqueness of Paris and of, say, Elkhart, Indiana—or of which Rome he was speaking, republican, imperial, medieval, renaissance, papal and baroque, fascist, or contemporary—each itself unique. Morton White summed up the dilemma when he said that the effort to define the essence of a city is dubious from a philosophical point of view.

Miss Thrupp was not ready to let this pass quite so easily. She seemed to insist that one should first try to distill an intellectual's definition of a city before trying to study his attitude toward it. To this, Mr. White retorted that intellectuals have had attitudes toward places called "cities" even when they lacked a clear conception of what they meant by cities. The lack of a clear conception did not inhibit a clear reaction.

But the thought that the city *ought* to be defined more explicitly before discussing it remained a nagging one. Thus there was much sympathy for Miss Thrupp's suggestion that the city is an idea.

Later on Miss Thrupp and Mr. Fitch provided further light. The idea of the city may become more elusive, Miss Thrupp suggested, under the pressure of unplanned population growth:

"If you think of the city as a fixed place, fixed people, everything else just fits; whereas there has always been flow in and flow out. In the Greek polis and in every other kind of city people live in the city only because they can get out of it. Even Mr. Lopez' high renaissance Italians spent the summer in the country and they found the city livable only for this reason. There is a symbiosis between the city and the country. Its nature depends partly on the nature of transportation. Take the great English country house in the eighteenth century. It was part of what maintained the countryside, for people maintained a huge staff of servants in these great houses. Yet its owners would also have a London house. When the population grows, the city grows out and encloses some of the suburbs, or suburban villages where smaller people used to go for the summer. Then they have to go out farther. Then some industry goes out also. The invention of the carriage, prior to the invention of the automobile, made for transportation tangles not unlike our own.

Miss Thrupp's notion about the new return to the city may not be well supported by the facts generally. But there is no doubt great confusion about what a city is today. For example, if a metropolis should include metropolitan cultural advantages, can it be said that a resident of Secaucus who never goes to Manhattan Island is really a part of the idea of New York? Or does the idea of New York now contain more facets than the "Garden of Ceres," many of them contradictory? Is there a new confusion of idea in the two-way flow of people morning and night where once the tide flowed in at dawn and ebbed at dusk?

Mr. Fitch sharpened this point. He said the conference was producing clues as to why "the average lay American has come to the conclusion that cities are no longer viable. . . . According to White and Schorske, one of the endemic attitudes in America toward the city is that it was evil, the source of evil. Certainly that was Frank Lloyd Wright's attitude. According to Wright nobody but usurers and men of ill-will and night life would occupy the city as a native habitat. The source of all real goodness came from the farm. But even Wright has to deal with the city, for at least in his young manhood it still produced a lot of the essential items of equipment. But now, I think, with the spread of urban amenities across the countryside, paved roads, ambulances, air-conditioning, TV, and all the rest of it, a great many people have come to the conclusion that they no longer need the city. They thought all along that it was evil, and now they conclude they don't even need it. And this is, I think, perfectly apparent in all the popular literature on the subject—the movies, TV programs, the radio, the women's magazines. You do not see Miss Thrupp's symbol of the city any more. It's all station wagons, country day schools, and cook outs. Actually I fear the laymen are following Dr. Gutkind in what I think is a misconception, because nobody asks, 'Who produces these things that are used in cookouts, station wagons, county day schools, and shopping centers?' Where do they come from? They come from urban centers. They don't come from farmyards. Here is the basic misapprehension. I think the role of the city has not altered a particle. I think it still is the generator of civilization, not merely the vehicle, but the generator of it! It is obvious that a great many Americans don't agree with me. And they may even succeed in killing the city before I have a chance to get heard. But that will not mean that they are correct. And this explains why it is so hard to mobilize popular opinion in the defense of any urban improvement. . . . Most people don't realize, don't think of themselves as any longer being involved with the city, despite the fact that their income, their furniture, their foam rubber, everything they utilize comes from the city. They are still under the illusion that they can do without it."

Interesting as this all was, it still left us without a common definition of a city to which we could all adhere and on which we could erect a systematic discussion. But perhaps, in truth, most of us were a little relieved that it was so, since any hammered-out definition promised to be so ponderous. Yet if the city cannot be defined, can it be usefully discussed? The unscientific answer has to be yes; but it must also be conceded that the absence of definition permits more or less unbridled discussion and the assertion of personal prejudice as fact—as the success of more than one recent and popular book about the city will testify.

Another question that went largely unasked was whether the study of urban history had any utility. This is simply one facet of the larger question about the usefulness of history in general. It is a question which has been banging about unresolved ever since Thucydides expressed his modest hopes. Do men relate their present conduct to what they think they know about the happy and the bitter experiences even of their ancestors, to say nothing of the ancestors of others? Or do they go their own blithe ways, shaping their courses as though there had been no history; or worse yet, do they shape their courses as they will and then select from history those episodes which conveniently support the present position? Despite the claims of a line of eminent men from Cicero to Lord Acton, does history have anything useful to teach us? Our past has surely conditioned our present; does a better understanding of our past affect how it might condition our present and our future? It cannot be proved but we have to believe it.

Not every one would necessarily demand even so much. Henry Millon gently noted that there is no compulsion for having a utilitarian value to history. I can applaud this for I myself find more variety and therefore more fun in the array of shades from Queen Hatshepsut to President Franklin Roosevelt than I do in the men who live today, even such different men as Nehru, Khrushchev, Bertrand Russell, and Albert Schweitzer. Anyhow one seems to know Pico della Mirandola and Henry of Navarre better than one knows Jack Kennedy—and there may be more to know. But this hedonistic view of history is in the end no more than the argument that George Leigh Mallory advanced for trying to ascend Mount Everest. It will not lead to funds for many expeditions if the funds have to be provided by pragmatists.

It is not much more satisfactory to look on history as consolation. The man locked in the frozen traffic of Piccadilly or driven mad by the nocturnal taxi horns of midtown Manhattan will scarcely be comforted by knowing of the deaths on the bridge at one of the Papal jubilees or recalling the remarks of Juvenal about how hard it was to sleep in Rome at night.

On the other end from Millon was Anthony Garvan's diatribe against the contemporary planners of contemporary Philadelphia. He assailed them for failures which he said they might have avoided had they consulted any first-year graduate student in history. This reminded me a little of Herbert Butterfield's account of the young history student who needs but five minutes of writing to reduce Bismarck to the position of a political simpleton; but who, himself, lacks sufficient political acumen to wheedle the loan of a sixpence from the hall porter. I do not mean by this to suggest that Ed Bacon, the Philadelphia planner, who knows a good deal of history, is a Bismarck; or that the Philadelphic achievement is free of fault; or that *some* historians, if not every graduate student, could not offer some useful knowledge to apply and some common sense about contemporary urban problems. What Garvan did not make clear, at least to me, was what conclusions from the earlier history of Philadelphia were relevant to Bacon's problems and in what specific ways these conclusions were either ignored or misapplied. This, to be sure, would have grown into a different conference and have needed a different cast of characters but it would no doubt be interesting to explore some time and in detail the history of a specific city and its region and to put this into close relation with a discussion of its present state and future plans.

I said "interesting" and I hope it would also be worth while. Any one who heard my preliminary remarks may remember that in this matter I am a skeptic. I reminded the audience of the notable crop of contemporary architects who join in a chorus of praise for the coherence of the Piazza San Marco of Venice whose history they know very well; and how these same designers, unlike the men, including Scamozzi, who built the Piazza San Marco over four hundred years ago, unlike the even more boisterous Romans Alberti, Bramante, Bernini, and Michelangelo, deny all the principles of urban harmony every time they build an important building while continuing to chant the praises of the urban masterpiece, Venice.

Probably the truth about the utility of urban history lies somewhere between these extremes. When Sir John Summerson entered on a defense of studying the suburb, he was effectively providing a defense of the utility of history as well as a prescription for the historian. The historian, he reminded us, must shut from his mind the idea that he will move things. He must be humble. The study of history is always slow and difficult and the historian is inevitably consigned to a modest role today. He does not know exactly what he is looking for—he wants a result and it is hard to define the result he wants.

It can be defined, I suppose, if we will settle for big words. He does want truth, or a part of it, however inconvenient it may turn out to be. Sir John was too gentle to remark that the one result that was not laudable was the location of enough confirmatory evidence of what had already been prejudged to be the truth, ignoring countervailing evidence or behaving like a prosecuting attorney, leaving its adduction to the defense. This is quite different, as all historians know, but not all practice, from starting with an hypothesis, hoping that nothing will turn up to deny it but being prepared, if necessary, to face the moment of truth. You cannot, for example, leave Rome out of a comprehensive urban history simply because you do not like it or because it contradicts your theories.

Sir John expressed a confidence, which in the end we must all share or our work is merely hobby, that some time, somewhere, some of the studies of urban history will have utility, even be influential; that "to know exactly how Camberwell happened is *perhaps* the best insurance against ever building a Camberwell again." It is a confidence which his experience may justify. Against it I refrain from citing my architectural aficionados of the Piazza San Marco who I believe know its history, or Garvan's Philadelphians who he believes are ignorant of theirs.

But if urban history is to be useful, it is still probable that some kinds of urban history will be more useful than other kinds, even if not so entertaining. A conference focused on the kinds of urban history that would be useful and the appropriate methods of such study might offer a sensible sequel to ours.

As it was, we said little about the methods of history. Some of the comments by nonhistorians made me think we owed them such an explanation. Perhaps historical study can be summed up by the commercial I hear most mornings with the radio news. It asks, "Who did it, how did they do it, and what in the world did they do?" It turns out in the commercial that "they" were "scientists," that they put the "men" in the menthol of a cigarette and that how they did it, if any one wants to know, will never be explained. There is, of course, a fourth part to the jingle as applied to history. This would go, "Why did they do it?"—a question that the poet laureates of the cigarette do not need to explain to us.

But this is only the beginning. We did not pursue very far the suggestion of Oscar Handlin that we needed more history of cities and less study of the city in history. This, I felt, was echoed by the papers of Summerson and Garvan and the comments of many others. The problem of who is good and bad as between the generalist and the monographer, we did not, fortunately, tackle. We probably need both but there will not be many safe generalizations without the monographs and there could be dangerously unsafe ones, as there already are. There is certainly some doubt on this score by those who do not read much history and who are often bored by the meticulous treatment of monographs. These doubters find general histories more entertaining than Summerson and Hitchcock, but entertainment may not be the point and broad assertions offer pitfalls for the untutored. Yet at the same time I would flinch, as I am sure Summerson would, at the prospect of monographs covering every Camberwell, and all arranged like Gilbert's dull M.P.'s in close proximity. This is not to be contemplated with any more equanimity than the prospect of interviewing the millions of Kilroys whom Douglas Haskell accused of making decisions every day while the historians were fiddling. Scientists evidently did once need a couple of hundred Ph.D. candidates to calibrate a thermometer down close to $-273\,°C$, one Ph.D. for each of the lower degrees Centigrade, but this is not the usually necessary scientific method, which does not pursue each vagrant electron and write a piece about it. Sampling methods refined by the social sciences, judicious selection of the exemplars to study, and then close examination of these mute inglorious sections is not only desirable but necessary. I doubt anybody really challenged it though some of us would shy away from too much organization of it.

I suppose my heart dropped a beat when it was proposed that the city might not be a suitable subject for historical research— some thought the canvas was much too vast while others thought it was not vast enough and that we ought to study urban civilization—in short, civilization itself, on the notion that if you cannot solve a small problem you improve by enlarging it. And although Lewis Mumford was not here, his shade was, and Senator Clark introduced it explicitly when he reminded us that Mumford had said there was not much use in speculating about the future of cities until we had settled the future of the bomb. All these counsels seem to me exaggerated although it is obvious that we must deal with the bomb and are not doing so.

In the end, good history of anything as complicated as the city (perhaps of anything) will have to depend on the careful putting together of the careful investigations of details such as those of Covent Garden or Camberwell. The interpretations and prophecies must come later. Detailed investigations can be and are best carried on with no determination to lay out the whole cosmic pattern although any historian can be forgiven a not unnatural glee if his study turns out to upset a current and popular myth.

But the point of view cannot be exorcised. I may be fascinated with the lives of, for example, Gabrielle d'Estrées or Catherine Howard, with no notion that I may gain wisdom in conducting my own love affairs therefrom. But what I look for in these charming women, whether or not they were bright, whether or not they were promiscuous, may surely be usefully influenced by whether I am trying to connect them to the private conduct of a monarch, the management of an international negotiation, or the planning of a city—and I see no reason why the life of a city may not be as good a thing to start from as anything else in the examination even of young ladies.

The real problem, of course, is whether the generalists can be kept at bay while the monographers are getting together enough more material to justify another generalization. We have to face it that most people will say they are too busy (which really means too lazy) to read the monographs and in this they are partly justified by the excessive jargon of many monographers. They turn then to what is more interesting; and the qualified truth is not always the most exciting thing to read, just as the balanced and inconclusive judgment is less satisfactory to many than the neatly wrapped conclusion. But is that really a problem? What is a generalized history? It is a statement of hypothesis whether it is *The Culture of Cities* or *Space, Time and Architecture*. We can hardly hope it to be unprejudiced. We have a right to expect that the prejudice be acknowledged and not cloaked in an appearance of omniscience. We have a right to ask that the account be honest, not wilfully ignoring or distorting evidence known to the writer, especially as in so doing he takes undue disadvantage of the untutored and lazy reader. The generalist has the responsibility to cite his sources explicitly so that the reader may test them if he wishes—and he has the responsibility to cite them accurately. But beyond this it is a case of *caveat lector*.

Some books do have an influence for good or bad which transcends the scale of their scholarship and their prejudice. We have to learn how to live with the Toynbees, the Spenglers, the Paretos, and the Beards—and of course with the Giedions and the Mumfords. We have the more difficult task of correcting their overly influential errors. It would be unfortunate if many accepted Mumford's strange interpretations of science and technology in the contemporary world; including his notion that there is something "natural" and therefore good in the use of night soil to support agriculture or that to die from plague in London in the seventeenth century was somehow less immoral than to die there from fallout in the twentieth. It is not easy to enter these corrections but to impose a moratorium on generalizations is not the way to solve the problem.

There will be more general books; they will be more fun for the public to read and therefore promoted more vigorously by the publishers; the most we can hope for is that they will be written by responsible and careful, even if opinionated, men, and not have influence beyond their merits.

That the city rather than a single suburb or the whole urban civilization in the pattern of Rasmussen's *London* is an appropriate subject, I have no doubt. Indeed, I suspect that more and more architectural history which has typically dealt with single buildings will move in the direction of groups of buildings if not to the whole city—how much of it will concern itself with what the writers think to be "bad" buildings or groups, and how often it can transcend the limited conditions of aesthetics to examine the social fabric as fully as the fabric of the façades, is hard to forecast.

There is going to be more urban history—it is a suitable heading under which to subsume many investigations—and it is likely to be of pragmatic as well as theoretical consequence.

One of the unresolved questions that kept cropping up swirled around urban data and its validity. Mr. Warner, who has done a good deal of microscopic study, and has first-hand experience with the quality of urban data, said there were two problems. "One is the research problem in tracking down the decisions which have gone into a large city scheme where no one person or small group decided to lay out the particular area. The material is just not available. I tried to work from building permits, which is about as basic a unit as you can use, but it is very difficult to find out who the John Smith on the building permit was. When you deal with thousands of permits, the task becomes even more difficult. So there is a real problem of data in studying the kind of anonymous developments which, it seems to me, are now most relevant.

"There is another question. The city may not be the appropriate unit of study. For Mr. Garvan the appropriate unit of study, or at least the basic unit, is England. Likewise, though Sir John crept around the Gothic arch, he did indicate that the broad emotional and historical popularity of the Gothic had relevance. I would think that this matter of scale is going to plague the whole field of urban history. The city is at once too small and too large a unit to be dissociated from the big economic developments that surround it. These developments in turn are often the crucial ones that disturb a past organization and create a new one. And so I think that if you are to make any kind of orderly progress, a kind of progress that could be lined up and used by planners later on, you would have the very difficult task of figuring out what the units of study are and how to relate the largest units to the smallest."

Dr. Gutkind reacted to this with the pessimistic view that, what with all the social scientists about making surveys, we could drown in data, "the assumption that was intriguing me when Millon asked if I understood him correctly, why were obelisks put up and not columns, and why were they put in this or that place. The answer may be 'Why not obelisks?' What I mean by this retort is that we are overwhelmed with historical documentation, to the point where I feel that documentation is almost useless. The documentation which is available tells you something about facts, so called facts, but I doubt whether you would ever find anything about the motives or at least any clear hint why these things were done, why obelisks were put up; in other words anything on the causes behind the facts. I believe we have to be Utopians in reverse and look at the situation as a whole to understand why, for instance, it was almost unavoidable to erect the obelisk as the center of the square. We don't find much explanation of the reasons in the documentations which are available to us. When you are writing, you can get so involved in all the documentary evidence that you simply don't know what to do with all of it. This approach is impossible because we tend to forget that behind all the data were men. The whole thing reminds me very much of—I want to be polite—let me call them 'social researchers,' who are running about with questionnaires and index cards, and in the end put silly questions to which they get silly answers. And why do they get silly answers? It is really not exclusively their fault, because most people don't know what they want or what they are talking about, and give as an explanation of their motives ideas which are irrelevant and misleading.

"What I want to express is my great skepticism of all so called 'documentary evidence.' Now I come to the second point which I think is even more important. I couldn't agree more with everything that Warner said, although I happen to be engaged at the moment in such a history of cities. If you look back in history, you will find that a city has never existed in isolation. To treat cities as isolated phenomena is entirely wrong. It is simply the invention of some historians. No medieval city existed without the surrounding hinterland; in other words, without the surrounding region. No city of antiquity existed without the surrounding hinterland. I feel that we are somewhat—I don't really know how to express it—on the wrong track, we can't look at the history of cities as isolated phenomena. In all periods of history all formative and essential decisions were made in cities; and out of cities came that new manifestation in a new form. We have reached a state where cities are at a decisive turning point."

If we are at such a turning point, the question posed by

Handlin and Summerson becomes even more cogent. They asked how many disciplines may be involved in the proper study of urban history. At least we need to remember how many different facets must be considered expertly and *simultaneously*. How this can be achieved is of course the big question of much modern advanced study. The problem of interdisciplinary collaboration is the central organizational problem of the scholarly world and about it a great deal is still uncertain.

But all this was surely not enough to satisfy at least some of the planners and critics who have got themselves into the happy American state where everything is in crisis and where it is feared that actions taken in urban redevelopment in the next year or two may ruin us for the next century. Not only do I doubt this very much, but if it is so I do not see why one should charge the historians with being the only ones slow to answer the bell. From the historians we have a right to ask some things, most of which they supply now.

If Schorske's hopes are realized, not too many historians will follow Plato's suggestion that time is the moving image of eternity, and be mere chroniclers too bemused by time. But at the same time not too many will be mere philosophers or social scientists (his words) too little concerned with time.

We have a right to hope that they do the kind of work Summerson described, quiet work, modest work, reliable work. But that is not quite enough, I suggest. We can ask that first-class critical reviews of the state of a specific field of historical study shall have high status for they are most necessary and they cannot be done well by second-rate people. And we have a right to hope that more historians, especially as they deal with specialized material, will find a way to preserve truth while writing well about it. There's never a dull thing on heaven or earth but writing makes it so.

But in turn we have a right to ask of the planners that they read history, the prose as well as the poetry, the statement as well as the oration. We might ask of the architects that they read more than the works of history which say what they like to hear, which are generally entertaining, but try to read sober stuff critically, which they are perhaps not qualified to do, by serious consideration of the important ways, if any, by which the conditions of their present problem differ from those of the historical example. If history may not teach them what to do, it can almost certainly help them to think more carefully about what they are proposing to do, and perhaps avoid the doing of some of it.

We had hoped that the conference would bring forth suggestions for future work and future conferences.

Mr. Tunnard supplied the most detailed statement as to what city planners need from history. "Histories of the city range from celebrations and memorials of local historians which are sometimes the only source we can use, to the side glances of travelers, like Henry James whose essay on Washington is a very subtle and a very beautiful evocation of the democratic process in the city. One cannot do without those, or without the accounts of earlier travelers in Latin America and China and other remote parts of the world. And lately, the social anthropologists have been helpful to us, as city planners, in turning their attention from African villages to cities like Timbuktu; sociologists also, who have become concerned with city life in modern Japan, as well as in New York. I would like to urge more attention to the history of physical planning and settlement patterns, of which we are woefully ignorant. We rely here mostly on the archeologists and on certain few classical scholars, Boethius, Wycherley, Brown, and others who have turned their attention to the city planning of special groups of cities or of individual cities. The kind of book which we find fascinating is Ferdinando Castagnoli's recent study of the origin and transfer of the orthogonal plan in classical times. Perhaps city planners themselves must turn their attention to these particular aspects because the archeological studies are so often made for other reasons, and we cannot expect them to pay attention to the physical form of the city. I would urge that some kind of construct is necessary for this attention to the physical plan. But I would also urge that the settlement patterns of the nation or of a region should be studied in connection with the city plan, including of course the value systems and the technologies of the society; that the morphology should be given great attention, the ground plan, and the uses of the city, and the build of the city which John Summerson has so excellently covered in his *Georgian London*; the block pattern, the hierarchy of street relationships and so on.

"And then I think perhaps almost the most important investigation for the city planner is the role of the institutions in the city, which seems to me to be the key to a great many puzzles. I believe that we need also rather special studies on urban design. Certainly, I agree that the city planner can be largely responsible for urban design; but for analysis, and for the separating out of the elements, as Professor Zucker has done so well in his recent book *Town and Square*, we need a somewhat different approach. Quality enters in much more strongly; we deal with the parts rather than with the whole, kinetics, movement of things, and people, and observers, and also qualitative measures of proportion. Perhaps this has to be done by art historians, architects and archeologists and city planners together. But I am reminded by the discussions today and by the various thoughts that they have prompted that most of our questions about the city are still unanswered."

There were many other fragmentary suggestions, but as I review my notes I can find no coherent way to report them and they will perhaps be best reflected in the way they influence the future thinking of those present.

The conference was strong on the verbal side and tended to ignore the visual. Another should perhaps have visual material, be interested in the views of artists, and much more specific about technology and its effects.

If the suggestions were followed, a subsequent conference might hear papers on at least the following subjects:

The Mind and the Viscera as Directors of Urban Organicism.	Creese
The Dynamics of Urban Decline (as opposed to those of growth).	Millon
Breaks in Urban Continuity and Systems.	Boulding
Some Differences between the Principles of Urban Growth in East and West.	Fleisher
A Comparison between the Lives of William Zeckendorf and the Earl of Bedford.	Anon
Artists' Views of the City as compared with the Views of Intellectuals.	by an intellectual
The Georgian Factory Building and the Georgian Machine (A Study of Contrasting Form).	Summerson
Quis ducet ipsos duces (A Study of the Influence if any of Urban Thinkers on Urban Actors).	Burchard

Most of us carried away some things to be put to use on personal occasions. If for no other reason than this, we can, I think, say this cross-disciplinary conference was worth while. Should it be repeated? Perhaps in five years. In the meantime and at least until the bigger fora for the explicit discussion of urban history are provided in the learned societies, there might be annual conferences each directed to a different, more explicit part of the whole field, each harrowed more deeply.

But is it too dangerous to wait so long? Will the city and history die in the interim? No. History and the city will survive, though it may not be our city or our history. Others will study our history and the regret may be that they too may pay no serious attention to the mistakes and successes of the Sumerians, the Egyptians, the Greeks, Romans, Byzantines, Italians, English, and Philadelphians, just as we usually do not. If they choose to study history and to comment upon it, they will study what interests and pleases them and they will interpret it not with a sublime objectivity but rather an Olympian subjectivity in terms of what they want to believe.

And as for the history we ourselves write, the question we need always to ask is, "Who's listening?" I put this in another context when I commented on Mr. White's paper. "For the moment let us not question who the leading intellectuals were or the extent of their unanimity." Then I ask whether further study would be productive or even possible along these lines: Could one locate the people who were the decision makers about the city in earlier days? Some of the cited intellectuals were, in a sense, decision makers; but most of them were talking about the city and thinking about it rather than acting upon it. So if one could locate the decision makers, could one then determine whether the decision makers were aware of what the intellectuals were saying? If they were aware of it, were they reacting with it or against it, and how much lag was involved in this process?

Now, Mr. Schorske has of course given us some of this in the notable and most obvious case of the Nazis, but it seems to me that there is a great deal of work that could be done for other times that is connected immediately with the needs of a city. All of us must desperately wonder how, in fact, any statement you may have heard comes to bear, let us say, on people who finally do make the decisions, if such people exist. Lewis Mumford talks and Robert Moses disposes; and one may then wonder whether the talk matters.

To this, a number of historians replied that there were at least good examples of listening. Mr. Schorske, for example, cited work that could be done. "One could trace the reciprocal influences between the feuilleton critics of the Paris plans and the further articulation of those plans. Chamber debates, for example, might contain very interesting clues with names dropped as to who has read whom and the like. I do not know whether this gets into the documents or not, but I have often wondered whether there could be any follow-up on a most interesting survey, which I believe Hobson mentions in his autobiography. At the time when the socialists first scored their big electoral victory, in 1906, Hobson says someone went around and asked the new M.P.s what had inspired them in a socialist direction, and their answer was overwhelmingly John Ruskin. Now, how much of the rest of Ruskin's lore was soaked up by socialist circles is still something which, to my knowledge, has not been fully investigated. It is a good line of inquiry again to attach the decision makers to the free-floating intelligentsia."

These were crumbs for one who wanted to believe that he knew how influential historians or philosophers might have been or might be in the forming of pragmatic policy. If we did know, it might be deflating or we might be projected to the stars. One who knows something of the reading habits of architects or of city planners, so different, one so romantically and falsely elated, the other so dogged and dreary, cannot have much hope unless it lies in the politicians who are steadily learning to read faster—and many to read better. But whether we can profit by knowing more about the follies and foresights of our urban ancestors, whether we can bring ourselves to paying more attention to serious, detailed, even microscopic history, with only occasional peregrinations to the broad canvas or the seashore, all this remains conjectural. One can only hope. Meanwhile serious historians will have to go on being as interesting as they can within the stubborn truths of what they know and let the greater glamor and royalties go elsewhere.

A Selection of Works Relating to the History of Cities

PHILIP DAWSON AND SAM B. WARNER, JR.

Urban history is a vast, sprawling, and complex field of study. We have not tried, in preparing this list of writings, to reduce it to order. Rather, we have sought a few notable works in the main subdivisions of historical study which would exemplify good scholarship on cities in history. We have kept in mind the needs of those, whether graduate students or amateurs of history, who might look for ways to begin learning about cities in the past. For continents or regions in which urban history has not been intensively cultivated, this seemed to require the inclusion of general works of history; these have been excluded from most of the sections relating to Europe and North America. Except for a few great cities like London, New York, and Paris, we have omitted all source material, in order to produce a list and not a library catalogue. Many works of merit are left out because they are extremely specialized, or because they resemble in method or subject matter works that are included. This list is a collection of examples more than a bibliography. Its usefulness, we believe, will come from the inclusion of many diverse historical fields. For this we are deeply grateful to many friends and colleagues who have been generous with suggestions and criticisms. Without the opportunity to draw on their expert knowledge, we could not have listed anything like this number of works of high quality.

GENERAL

CHILDE, V. GORDON. "The Urban Revolution," *Town Planning Review.* XXI, 1950, 3–17. Common features of the first cities known to archaeologists.

GEDDES, PATRICK. *Cities in Evolution.* London, 1915; 2nd ed., 1949, omits some material, contains additions.

GIEDION, SIGFRIED. *Mechanization Takes Command.* Cambridge, 1948.

———. *Space, Time and Architecture.* 4th ed., Cambridge, 1962.

GUTKIND, ERWIN A. *The Twilight of Cities.* New York, 1962.

———. *Our World from the Air.* New York, 1950.

KORN, ARTHER. *History Builds the Town.* London, 1953. Handy brief illustrated survey of town form from the Neolithic to the present.

LAVEDAN, PIERRE. *Histoire de l'urbanisme.* 3 vols., Paris, 1926–1952.

MUMFORD, LEWIS. *The City in History. Its Origins, Its Transformations, and Its Prospects,* New York, 1961.

———. *The Culture of Cities.* New York, 1938.

———. *Technics and Civilization.* New York, 1934.

PFEIL, ELISABETH. *Grossstadtforschung; Fragestellungen, Verfahrensweisen und Ergebnisse einer Wissenschaft die dem Neubau von Stadt und Land von Nutzen sein könnte.* Bremen, 1960.

RASMUSSEN, STEEN EILER. *Towns and Buildings.* Cambridge, 1951.

SALINARI EMILIANI, MARINA. "Bibliografia degli scritti di geografia urbana," *Memorie di Geografia Antropica* (Consiglio Nazionale delle Ricerche e Istituto di Geografia della Università di Roma). II (1947) fasc. 2; XI (1956). Lists publications of the years 1901–1954 concerning cities all over the world, includes a considerable number of works not strictly geographical.

SOCIÉTÉ JEAN BODIN. *Recueils,* VI–VIII (1954–1956). *La ville.* World-wide survey of administrative and judicial institutions, economic and social institutions, and private law, ranging from ancient times to nineteenth century. Wide variations in quality.

THOMAS, WILLIAM L., JR., (ed.). *Man's Role in Changing the Face of the Earth.* Chicago, 1956. Symposium which summarizes geographers' approach. Papers from prehistoric time on. Notes and illustrations.

PLANNING AND URBAN FORM

Bibliography

BESTOR, GEORGE C. AND HOLWAY R. JONES. *City Planning: A Basic Bibliography of Sources and Trends.* Sacramento, 1962.

DAHIR, JAMES. *The Neighborhood Unit Plan: Its Spread and Acceptance. A Selected Bibliography with Interpretive Comments.* New York, 1947.

MCNAMARA, KATHERINE. *Bibliography of Planning, 1928–1935.* Cambridge, 1936.

SPIELVOGEL, SAMUEL. *A Selected Bibliography in City and Regional Planning.* Washington, 1951.

UMLAUF, JOSEF. *Deutsches Schrifttum zur Stadtplanung; Nachweis bis Anfang 1950*. Düsseldorf, 1953.

History

ADAMS, JAMES W. R. *Modern Town and Country Planning; a history of and introduction to the study of the law and practice of modern town and country planning in Great Britain*. London, 1952.

ASHWORTH, WILLIAM. *The Genesis of Modern British Town Planning; a Study in Economic and Social History of the 19th and 20th centuries*. London, 1954.

BRINCKMANN, ALBERT E. *Platz und Monument; Untersuchungen zur Geschichte und Ästhetik der Stadtbaukunst in neurer Zeit*. Berlin, 1908. Influential book stressing the social and economic influences upon physical form.

HAAR, CHARLES M. *Land Planning Law in a Free Society; a Study of the British Town and Country Planning Act*. Cambridge, 1951.

HARTOG, RUDOLF I. *Stradterweiterungen im XIX. Jahrhundert*. Stuttgart, 1951. Survey of planning and housing reform, emphasis on Germany. Illustrations, maps, bibliography.

PAVLSSON, THOMAS. *Den glömda staden, Svensk stadsplanering under 1900-talets början särskild hänsyn till Stockholm isehistoric, teori och prakbk*. Stockholm, 1959. Survey of Swedish town planning in first thirty years of the twentieth century. Traces German influences. Illustrations and bibliography, English summary 165-175.

PRITCHETT, C. HERMAN. *The Tennessee Valley Authority: A Study in Public Administration*. Chapel Hill, N.C., 1943.

RODWIN, LLOYD. *The British New Towns Policy: Problems and Implications*. Cambridge, 1956.

SITTE, CAMILLO. *Der Städtebau nach seinen kunstlerichen Grundsätzen*. Vienna, 1899; 5th ed., 1922; abridged transl. 1935.

STEIN, CLARENCE S. *Toward New Towns for America*. Rev. ed., New York, 1957. Review of American garden city experiments.

TUNNARD, CHRISTOPHER. *The City of Man*. New York, 1953.

U.S. Commissioner of Labor. *8th Special Report: The Housing of the Working People*. Washington, 1895. Pictures and plans of model philanthropic housing in the United States and Europe and discussion of contemporary housing rationale.

U.S. Works Progress Administration. *Urban Housing, Summary of Real Property Inventories Conducted as Work Projects, 1934-36* (Peyton Stapp, ed.). Washington, 1938. A guide to an essential source for studies of past city life, includes a finding list.

VIOLICH, FRANCIS. *Cities of Latin America*. New York, 1944. Describes urban planning and housing.

DEMOGRAPHY

BOGUE, DONALD J. *Population Growth in Standard Metropolitan Areas: 1900-1950*. Washington, 1953.

KUZNETS, SIMON AND DOROTHY THOMAS, *et al*. *Population Redistribution and Economic Growth, United States, 1870-1950*. 2 vols., Philadelphia, 1957, 1960.

WEBER, ADNA F. *The Growth of Cities in the 19th Century*. New York, 1899.

GOLDSTEIN, SIDNEY. *Patterns of Mobility, 1910–1950; the Norristown Study*. Philadelphia, 1958.
Careful analysis of migration of population in a small industrial city.
MOLS, ROGER. *Introduction à la démographie historique des villes d'Europe du
XIVe au XVIIIe siècle*. 3 vols., Louvain, 1954–1956. First volume: research
problems. Second volume: results. Third volume: appendices.
University of California, Institute of International Studies, *The World's Metropolitan Areas*. Berkeley and Los Angeles, 1959. Essay on statistical problems
of determining metropolitan areas, guide to sources, and tabulation of population of all cities over 100,000 population c. 1955.
WOYTINSKY, WLADIMIR S., AND EMMA S. WOYTINSKY. *World Population and Production*. New York, 1953. Each chapter includes references to statistical
sources and lists of secondary works.

AFRICA SOUTH OF THE SAHARA

Precolonial East Africa

FREEMAN-GRENVILLE, G. S. P. *The Medieval History of the Coast of Tanganyika*.
London, 1962. Includes information on the city of Kilwa.
KIRKMAN, JAMES. *The Arab City of Gedi; Excavations at the Great Mosque, Archi-
tecture and Finds*. London, 1954.
MATHEW, GERVAISE, AND ROLAND OLIVER. *History of East Africa*. (forthcoming).

Precolonial West Africa

EGHAREVBA, JACOB. *A Short History of Benin*. Benin, 1953.
MAUNY, RAYMOND. "The Question of Ghana," *Africa*, no. 24 (1954), 200–212.

Modern Africa

BIBLIOGRAPHY

VERHAEGEN, PAUL. "L'urbanisation de l'Afrique noire: son cadre, ses causes et ses
conséquences économiques, sociales et culturelles," Centre de Documentation
Économique et Sociale Africaine (Brussels), *Enquêtes Bibliographiques*, IX
(1962), 1–385. Urban Studies, by regions.

CONGO

BALANDIER, GEORGES. *Sociologie des Brazzavilles noires*. Paris, 1955.
PONS, V. G., and others. "Effets sociaux de l'urbanisation a Stanleyville," in *Social
Implications of Industrialization and Urbanization in Africa South of the
Sahara*. Paris (UNESCO for the International African Institute, London),
1956.

GHANA

BUSIA, K. A. *Report on a Social Survey of Sekondi-Takoradi*. London, 1950.

A Selection of Works / 273

NATAL

WATTS, H. L., LEO KUPER, AND R. DAVIES. *A Study in Racial Ecology* [of Durban]. London, 1958.

NIGERIA

PARRINDER, GEOFFREY. *Religion in an African City* [Ibadan]. New York, 1953.

RHODESIA

WILSON, GODFREY. *The Economics of Detribalization in Northern Rhodesia.* 2 fascicules, Livingstone, 1941–1942. On the city of Broken Hill.

SIERRA LEONE

BANTON, MICHAEL. *West African City; a Study of Tribal Life in Freetown.* London, 1957.

UGANDA

SOFER, C. AND R. *Jinja Transformed; a Social Survey of a Multi-Racial Township.* Kampala, 1956.

SOUTHALL, AIDAN W., AND PETER C. W. GUTKIND. *Townsmen in the Making; Kampala and Its Suburbs.* Kampala, 1956.

ASIA

Bibliography and General Studies

GINSBURG, NORTON S. "The Great City in Southeast Asia," *American Journal of Sociology,* LX (March, 1955), 455–462.

HAUSER, PHILIP M. (ed.). *Urbanization in Asia and the Far East; Proceedings of the Joint UN/UNESCO Seminar in Cooperation with the International Labor Office.* Calcutta, 1957.

Human Relations Area Files, Inc., New Haven, Conn. "Subcontractors Monographs," 1955–1956. A multilithed series of anthropological surveys of Afganistan, British Borneo, Burma, Cambodia, China, India, Indonesia, Laos, Malaya, Mongolia, Nepal, Pakistan, Taiwan, and Thailand. Each volume is a summary of the material which is classified in the central files and each contains an historical survey, notes, and bibliographic guides.

PATTERSON, MAUREEN L. P., AND RONALD B. INDEN. *South Asia: An Introductory Bibliography.* Chicago, 1962.

Research Institute of Humanistic Sciences. *Annual Bibliography of Oriental Studies 1946–.* Kyoto, 1952–. About a third of this continuing bibliography is devoted to books and articles on social and economic history.

China

BURGESS, JOHN S. *The Guilds of Peking.* London, 1928.

CH'U T'UNG-TSU. *Local Government in China under the Ch'ing.* Cambridge, 1962.

FAIRBANK, JOHN K. *Trade and Diplomacy on the China Coast: The Opening of the Treaty Ports, 1842–1854.* 2 vols., Cambridge, 1954.

GAMBLE, SIDNEY D., AND JOHN S. BURGESS. *Peking: A Social Survey.* New York, 1921.

GERNET, JACQUES. *Daily Life in China, on the Eve of the Mongol Invasion, 1250–1276* (H. M. Wright, trans.). New York, 1962.

HO PING-TI. *Studies on the Population of China, 1368–1953.* Cambridge, 1953.

MOULE, ARTHUR C. *Quinsai with Other Notes on Marco Polo.* Cambridge, 1957.

MURPHEY, RHOADS. *Shanghai, Key to Modern China.* Cambridge, 1953.

SHIGERU, KATO. "On the *hang* or the Association of Merchants in China," *Memoirs of the Research Department of the Toyo Bünko,* VIII (1936), 45–83.

SIRÉN, OSVALD. *A History of Early Chinese Art.* 4 vols., London, 1930. "Architecture," volume four, contains a short essay and many maps and illustrations.

———. *The Imperial Palace of Peking.* 3 vols., Paris, 1924–26.

YANG LIEN-SHENG. *Studies in Chinese Institutional History.* Cambridge, 1961.

India

For the precolonial period there is a growing archaeological literature, some of which is indicated here. In the modern period the British Civil Service wrote a mass of reports. Also, the nineteenth century abounds with travelers' reports and descriptions of all kinds. For instance, Walter Hamilton's two-volume *East-India Gazetteer,* 2nd. ed., London, 1828, was followed by the massive *Imperial Gazetteer* of 1881 and 1907. In the twentieth century both English and English-trained Indians wrote numerous economic studies. In short, though the quality is often disappointing the material for satisfactory urban history is plentiful.

PRECOLONIAL INDIA

BROWN, PERCY. *Indian Architecture (Buddhist and Hindu Periods).* Bombay, 1956.

———. *Indian Architecture (The Islamic Period).* 2nd ed., Bombay, n.d.

DUTT, BINODE B. *Town Planning in Ancient India.* Calcutta, 1925. Introductory note by Patrick Geddes.

MARSHALL, SIR JOHN. *A Guide to Taxila.* Cambridge, 1960. An Indian trading city, later a Hellenistic city. Description of the history and ruins, fifth century B.C. to 800 A.D. This author published a three-volume account in 1951.

PANIGRAHI, KRISHNA C. *Archaeological Remains at Bhubaneswar.* Bombay, 1961.

PIGGOTT, STUART. *Some Ancient Cities of India.* London, 1945.

ROWLAND, BENJAMIN. *The Art and Architecture of India (Pelican Histoy of Art, II).* 2nd ed., Baltimore, 1959.

MODERN INDIA

BOGLE, JAMES M. L. *Town Planning in India.* London, 1929.

CRANE, ROBERT I. "Urbanism in India." *American Journal of Sociology,* LX (March 1955), 463–470.

DAVIS, KINGSLEY. *The Population of India and Pakistan.* Princeton, 1951.

GADGIL, DHANAJAYA R. *Poona, a Socio-economic Survey.* Poona, 1945. In the 1950's a number of surveys of Indian cities were made: Delhi, Hubli, Baroda, Jameshedpur, Kolhapur, and Bangalore. Poona was resurveyed ten years after the first study: N. V. Sovani, D. P. Apte, and R. G. Pendse, *Poona: A Re-Survey.* Poona, 1956.

MEHTA, S. D. *The Cotton Mills of India, 1854–1954.* Bombay, 1954.

RAMESA-CHANDRA, MAJUMDAR, H. C. RAYCHAUDHURI, AND KALIKINKAR DATTA. *An Advanced History of India.* 2nd ed., London, 1950.

SPATE, OSCAR H. K., AND ENAYAT AHMAD. "Five Cities of the Gangetic Plain, A Cross-

Section of Indian Cultural History." *Geographical Review*, XL (April 1950), 260–278. Cawnpore, Lucknow, Agra, Benares, and Allahabad, with maps.

SPATE, OSCAR H. K. *India and Pakistan, A General Regional Geography*. New York and London, 1954. A great deal of material on cities, maps and notes; short bibliographies follow each major section.

TURNER, ROY (ed.). *India's Urban Future*. Berkeley, 1962.

TYRWHITT, JACQUELINE, (ed.). *Patrick Geddes in India*. London, 1947. Extracts from the reports of Geddes' 1915–1919 visit, bibliography.

JAPAN

BORTON, HUGH, et al. *A Selected List of Books and Articles on Japan in English, French and German*. Cambridge, 1954.

DORE, RONALD P. *City Life in Japan. A Study of a Tokyo Ward*. Berkeley, 1958.

HALL, JOHN W. "The Castle Town and Japan's Modern Urbanization," *Far Eastern Quarterly*, XV (1955), 37–56.

LOCKWOOD, WILLIAM W. *The Economic Development of Japan; Growth and Structural Change*. Princeton, 1954.

PAINE, ROBERT T., AND ALEXANDER SOPER. *The Art and Architecture of Japan (Pelican History of Art, VIII)*. Baltimore, 1955.

SMITH, THOMAS C., (ed.). "City and Village in Japan," *Economic Development and Cultural Change*, IX (1960), Number 1, part 2 entire. Includes articles on urbanization and population change, urban-rural differences, preindustrial urban life.

TAKEKOSHI, YOSOBURO. *The Economic Aspects of the History of the Civilization of Japan*. 3 vols., New York, 1930.

TREWARTHA, GLENN T. "Japanese Cities, Distribution and Morphology," *Geographical Review*, XXIV (1924), 404–422.

TSURU, SHIGETO. *Essays on Japanese Economy*. Tokyo, 1958.

EUROPE

Greece and Rome in Antiquity

FUSTEL DE COULANGES, NUMA DENIS. *La cité antique; étude sur le culte, le droit, les institutions de la Grèce et de Rome*. Paris, 1864; 7th ed., 1898. Transl. as *The Ancient City*. Marked a new stage in the study of its subject, but emphasis on religion now regarded as overstated.

Greece

GERKAN, ARMIN VON. *Griechische Städteanlagen*. Berlin, 1924.

HILL, IDA THALLON. *The Ancient City of Athens; Its Topography and Monuments*. London, 1953.

JONES, ARNOLD H. M. *The Greek City from Alexander to Justinian*. Oxford, 1940.

MARTIN, ROLAND. *L'urbanisme dans la Grèce antique*. Paris, 1956.

MYLONAS, GEORGE E. *Ancient Mycenae; the Capital City of Agamemnon*. Princeton, 1957.

WYCHERLEY, RICHARD E. *How the Greeks Built Cities*. 2nd ed., London, 1962.

TARN, W. W. *Hellenistic Civilization*. 3rd ed., London, 1952. Chapter on cities.

ZIMMERN, ALFRED E. *The Greek Commonwealth.* 5th ed., Oxford, 1931. The geographical, political, and economic setting of Athens in the fifth century, B.C.

Rome

FOWLER, WILLIAM WARDE. *Social Life at Rome in the Age of Cicero.* London, 1908.

FRANK, TENNEY (ed.). *An Economic Survey of Ancient Rome.* 6 vols., Baltimore, 1933–1940, reprinted Paterson, 1959. Summarizes and comments on ancient evidence; first and fifth volumes cover Rome and Italy, second and fourth volumes on the provinces.

FRIEDLÄNDER, LUDWIG. *Darstellungen aus der Sittengeschichte Roms in der Zeit von August bis zum Ausgang der Antonine.* 10th ed., 4 vols., Leipzig, 1922–1923; 7th ed. transl. as *Roman Life and Manners under the Early Empire,* 4 vols., 1908–1913. Fullest treatment of its subject.

HOMO, LÉON. *Rome impériale et l'urbanisme dans l'antiquité.* Paris, 1951.
Cities in the Roman provinces have generally been studied in connection with provincial history. A good recent example of the latter is David Magie, *Roman Rule in Asia Minor to the End of the 3rd Century after Christ,* 2 vols., Princeton, 1950. But a few cities other than Rome have been studied as such. For example: DOWNEY, GLANVILLE. *A History of Antioch in Syria, from Seleucus to the Arab Conquest.* Princeton, 1961.

MEIGGS, RUSSELL. *Roman Ostia.* Oxford, 1960.

SCHULTEN, ADOLF. *Geschichte von Numantia.* Munich, 1953.
By an expert on Spain in ancient times.

TANZER, HELEN H. *The Common People of Pompeii; a Study of the Graffiti.* Baltimore, 1939.

MEDIEVAL EUROPE

General

In the bibliographical notes for his paper in this volume, Professor Lopez comments on a number of the following and mentions other works.

La città nell'alto medioevo. Spoleto (Centro Italiano di Studi sull'Alto Medioevo, *Settimane de Studi,* VI), 1959.

Studien zu den Anfängen des europäischen Städtewesens. Lindau and Constance (Institut für Geschichtliche Landesforschung des Bodenseegebietes in Konstanz, *Vorträge und Forschungen,* IV), 1958. Studies of Magdeburg, Regensburg, Salzburg, and Würzburg, and more general essays.

ENNEN, EDITH. *Frühgeschichte der europäischen Stadt.* Bonn, 1953.

PIRENNE, HENRI. *Medieval Cities; Their Origins and the Revival of Trade.* Princeton, 1925.
A classic, but its main theme is subject to considerable revision and qualification.

ENGLAND (FOR LONDON, SEE PAGE 279).

On the whole, scholarly opinion regards James Tait, *The Medieval English Borough: Studies on Its Origins and Constitutional History,* Manchester, 1936, as better than Carl Stephenson, *Borough and Town; a Study of Urban Origins in England,* Cambridge, Massachusetts, 1935. One should not overlook Frederic William Maitland, *Township and Borough,* Cambridge, 1898.

FRANCE (FOR PARIS, SEE PAGE 280).

The legal status of cities is the subject of Charles Petit-Dutaillis, *Les communes françaises*, Paris, 1947, and Achille Luchaire, *Les communes françaises*, 2nd ed. (ed. Louis Halphen), Paris, 1911. Their physical extension is treated by François-Louis Ganshof, *Le développement des villes entre Loire et Rhin au moyen âge*, Paris and Brussels, 1943. A major study of a Flemish city is that by Georges Espinas, *La vie urbaine de Douai au moyen âge*, 4 vols., Paris, 1913; the third and fourth volumes consist of documents. Another northern town has been studied by Jean Lestocquoy, *Les dynasties bourgeoises d'Arras du XIe au XVe siècle; patriciens du moyen âge*, Arras, 1945; and by Marie Ungureanu, *La bourgeoisie naissante; société et littérature bourgeoises d'Arras aux XIIe et XIIIe siècles*, Arras, 1955. The urban life of Troyes, Provins, Bar-sur-Aube, and Lagny is described by Elizabeth Chapin, *Les villes de foires de Champagne des origines au début du XIVe siècle*, Paris, 1937, and the rise and fall of their economic importance is analyzed by Robert-Henri Bautier, "Les principales étapes du développement des foires de Champagne," *Comptes-Rendus de l'Académie des Inscriptions et Belles-Lettres*, Année 1952, 314–326. For a southern city there are the works of John Hine Mundy, *Liberty and Political Power in Toulouse, 1050–1240*, New York, 1954, and Philippe Wolff, *Commerces et marchands de Toulouse, vers 1350–vers 1450*, Paris, 1954. On the new southwestern towns of the thirteenth and fourteenth centuries, see Charles Higounet, "Bastides et frontières," *Le Moyen Age*, LIV (1948), 113–130.

GERMANY

A general account is Hans Planitz, *Die deutsche Stadt im Mittelalter von der Römerzeit bis zu den Zunftkämpfer*, Graz-Köln, 1954. Greater emphasis on the physical form of the city is provided by Karl Gruber, *Die Gestalt der deutschen Stadt; ihr Wandel aus der geistigen Ordnung der Zeiten*, 2nd ed., Munich, 1952; and by Ernst Hamm, *Die deutsche Stadt im Mittelalter*, Stuttgart, 1935. For the Hanse towns, see the works of Fritz Rörig, most recently *Wirtschaftskräfte im Mittelalter; Abhandlungen zur Stadt und Handelsgeschichte* (ed. Paul Kaegbein), Köln, 1959; also the essays by various scholars in the *Gedächtnisschrift für Fritz Rörig* (ed. Ahasver von Brandt and Wilhelm Koppe), Lübeck, 1953. An episcopal town has been studied by Jean Schneider, *La ville de Metz aux XIIIe et XIVe siècles*, Nancy, 1950. Frontier towns are the subject of Eduard Jobst Siedler, *Märkischer Städtebau im Mittelalter; Beiträge zur Geschichte der Entstehung, Planung und baulichen Entwicklung der märkischen Städte*, Berlin, 1914.

Italy

BRAUNFELS, WOLFGANG. *Mittelalterliche Stadtbaukunst in der Toskana*. Berlin, 1953.
CAGGESE, ROMOLO. *Firenze della decadenza di Roma al Risorgimento d'Italia*. 3 vols., Florence, 1912–1921.
MARINOTTI, PAOLO, and others. *Storia di Venezia*. Venice, 1957– (in progress).
RUSSO, GIOVANNI, *La città di Napoli dalle origini al 1860*. Naples, 1960.
TRECCANI DEGLI ALFIERI, GIOVANNI (ed.). *Storia di Milano*. 15 vols., Milan, 1953–1962. From the origins to 1900.

Spain

CARANDE, R. "Sevilla, fortaleza y mercado," *Anuario de Historia del Derecho Espanol*, II (1925), 234–401.

TIKHOMIROV, MIKHAIL N. *The Towns of Ancient Russia* (trans. Y. Sdobnikov, ed. D. Skvirsky). Moscow, 1959.

U.S.S.R. Society for Cultural Relations with Foreign Countries, *The Five Largest Towns of the Soviet Union.* Moscow, 1925. Guidebook to Moscow, Leningrad, Kharkov, Kiev, and Odessa.

EUROPE SINCE THE FIFTEENTH CENTURY

A comparative geographic interpretation is given by Robert E. Dickinson, *The West European City,* London, 1950.

Britain

LONDON

(For comments on a number of the following, see the paper by Sir John Summerson in this volume.) There is a sensitive general essay by Steen Eiler Rasmussen, *London, the Unique City,* London and New York, 1937. Different aspects as well as different periods of medieval London are treated by Sir Frank Stenton, "Norman London," in *Social Life in Early England* (Geoffrey Barraclough ed.), London, 1960, by Gwyn A. Williams, *Medieval London, from Commune to Capital,* London, 1963, and by Sylvia L. Thrupp, *The Merchant Class of Medieval London, 1300–1500,* Chicago, 1948; see also Marjorie B. Honeybourne, *Sketch Map of London under Richard II,* London, 1960.

For the seventeenth century, Norman G. Brett-James, *The Growth of Stuart London,* London, 1935, and Thomas F. Reddaway, *The Rebuilding of London after the Great Fire,* London, 1940, and for social and political history, Valerie Pearl, *London and the Outbreak of the Puritan Revolution,* London, 1961. For the eighteenth century, Sir John Summerson, *Georgian London,* London, 1945, on the physical form of the city, and Mary Dorothy George, *London Life in the 18th Century,* London, 1925, on the lower classes; it is enlightening to compare with the latter the recent study of riots by George Rudé, *Wilkes and Liberty,* Oxford, 1962; see also Lucy Sutherland, "The City of London in 18-Century Politics," in the *Essays Presented to Sir Lewis Namier* (ed. Richard Pares, and A. J. P. Taylor), London, 1956. Other more localized studies are: Sir Joseph Broadbank, *History of the Port of London,* 2 vols., London, 1921; Millicent Rose, *The East End of London,* London, 1951, on social history in the eighteenth and nineteenth centuries; Michael Young and Peter Willmott, *Family and Kinship in East London,* London, 1957, a study of contemporary Bethnal Green; and Harold J. Dyos, *Victorian Suburb; a Study of the Growth of Camberwell,* Leicester, 1961, based on the records of the individuals who carried out the original subdivisions.

A major social survey is that by Charles Booth and others, *Life and Labour in London,* 17 vols., 1902–1903, in three series: *Poverty,* 4 vols., *Industry,* 5 vols., and *Religion,* 7 vols.; a one-volume *Summary* concludes the whole work. (Preliminary results had been published as *Life and Labour of the People,* 2 vols., London, 1889–1891, and Booth later prepared a *New Survey of London Life and Labour,* 9 vols., London, 1930–1935.) A modern physical survey is that of the Committee for the Survey of the Memorials of Greater London, *Monographs,* 9 vols., London, 1896–1908, continued as the London Survey Committee, *Monographs*, 21 vols., London, 1916– (in progress).

OTHER CITIES

A general treatment has recently been attempted by Asa Briggs, *Victorian Cities*, London, 1963. Valuable studies of Cambridge, Leicester, Salisbury and Wilton, and York are included in the *Victoria History of the Countries of England*.

For Birmingham, see Conrad Gill and Asa Briggs, *History of Birmingham*, 2 vols., London, 1952, and George Cyril Allen, *The Industrial Development of Birmingham and the Black Country, 1860–1927*. London, 1929.

For Manchester, the works of Arthur Redford and others, *History of Local Government in Manchester*, 3 vols., London, 1939–1940, and *Manchester Merchants and Foreign Trade* [1794–1935], 2 vols., Manchester, 1934–1956.

BARKER, THEODORE C., AND J. R. HARRIS. *A Merseyside Town in the Industrial Revolution: Saint Helens, 1750–1900*. 2nd ed., London, 1959.

CHALONER, WILLIAM H. *The Social and Economic Development of Crewe, 1780–1923*. Manchester, 1950.

MACKENZIE, HUGH. *The City of Aberdeen*. Edinburgh, 1953.

PATTERSON, ALFRED TEMPLE. *Radical Leicester; a History of Leicester, 1780–1850*. Leicester, 1954.

France

PARIS

The entire history of the city is considered by Marcel Poëte, *Une vie de cité: Paris de sa naissance à nos jours*, 4 vols., Paris, 1924–1931. Two very short but masterly surveys are by the geographer Albert Demangeon, *Paris, la ville et sa banlieue*, Paris, 1933, and the historian of urbanism, Pierre Lavedan, *Histoire de Paris*, 2nd ed., Paris, 1947. The origins and evolution of the parish boundaries are described in the thesis of Adrien Friedmann, *Paris, ses rues, ses paroisses, du moyen âge à la Révolution*, Paris, 1959. A medieval suburb is the subject of Françoise-Marie Lehoux, *Le bourg Saint-Germain-des-Prés depuis ses origines jusqu'à la guerre de cent ans*, Paris, 1951. From the large number of memoirs by Parisians may be selected Pierre de l'Estoile, *Mémoires-journaux* (Louis-Raymond Lefèbre, ed.), 3 vols., Paris, 1948–1960, covering the years 1589–1611, and Louis-Sébastien Mercier, *Tableau de Paris*, 8 vols., Paris, 1782–1783; selections from each have been published in English translations. The *Atlas des anciens plans de Paris; réproduction en fac-simile des originaux les plus rares et les plus intéressants pour l'histoire de la topographie parisienne*, Paris, 1880, forms part of the *Histoire générale de Paris* under the auspices of the Conseil municipal de Paris. On particular points, the publications of the scholarly societies of the various arrondissements are often helpful; these are listed in the volumes for the department of the Seine in the *Bibliographie des travaux d'histoire et d'archéologie publiés par les sociétés savantes de la France*, begun by Robert Lasteyrie and continued by René Gandilhon.

A major social study of the Paris region in the mid-nineteenth century, submitted by Louis Chevalier as his main thesis, has not yet been published, but see his *La formation de la population parisienne au XIXe siècle*, Paris, 1950, and *Classes laborieuses et classes dangereuses à Paris pendant la première moitié du XIXe siècle*, Paris, 1958. The work of Haussmann has been re-examined by David H. Pinkney, *Napoleon III and the Re-Building of Paris*, Princeton, 1958.

For the mid-twentieth century city, there is the work of Paul Chombart de Lauwé and others, *Paris et l'agglomération parisienne*, 2 vols., Paris, 1952, describing the agglomeration, its social structure as a whole, and local structures; the second volume is devoted to research methods.

LYON

An original treatment of urban social and intellectual life in the late eighteenth and early nineteenth century is that by Louis Trenard, *Lyon de l'Encyclopédie au Préromantisme; histoire sociale des idées*, 2 vols., Paris, 1958. Changes in the physical form of the city have been studied briefly by Félix Rivet, *Le quartier Perrache, 1766–1946*, Lyon, 1951, and *Une réalisation d'urbanisme à Lyon: le quartier Grôlée, 1887–1908*, Trévoux, 1955, as well as by Charlene Marie Leonard, *Lyon Transformed; Public Works of the Second Empire, 1853–1864*, Berkeley and Los Angeles, 1961. A plan for a satellite town, based on experience at Lyon, was proposed by Tony Garnier, *Une cité industrielle; étude pour la construction des villes*, Paris, 1918. Economic organization is analyzed with historical perspective by Michel Laferrère, *Lyon, ville industrielle; essai d'une géographie urbaine des techniques et des entreprises*, Paris, 1960.

MARSEILLE

A general history is contained in the fourteenth volume of *Les Bouches-du-Rhône; encyclopédie départementale* (Paul Masson, ed.), 16 vols., Marseille, 1921–1937. A study of the urban geography was done by Gaston Rambert, *Marseille*, Marseille, 1937; he is also editor of the *Histoire du commerce de Marseille*, 6 vols., Paris, 1949– (in progress), of which the first four volumes go to 1660, the fifth covers the Levant trade from 1660 to 1799, and the sixth covers the colonial trade from 1660 to 1789.

OTHER CITIES

Two notable studies of seventeenth century urban history: Pierre Goubert, *Beauvais et le Beauvaisis de 1600 à 1730; contribution à l'histoire sociale de la France au XVIIe siècle*, 2 vols., Paris, 1960, the second volume consisting of eleven maps, fifty-one graphs of demographic data, and eighty-one graphs of prices and other economic data; and Gaston Roupnel, *La ville* [de Dijon] *et la campagne au XVIIe siècle; étude sur les populations du pays dijonnais*, Paris, 1922, an essay centering on the urban patriciate of judges and royal officeholders, and the part they played in the countryside as landowners. For the eighteenth century, Maurice Braure, *Lille et la Flandre wallonne au XVIIIe siècle*, Lille, 1932, treats administrative organization, economic activity, intellectual and social life; Pierre Lelièvre, *Nantes au XVIIIe siècle; urbanisme et architecture*, Nantes, 1942, depicts changes in physical form; Franklin L. Ford, *Strasbourg in Transition, 1648–1789*, Cambridge, 1958, studies the adaptation of a former German free city to the political control and cultural life of France. On Versailles, see J. Hugueney, "L'urbanisme a Versailles au temps du despotisme eclaire," in *Urbanisme et architecture; études en l'honneur de Pierre Lavedan*; and Fernand Évrard, *Versailles, ville du roi (1770–1789)*; *étude d'économie urbaine, suivie du texte des cahiers des corps et communautés des métiers de Versailles*, Paris, 1935.

The following are a few of the many studies of French cities emphasizing the period since industrialization.

COPPOLANI, JEAN. *Toulouse, étude de géographie urbaine*. Toulouse, 1954. Historical summary; modernization of the economy; present problems.

GOUHIER, JEAN. *Naissance d'une grande cité: Le Mans au milieu du XXe siècle*.

Paris, 1953. Brief study of results of sudden transfer of factories from Paris area to Le Mans.

PERRIN, MAXIME. *Saint-Étienne et sa région économique; un type de la vie industrielle en France.* Tours, 1937. Economic geography and demography.

ROCHEFORT, MICHEL. *L'organisation urbaine de l'Alsace.* Paris, 1960. Emphasizes interdependence of cities in the region, describes present urban organization, development of urban network since mid-eighteenth century, and types of cities.

Germany

Recent publications are described by Erich Keyser, "Neue Veröffentlichungen über deutsche Städtegeschichte," *Blätter für Deutsche Landesgeschichte*, XCVII (1961), 228–259, sixth in a series of biennial articles. An effort at synthesis has been made by Hans Mauersberg, *Wirtschafts- und Sozialgeschichte zentraleuropäischer Städte in neurer Zeit, dargestellt an den Beispielen von Basel, Frankfurt am Main, Hamburg, Hannover und München,* Göttingen, 1960, covering the fifteenth to nineteenth centuries.

BERLIN

HEGEMANN, WERNER. *Das steinerne Berlin. Geschichte der grössten Mietkasernenstadt der Welt.* Berlin, 1930.

Institut für Raumforschung, Bonn. *Die unzerstörbare Stadt.* Cologne and Berlin, 1953.

LEYDEN, F. *Gross Berlin; Geographie der Weltstadt.* Breslau, 1933.

WINZ, H. *Sozialgeographische Karten von Gross Berlin.* Berlin, 1950.

FRANKFURT

VOELCKER, HEINRICH, ed. *Die Stadt Goethes Frankfurt am Main im XVIII. Jahrhundert.* Frankfurt am Main, 1932.

HAMBURG

BOLLAND, JÜRSEN. *Die Hamburgische Bürgerschaft in alter und neuer Zeit.* Hamburg, 1959.

MÖLLER, ILSE. *Die Entwicklung einer Hamburger Gebietes von der Agrar- zur Grossstadtlandschaft.* Hamburg, 1959.

LÜBECK

FAHL, J. *Lübecks Strukturwandel von einen Handels- zu einen Industriestadt, 1862–1933.* Lübeck, 1947.

PIEPER, H. *Lübeck; städtebauliche Studien zum Wiederaufbau einer historischen deutschen Stadt.* Hamburg, 1947.

Italy

BERENGO, MARINO. *La società veneta alla fine del settecento.* Florence, 1956.

CAGGESE, ROMOLO. *Firenze della decadenza di Roma al Risorgimento d'Italie.* 3 vols., Florence, 1912–1921.

CARACCIOLO, ALBERTO. *Roma capitale, dal Risorgimento alla crisi dello stato liberale.* Rome, 1956.

COCCHIA, CARLO. *L'edilizia a Napoli dal 1918 al 1958*. Naples, 1960.

COGNASSO, FRANCESCO. *Storia di Torino*. Milan, 1960.

COMPAGNA, FRANCESCO (ed.). *La pianificazione urbanistica del Mezzogiorno* (Fondazione Aldo della Rocca, *Studi Urbanistici*, II), Milan, 1960.

MURATORI, SAVERIO. *Studi per una operante storia urbana di Venezia*. 2 vols., Rome, 1960.

PICCINATO, LUIGI (ed.). *Problemi urbanistici di Roma* (Fondazione Aldo della Rocca, *Studi Urbanistici*, I), Milan, 1960.

QUARONI, LUDOVICO, "Una città eterna ⸺ quattro lezioni da 27 secoli." *Urbanistica*, No. 27 (June 1959), 6–73. First of a series of articles on Rome in this and the next issue (October 1959); bibliographies.

QUARONI, LUDOVICO. "Una città eterna—quatto lexioni da 27 secoli."

ROCHEFORT, RENÉ. *Le travail en Sicile*. Paris, 1962.

RUSSO, GIOVANNI. La Città di Napoli dalle origini al 1860. Naples, 1960.

RUSSO, GIUSEPPE, *Il risanamento e l'ampliamento della città di Napoli*. Naples, 1960.

TRECANI DEGLI ALFIERI, GIOVANNI (ed.). *Storia di Milano* 15 vols., Milan, 1953–1962. From the origins to 1900.

Russia

BILL, VALENTINE T. *The Forgotten Class; the Russian Bourgeoisie from the earliest beginnings to 1900*. New York, 1959.

BLUMENFELD, HANS. "Russian City Planning of the 18th and Early 19th Centuries." *Journal of the Society of Architectural Historians*, IV (January 1944), 22–23.

BUNIN, ANDREI V. *Istoriia gradostroitel'nogo iskusstva*. Moscow, 1953.

⸺. *Geschichte des russischen Städtebaues bis zum XIX. Jahrhundert* (trans. Maria Fischer). Berlin, 1961.

HAMILTON, GEORGE H. *The Art and Architecture of Russia* (*Pelican History of Art*, VI). Baltimore, 1954.

LORIMER, FRANK. *The Population of the Soviet Union*. Geneva, 1946. Analysis of ethnic and other population trends using the censuses of 1897, 1926, and 1938.

LYALL, ROBERT. *The Character of the Russians, and a Detailed History of Moscow*. London, 1823.

PARKINS, MAURICE F. *City Planning in Soviet Russia; with an Interpretative Bibliography*. Chicago, 1953.
The essay on planning includes some historical background and maps of Russian cities. The bibliography includes annotations and a finding list for American libraries.

SHAPIRO, DAVID. *A Select Bibliography of Works in English on Russian History, 1801–1917*. Oxford, 1962.

Spain

CAMPUZANO, MIGUEL MOLINA. *Planos de Madrid de los siglos XVII y XVIII*. Madrid, 1960. Detailed account of topographical changes. Illustrated.

CARRERAS I CANDI, F. *La ciutat de Barcelona*. Barcelona (*Geografia general de Catalunya*), n.d. [circa 1910]. A detailed survey of all aspects of the city.

KUBLER, GEORGE, AND MARTIN SORIA. *Art and Architecture in Spain and Portugal and their American Dominions, 1500 to 1800*. (Pelican History of Art, XVII). Baltimore, 1959.

TORRES BALBAS, LEOPOLDO (ed.). *Resumen historico del urbanismo en España*. Madrid, 1954.

Other Countries

BURKE, GERALD L. *The Making of Dutch Towns; a Study in Urban Development from the 10th to the 17th Centuries*. London, 1956.

JOLLES, HIDDO M. *Wien, Stadt ohne Nachwuchs; sozialwissenschaftliche Betrachtungen über den Geburtenrückgang in der alten Donaustadt*. Assen, 1957.

København Stadsingeniorens Direktorat. *København*. Copenhagen, 1947. Illustrated history from middle ages to the present; maps of city and illustrations of housing.

LETTMAYER, FERDINAND. *Wien um die Mitte des XX. Jahrhunderts; ein Querschnitt durch Landschaft, Geschichte, soziale und technische Einrichtungen, wirtschaftliche und politische Stellung, und durch das kulturelle Leben*. Vienna, 1958.

NEAR EAST AND NORTH AFRICA

Near East before Industrialization

ALBRIGHT, WILLIAM F. *The Archaeology of Palestine*. Revised ed., Harmondsworth, 1954.

DOWNEY, GLANVILLE. *A History of Antioch in Syria, from Seleucus to the Arab Conquest*. Princeton, 1961.

FRANKFORT, HENRI. *Art and Architecture of the Ancient Orient (Pelican History of Art, VII)*. Baltimore, 1955.

KRAELING, CARL H., AND ROBERT M. ADAMS (eds.). *City Invincible: a Symposium on Urbanization and Cultural Development in the Ancient Near East*. Chicago, 1960.

MACKAY, ERNEST. *Early Indus Civilizations*. 2nd ed., London, 1948.

WOOLLEY, SIR CHARLES LEONARD. *Ur Excavations*. vs. 1–5 and 10, London, 1927– (in progress).

———. *Excavations at Ur; a Record of Twelve Years' Work*. London, 1955.

ISLAM

CAHEN, CLAUDE. "Mouvements populaires et autonomisme urbaine dans l'Asie musulmane du moyen âge," *Arabica*. V (1958), 225–250; VI (1959), 25–26, 223–265.

CRESSWELL, K. A. C. *A Short Account of Early Muslim Architecture*. Baltimore, 1958.

GARDET, LOUIS, pseud. *La cité musulmane; vie sociale et politique*. 2nd ed., Paris, 1961.

GRUNEBAUM, GUSTAVE VON. *Islam: Essays in the Nature and Growth of a Cultural Tradition. Memoir #81, American Anthropological Association*. Menasha, 1955. Social institutions of Islamic cities.

LE TOURNEAU, ROGER. *Les villes musulmanes de l'Afrique du Nord*. Alger, 1957. Social institutions.

———. *Fez in the Age of the Marinides* (B. A. Clement, trans.). Norman, Okla., 1961. Fourteenth and fifteenth century Moroccan city.

LOCKHART, LAURENCE. *Famous Cities of Iran*. Brentford, 1939.

SAUVAGET, JEAN. *Alep: essai sur le développement d'une grand ville syrienne, des origines* au milieu du XIXe siècle. 2 vols., Paris, 1941.

ZIADEH, NICOLA. *Urban Life in Syria under the Early Mamluks*. Beirut, 1953.

284 / Philip Dawson and Sam B. Warner, Jr.

Modern Period

ALGERIA

LESPÈS, RENÉ. *Alger; étude de géographie et d'histoire urbaines.* Paris, 1930.
————. *Oran; étude de géographie et d'histoire urbaines.* Paris, 1938.

EGYPT

ABU-LUGHOD, JANET. "Migrant Adjustment to City Life: The Egyptian Case." *American Journal of Sociology.* LXVII (July, 1961), 22–32.
CLERGET, MARCEL. *Le Caire: étude de géographie urbaine et d'histoire économique.* 2 vols., Cairo, 1934.
FORSTER, EDWARD M. *Alexandria: A History and a Guide.* 3rd ed., New York, 1961.
JOMARD, EDME. "Description abrégée de la ville et de citadelle de Kaire," in section entitled *Déscriptions* of report entitled *Déscription de l'Egypte, ou, Recueil des observations et des recherches qui ont été faites en Egypte pendant l'expédition de l'armée française* . . . 13 vols in 10, Paris, 1809–1828.
LANE-POOLE, STANLEY. *The Story of Cairo.* London, 1918.
SAATY, HASSAN EL, AND GORDON HIRAYBAYASHI. *Industrialization in Alexandria.* Cairo, 1959.
United Arab Republic, Ministry of Municipal Affairs and the Municipality of Cairo, *Master Plan of Cairo.* 2 vols., Cairo, 1956. Unavailable at present, not released by government.

JORDAN

HACKER, JANE M. *Modern Amman; a Social Study.* (J. I. Clarke, ed.). Durham (University of Durham, Department of Geography, Research Papers Series 3), 1960.

PALESTINE

JOIN-LAMBERT, MICHEL. *Jerusalem* (C. Haldane, trans.). New York, 1958.

SYRIA

SAUVAGET, JEAN. "Esquisse d'une histoire de la ville de Damas." *Révue des Études Islamiques,* VIII (No. 4, 1934), 421–480.

TURKEY

AKÇURA, TUGRUL. "Ankara; ses fonctions urbaines," and "Les fonctions d'Ankara sous la République." *La Vie Urbaine,* January–March 1960, 35–64; April–June, 1960, 89–128.
BIRGE, JOHN K. *A Guide to Turkish Area Study.* Washington, 1949.
An annotated bibliography which includes a chronology of Turkish history from 1037. There is no single first-rate book on cities.

SOUTH AMERICA

Bibliography

HARDOY, JORGE E. *Bibliography on the Evolution of Cities in Latin America* (Mimeo, Council of Planning Libraries, Exchange Bibliography, # LA3). Oakland, 1962.

HUMPHREYS, R. A. *Latin American History, a Guide to the Literature in English.* London, 1958.

General

DIFFIE, BAILEY W. *Latin American Civilization.* Harrisburg, 1945. Social and economic background of the colonies.

JAMES, PRESTON. *Latin America.* New York, 1959.

MORSE, RICHARD M. "Some Characteristics of Latin American Urban History." *American Historical Review,* LXVII (January, 1962), 217–338.

Archaeology

Instituto Nacional de Anthropología e Historia, *Guias Oficiales.* Mexico, 1958– (in progress). Guides to Mexican sites, including maps of ruins.

KUBLER, GEORGE C. *Architecture in Ancient America; the Mexican, Mayan and Andean Peoples (Pelican History of Art, XXI).* Baltimore, 1961.

MORLEY, S. GRISWOLD. *The Inscriptions of Petén* (Carnegie Institution of Washington. Publication No. 437). vol. 5, pt. 2, Washington, 1938.

TOUSSAINT, MANUEL, FEDERICO GOMÉZ DE OROZCO, AND FERNÁNDEZ JUSTINO. *Planos de la Ciudad de Mexico, Siglos XVI y XVII.* Mexico, 1938. Important maps of Tenochtitlan.

WILLEY, GORDON R. *Prehistoric Settlement Pattern in the Viru Valley.* Washington, 1953. 5,000 years of urban evolution in Peru.

———. *Prehistoric Settlement Patterns in the New World.* New York, 1956.

Colonial

ANGULO IÑIGUEZ, DIEGO. *Historia del Arte Hispanoamericano.* 3 vols., Barcelona, 1945–50.

AZEVEDO, AROLDO DE. *Vilas e Cidades do Brasil Colonial. Geografia No. 11.* Sao Paulo, 1956. History of changes in Brazilian cities from trading posts to late colonial forms.

Instituto de Estudios de Administracion local, Madrid. *Planos de Ciudades Iberoamericanas y Filipinas Existentes en el Archivo de Indias.* 2 vols., Madrid, 1951. Compilation of maps of seventeenth and eighteenth century cities and some comments.

KUBEER, GEORGE. *Mexican Architecture of the Sixteenth Century,* Chap. II, "Urbanism," Chap. V, "Civil Architecture." New Haven, 1948.

Ordenanzas del Descubrimento y Poblacion, dadas por Felipe II en 1573. Reprinted in, Rafael Altamira y Creven, *Ensayo Sobre Felipe II Hombre de Estedo, su Psicologia General y su Individualidad Humana.* Mexico, 1950. Includes the 148 colonial ordinances on planning and administration of the Spanish colonies.

"Planos de la Ciudad de Mexico." *Boletin de la Sociedad Mexicana de Geografia y Estadistica* LVII (March–June 1949). Collection of existing maps of Mexico City.

Recopilacion de Leyes de los Reynos de las Indias: Mandadas Imprimir y Publicar por la Majestad Catolica del Rey Don Carlos II, Nuestro Señor. 4 vols., 3rd ed., Madrid, Andrés Ortega, 1774. Massive compilation of 6385 laws; all the legislation on land planning, water rights, municipal government and town design are included.

Modern

BROMLEY, JUAN AND JOSE BARBAGELATA. *Evolucion Urbana de la Ciudad de Lima.* Lima, 1940.

MARCO DORTA, ENRIQUE. *Cartagena de Indies* (Alfonso Amadó, ed.). Cartagena, 1960.

RAZORI, AMÍLCAR. *Historia de la Cuidad Argentina.* 3 vols., Buenos Aires, 1945.

RAZORI, AMÍLCAR. *ria de la Cuidad Argentina.* 3 vols., Buenos Aires, 1945.

TOUSSAINT, MANUEL. *Patzcuaro.* Mexico, 1942. Old colonial city, architecture and history.

UNITED STATES

Bibliography

American Historical Association, Urban History Group. *Newsletter* (present publisher, State Historical Society of Wisconsin, Madison). 1953–.

MCKELVEY, BLAKE. "American Urban History Today." *American Historical Review*, LVII (1952), 919–929.

Colonial Period

BAILYN, BERNARD AND LOTTE BAILYN. *Massachusetts Shipping, 1697–1714: A Statistical Study.* Cambridge, 1959. A study of trade statistics which suggests methods for studying business in colonial cities.

BRIDENBAUGH, CARL. *Cities in the Wilderness: The First Century of Urban Life in America, 1625–1742. Cities in Revolt: Urban Life in America, 1743–1776.* 2 vols., New York, 1938, 1950.

FORD, AMELIA C. *Colonial Precedents of Our National Land System as it Existed in 1800.* Madison, 1910.

GARVAN, ANTHONY N. B. *Architecture and Town Planning in Colonial Connecticut.* New Haven, 1951.

GRIFFITH, ERNEST S. *History of American City Government.* New York, 1938. Colonial municipal government.

HALLER, WILLIAM. *The Puritan Frontier: Town-planting in New England Colonial Development, 1630–1660.* New York, 1951.

LABAREE, BENJAMIN W. *Patriots and Partisans, the Merchants of Newburyport, 1764–1815.* Cambridge, 1962. Contains an occupational survey of the town from old legal records.

REPS, JOHN W. "Town Planning in Colonial Georgia." *Town Planning Review*, XXX (January, 1960), 273–285.

TREWARTHA, GLENN T. "Types of Rural Settlement in America," *Geographical Review*, XXXVI (1946), 568–596. A useful summary of the settlement patterns of the thirteen colonies.

SELLERS, LEILA. *Charlestown Business on the Eve of the American Revolution.* Chapel Hill, 1934.

TOLLES, FREDERICK B. *Meetinghouse and Countinghouse; the Quaker Merchants of Colonial Philadelphia.* Durham, 1948.

Modern Period

GENERAL

ALEXANDERSSON, GUNNAR. *The Industrial Structure of American Cities. A Geographic Study of Urban Economy in the United States.* Lincoln, Nebr., 1956. Though based on the 1950 Census the statistical method would be very useful for historical studies.

BURCHARD, JOHN E. AND ALBERT BUSH-BROWN. *The Architecture of America; a Social and Cultural History.* Boston, 1961.

GOLDMAN, ERIC F., ed. *Historiography and Urbanization.* Baltimore, 1941.

GOODRICH, CARTER. *Government Promotion of American Canals and Railroads, 1800–1890.* New York, 1960.

GREEN, CONSTANCE M. *American Cities in the Growth of the Nation.* London, 1957.

HAMLIN, TALBOT F. *Greek Revival Architecture in America.* New York, 1944.

HAWLEY, AMOS H. *The Changing Shape of Metropolitan America: Deconcentration Since 1920.* Glencoe, Ill., 1956.

KIRKLAND, EDWARD C. *Men, Cities and Transportation: A Study in New England History, 1820–1900.* 2 vols., Cambridge, 1948.

LAMPARD, ERIC E. "American Historians and the Study of Urbanization." *American Historical Review,* LXVII (October, 1961), 49–61.

MCKELVEY, BLAKE. *The Urbanization of America: 1860–1915.* New Brunswick, 1963. Includes an extensive bibliography.

MEIER, RICHARD L. *A Communications Theory of Urban Growth.* Cambridge, 1962.

PERLOFF, HARVEY S. *et al. Regions, Resources and Economic Growth.* Baltimore, 1960.

QUIETT, GLENN C. *They Built the West; an epic of rails and cities.* New York, 1934.

SCHLESINGER, ARTHUR M. *The Rise of the City: 1878–1898.* New York, 1933.

STRAUSS, ANSELM. *Images of the American City.* Glencoe, Ill., 1961.

WADE, RICHARD C. *The Urban Frontier: The Rise of Western Cities 1790–1830.* Cambridge, 1960. Pittsburgh, Cincinnati, Louisville, Lexington, and St. Louis.

WHITE, MORTON AND LUCIA WHITE. *The Intellectual and the City: From Thomas Jefferson to Frank Lloyd Wright.* Cambridge, 1962.

WISSINK, G. A. *American Cities in Perspective, with Special Reference to the Development of Fringe Areas.* Assen (Holland), 1962. Comparison of American and European cities from 1850 to the present. Written in terms of modern economic geography.

BOSTON

In recent years Boston has been the subject of some unusual social and economic analysis. Oscar Handlin's *Boston's Immigrants, 1790–1880; A Study in Acculturation,* rev. ed., Cambridge, 1959, is a classic whose scholarship underlies many of the later studies. Walter Firey, *Land Use in Central Boston,* Cambridge, 1947, is a sociologist's history of the downtown section of the city; it should be accompanied by Sam B. Warner, Jr., *Streetcar Suburbs; The Process of Growth in Boston 1870–1900,* Cambridge, 1962, a description of suburban development derived from an analysis of building permits. Both the foregoing should be read with Walter M. Whitehill, *Boston: A Topographical History,* Cambridge, 1959. Lloyd Rodwin's *Housing and Economic Progress: A Study of the Housing Experiences of Boston's Middle Income Families,* Cambridge, 1961, gives an unusual portrait of the city. Also, Boston was the place of William I. Whyte's pioneering *Streetcorner Society; The Social Structure of an Italian Slum,* 2nd ed., Chicago, 1955.

CHICAGO

The literature of Chicago history is enormous. Bessie L. Pierce, *As Others See Chicago; Impressions of Visitors 1673-1933*, Chicago, 1933, summarizes some of it. Her *History of Chicago*, 3 vols., in progress, New York, 1937-, is a model full-scale history. Wyatt W. Belcher, *The Economic Rivalry between St. Louis and Chicago, 1850-1880*, New York, 1947, takes up the struggle of Chicago to become the midland capital of the United States. Jane Addams *et al., Hull-House Maps and Papers, A Presentation of Nationalities and Wages in a Congested District of Chicago*, New York, 1895, demonstrates the settlement house analysis of the city. St. Clair Drake and Horace R. Clayton, *Black Metropolis*, New York, 1945, and Louis Wirth, *The Ghetto*, Chicago, 1928, present the city in terms of the "Chicago school" of urban sociology. For a modern picture of the functioning of the city, Martin Meyerson and Edward C. Banfield, *Politics, Planning and the Public Interest; The Case of Public Housing in Chicago*. Glencoe, 1955.

NEW YORK

The variety of material on New York makes this city the best place for a beginner to commence the study of American urban history. Two excellent illustrated surveys are John A. Kouwenhoven, *The Columbia Historical Portrait of New York*, Garden City, 1953, and Isaac N. P. Stokes, *The Iconography of Manhattan Island, 1498-1909*, 6 vols., New York, 1915-1918. The latter includes a detailed chronology of the city's history. Bayrd Still has gathered together contemporary accounts of the city which he introduces with useful interpretive notes, *Mirror for Gotham, New York as Seen by Contemporaries from Dutch Days to the Present*, New York, 1956. For the early federal city: Sydney I. Pomerantz, *New York; an American City, 1783-1803; a Study in Urban Life*, New York, 1938. For economic history, Robert G. Albion, *The Rise of the New York Port, 1815-1860*, New York, 1939, should be followed by the massive, Committee on Regional Plan of New York and Its Environs, *Regional Survey*, 8 vols., New York, 1927-1929, and the equally ambitious up-to-date study, Raymond Vernon *et al., New York Metropolitan Regional Study*, 8 vols., Cambridge, 1959-1960. Some planning highlights: Roy Lubove, *Progressives and Slums: Tenement House Reform in New York City, 1890-1917*, Pittsburgh, 1962, opens up the extensive literature of housing reform; and the pioneering metropolitan plan, Committee on Regional Plan of New York and Its Environs, *The Graphic Regional Plan*, and *The Building of the City*, 2 vols., New York, 1929-1931. Immigrant life, Robert Ernst, *Immigrant Life in New York City, 1825-1863*, New York, 1949, and Moses Rischin, *The Promised City: New York's Jews, 1870-1914*, Cambridge, 1962. These should be followed by a look at Eugene L. Armbruster's *Brooklyn's Eastern District*, Brooklyn, 1942, which is an unusual antiquarian history constructed from a lifetime of title searching. Thomas C. Cochran, *et al., The Greater City, New York, 1898-1948*, New York, 1948, surveys the modern period. Finally, Caroline F. Ware, *Greenwich Village, 1920-1930; a Comment on American Civilization in the Post-War Years*, Boston, 1935, is an application of "Chicago school" sociology to one of the city's most interesting districts.

PHILADELPHIA

One of the largest industrial cities in America, Philadelphia has been depicted by an interesting series of social studies. William E. B. DuBois, *The Philadelphia Negro*, Philadelphia, 1899, analyzes Negro life and lower class settlements of the city; Wallace W. Weaver, *West Philadelphia: A Study of Natural Social Areas*, Philadelphia, 1930, is a "Chicago school" study of one of the largest residential areas of the city; E. Digby Baltzell, *Philadelphia Gentlemen. The Making of a*

National Upper Class, Glencoe, 1958, gives a social history of Philadelphia's leading families from colonial times. For an excellent statistical study of the twentieth century, Gladys L. Palmer, *Philadelphia Workers in a Changing Economy*, Philadelphia, 1956.

OTHER U.S. CITIES

Titles in this section are listed alphabetically by cities.

SHLAKMAN, VERA. *Economic History of a Factory Town: A Study of Chicopee, Massachusetts*. Northampton, 1935. A classic.

GREEN, CONSTANCE M. *Holyoke, Massachusetts; A Case History of the Industrial Revolution in America*. New Haven, 1939.

GLAAB, CHARLES N. *Kansas City and the Railroads*. Madison, 1962.

NADEAU, REMI A. *Los Angeles: From Mission to Modern City*. New York, 1960.

COOLIDGE, JOHN. *Mill and Mansion, a Study of Architecture and Society in Lowell, Massachusetts, 1820–1865*. New York, 1942.

CAPERS, GERALD M., JR. *The Biography of a River Town Memphis: Its Heroic Age*. Chapel Hill, 1939.

HAMMING, EDWARD. *The Port of Milwaukee*. Rock Island, 1953.

STILL, BAYRD. *Milwaukee, the History of the City*. Madison, 1948.

HARTSOUGH, MILDRED L. *The Twin Cities as a Metropolitan Market. A Regional Study of the Economic Development of Minneapolis and St. Paul*. Minneapolis, 1925.

SCHMID, CALVIN F. *The Social Saga of Two Cities: An Ecological and Statistical Study of the Economic Development of Minneapolis and St. Paul*. Minneapolis, 1925.

LYND, ROBERT S. AND HELEN M. *Middletown*. New York, 1929. Pioneer sociological study.

OSTERWEIS, ROLLIN G. *Three Centuries of New Haven: 1638–1938*. New Haven, 1953.

FOSSIER, ALBERT E. *New Orleans, the Glamour Period 1800–1840*. New Orleans, 1957. An antiquarian's social reconstruction from a careful newspaper search.

WERTENBAKER, THOMAS J. AND MARVIN W. SCHLEGEL. *Norfolk, Historic Southern Port*. Durham, 1962.

KELLOGG, PAUL V. *The Pittsburgh Survey*. 6 vols., New York, 1909, 1914. Detailed study of working-class life with photographs.

MCLAUGHLIN, GLENN E. *Growth of American Manufacturing Areas. A Comparative Analysis with Special Emphasis on Trends in the Pittsburgh District*. Pittsburgh, 1938.

REISER, CATHERINE E. *Pittsburgh's Commercial Development, 1800–1850*. Harrisburg, 1951.

DOTY, (MRS.) DUANE. *The Town of Pullman: Its Growth with Brief Accounts of Its Industries*. Pullman, Ill., 1893. Description before the great strike.

KIRKER, HAROLD. *California's Architectural Frontier; Style and Tradition in the 18th Century*. San Marino, 1960.

SCOTT, MELLIER G. *The San Francisco Bay Area: A Metropolis in Perspective*. Berkeley, 1959. Illustrated.

NESBIT, ROBERT C. *He Built Seattle, A Biography of Judge Thomas Burke*. Seattle, 1961.

MCKELVEY, BLAKE. *Rochester*. 4 vols., Cambridge and Rochester, 1945–1961. History spans the years 1812–1961.

GREEN, CONSTANCE M. *Washington*. 2 vols., Princeton, 1962– (in progress).

CANBY, HENRY SEIDEL. *The Age of Confidence*. New York, 1934. Upper class life in Wilmington, Delaware, 1880–1900.

Index

Front Street, Phila., 194
Fulton, Robert, 65

Garvan, Anthony, 64n., 210, 214, 253, 258–260, 263
Gay, John, 20
Geddes, Patrick, 167, 203, 204
Geneva, Switzerland, 30
Genoa, Italy, 36–39
Gerald of Wales, 125
Germans abroad, 162, 188
Germantown, Pa., 187
Germany, 31, 58, 100–104, 108, 125, 128, 148, 150, 154, 155, 227
Ghent, Belgium, 35
Giedion, Sigfried, 211, 262
Glaber, Raoul, 39
Glasgow, Scotland, 146, 152, 154n., 156n., 161
Goethe, J. W. von, 11
Goldsmith, Oliver, 102, 151
Gomorrah, 102
Gorki, Maxim, 104
Gottmann, Jean, 250
Grady, Henry, 117
Great Britain, 152, 157, 159, 161, 162, 227, 239, *See also* England
Greece, 28, 33, 97, 100, 101, 124, 160, 175, 218
Green, Constance M., 249
Greenock, Scotland, 154n.
Gromort, Georges, 223
Gutenberg, Johann, 30
Gutkind, E. A., 256, 263

Hamburg, Germany, 137
Hampstead, London, 171, 203
Handlin, Oscar, 71, 118, 260, 265, 338
Hanseatic League, 217n.
Hardy, Thomas, 162
Harrison, N.J., 13
Hartford, Conn., 29, 64, 152
Haskell, Douglas, 260
Hatshepsut, Queen, 257
Haussmann, Baron, 21
Havana, Cuba, 26
Haverford, Pa., 188
Hawthorne, Nathaniel, 84, 85, 90
Hay, John, 89
Hegel, G. W. F., 86, 101
Hegemann, Werner, 223
Henry of Navarre, 258

Henry VIII of England, 174
Hicksville, N.Y., 80
Hippodamus, 220
Hirschman, A. O., 47, 51
Hitchcock, H. R., 260
Hobson, John A., 269
Hofstadter, Richard, 89
Hogarth, William, 20
Hölderlin, F., 101
Holford, Sir William, 203
Holme, Thomas, 186, 188n., 190–195, 197, 201, 214
Howard, Ebenezer, 21
Howells, William Dean, 84, 85, 88, 90–93
Hudson River tunnels, 12, 13

Idlewild Airport, 12
India, 118
Indonesia, 140
Indus River, 133
Inversie, barony of, 186n.
Iowa, 143, 151, 162
Ireland and the Irish, 125, 151, 181, 182, 185, 190–192, 197
Isaiah, 123
Isard, Walter, 75n.
Isidore of Seville, 29
Italy, 34, 36, 50, 125, 130, 159, 220, 240

Jakarta, Indonesia, 140
Jamaica, Long Island, 13
James II of England, 186
James, Henry, 84–93 *passim*, 218, 266
Japan, 5, 24, 44n., 48, 155, 266
Jefferson, Thomas, 84–86, 102, 115, 163
Jenks, Alfred, 67
Jeremiah, 134
Jerusalem, 129, 135, 144
Jews in Manchester, 162
Johannesburg, South Africa, 5, 22
Johnson, Dr. Samuel, 150, 151
Jones, A. J. H., 218
Jones, Inigo, 172–174, 205
Judaic tradition, 124
Juvenal, 148, 151, 258

Kansas, 117
Karlsruhe, Germany, 100, 150, 254
Kennedy, (John F.), Jack, 258
Kensington, Phila., 68
Khrushchev, Nikita, 257

THE M.I.T. PRESS PAPERBACK SERIES